RESIDUAL FUTURES

Studies of the Weatherhead East Asian Institute,
Columbia University

STUDIES OF THE WEATHERHEAD EAST ASIAN INSTITUTE,
COLUMBIA UNIVERSITY

The Studies of the Weatherhead East Asian Institute of Columbia University were inaugurated in 1962 to bring to a wider public the results of significant new research on modern and contemporary East Asia.

Residual Futures

*The Urban Ecologies of Literary and
Visual Media of 1960s and 1970s Japan*

Franz Prichard

Columbia University Press   New York

This publication has been funded in part by the Princeton University Committee on Research in the Humanities and Social Sciences.

This publication is made possible in part from the Barr Ferree Foundation Fund for Publications, Department of Art and Archaeology, Princeton University

Columbia University Press
Publishers Since 1893
New York   Chichester, West Sussex
cup.columbia.edu
Copyright © 2019 Columbia University Press
All rights reserved

Cataloging-in-Publication Data available from the Library of Congress
LCCN 2018056373
ISBN 978-0-231-19130-2 (cloth)
ISBN 978-0-231-19131-9 (paper)
ISBN 978-0-231-54933-2 (electronic)

Columbia University Press books are printed on permanent and durable acid-free paper.
Printed in the United States of America

Cover design: Chang Jae Lee
Cover photographs: Takuma Nakahira © Gen Nakahira Courtesy of Osiris

Contents

Acknowledgments   vii

Introduction   1

CHAPTER ONE
Prelude to the Traffic War: Infrastructural Aesthetics
of the Cold War   20

CHAPTER TWO
Disappearance: Topological Visuality in Abe Kōbō's
Urban Literature   48

CHAPTER THREE
Landscape Vocabularies: *For a Language to Come* and the
Geopolitics of Reading   81

CHAPTER FOUR
An Illustrated Dictionary of Urban Overflows   113

CHAPTER FIVE
Photography as Threshold and Pathway After Reversion   150

CHAPTER SIX
Residual Futures   192

Notes   209
Index   257

Acknowledgments

The extensive notes at the end of this volume offer a partial mapping of the intellectual genealogies at play in these chapters. However, I would like to briefly acknowledge the contributions and generosity of so many who made this work possible and enjoyable along the way.

At UCLA, I had the chance to study with many great teachers, including George Baker, William Bodiford, Namhee Lee, Donald McCallum, William Marotti, Amir Mufti, Thu-Huong Ngyuyen-Vo, Mariko Tamanoi, and to learn together with a host of inspiring cohorts, friends, and fellow travelers: Emily Anderson, Brian Bernards, Caleb Carter, Carlos Prado-Fonts, Timothy Unverzagt Goddard, Koichi Haga, Chris Hanscom, Natilee Harren, Todd Henry, Nathaniel Isaacson, Mari Ishida, Spencer Jackson, Howard Kahm, Elli Kim, Aynne Kokas, Hieyoon Kim, Gabriel Ritter, Youngju Ryu, Ken Shima, Hijoo Son, Serk-Bae Suh, Chinghsin Wu, and Mika Yoshitake. At Waseda University, with the invaluable support of the Fulbright-Hays Dissertation Research Fellowship, Keiko Kanai made it possible to conduct my dissertation fieldwork, generously sharing her sense of the literary as a living form, and a way of life. Most of all, without the tireless encouragement and deep musical sensibility of Michael Bourdaghs and the limitless generosity, wisdom, and guidance of Seiji Lippit, this work would have never been possible.

As a postdoctoral fellow at the Reischauer Institute of Japanese Studies at Harvard University, this work benefited in substantial ways from insightful feedback and shared meals with fellow postdocs Molly Des Jardin, Nick Kapur, Halle O'Neal, and Jeremy Yellen. I was fortunate to learn from the bold thinking of Julia Alekseyeva, Andrew Campana, Andrew Littlejohn, and Teng-Kuan Ng in my seminar. I had the opportunity to have many thoughtful discussions in and outside the halls of the CGIS building with Peter Bernard, Ryoko Kosugi, Misook Lee, Jooeun Noh, Hansun Hsiung, Shi-Lin Loh, Esra Gokce Sahin, Hannah Shepherd, and Eric Swanson. I am eternally grateful for librarian Kuniko Yamada McVey's encyclopedic knowledge and humor, Stacie Matsumoto's diligence, support, and kindness, and the generosity and inspiring work of the many faculty and associated faculty in the Cambridge/ Boston area that have made a decisive impact on my work, including Ted Gilman, Shigehisa Kuriyama, Yukio Lippit, and Melissa McCormick at Harvard University, Ian Condry and Hiromu Nagahara at MIT, Matthew P. Fraleigh and Ellen Schattschneider at Brandeis University, Marié Abe, Sarah Frederick, and Keith Vincent at Boston University, and Eve Zimmerman and Quinn Slobodian at Wellesley College.

As participants in an author's conference organized by Tomiko Yoda, the thorough feedback and generative questions of Tom LaMarre, Tom Looser, Chris Nelson, and Alex Zahlten profoundly impacted the development of this work; their own work continues to inspire. The conversations with Hayden Guest, Kazunori Mizushima, Alex Zahlten, and Tomiko Yoda continue to shape my work in untold ways, and I am particularly grateful for Tomiko's intellectual generosity and invigorating spirit of inquiry.

At the University of North Carolina at Charlotte, I enjoyed the contagious enthusiasm and inexhaustible intellectual curiosity of many students, as well as the kindness and solidarity of many colleagues, including Giseung Lee.

At Princeton's Department of East Asian Studies, I have benefited from the admirable leadership and support of Martin Kern, David Leheney, and Anna Shields, as well as a host of estimable colleagues, including Amy Borovoy, who generously hosted a departmental Hegel reading group and provided helpful suggestions for this book. The unwavering intellectual inspiration and camaraderie of Steven Chung,

Erin Huang, Paize Keulemans, Federico Marcon, and Atsuko Ueda have each in their own way catalyzed key aspects of this work. What's more, the collegiate spirits of He Bian, Ksenia Chizhova, Brian Steininger, and Xin Wen have made for many enjoyable conversations and gatherings. The boundless collaborative spirits of Steven and Erin have made for an especially generative and rewarding experience that has profoundly shaped my work, offering many crucial suggestions and their inspiring commitments to the vocation of inquiry. This study has benefited from working with many exceptional graduate students, including David Boyd, Chan Yong Bu, Junnan Chen, Kimberly Hassel, Claire Kaup, Jessica LeGare, Nicholas Risteen, Bernard Shee, Tomoko Slutsky, and Ajjana Thairungroj. I am eternally grateful for the indispensable efforts of department staff Lisa Ball, Brandon Ermita, Jeff Heller, Amber Lee, Donna M. Musial-Manners, Sean Miller, and Margo Orlando. This work has also benefited from the suggestions and support of many colleagues beyond the department, including Andrew Watsky in Art and Archeology, Aaron Shkuda in the Princeton-Mellon Initiative in Architecture, Urbanism, and the Humanities, Stephen Teiser and the generous assistance of the East Asian Studies Program, the librarians and staff of the East Asian Library, especially Setsuko Noguchi whose unflagging efforts have contributed to this work in many ways.

Parts of this study were developed in participation in a number of conferences, publications, talks and workshops. Chapter 5 of this volume was first shared at the "Space of Possibility: In, Between, and Beyond Korea and Japan" conference organized by Andrea Gevurtz Arai and Clark Sorensen at the University of Washington, and I gained many insightful readers' comments as a chapter in the resultant edited volume. Nakamori Yasufumi invited me to participate in a series of symposia and events related to the exhibition *For a New World to Come* at the Museum of Modern Art, Houston. Many conspirators and collaborators in conference panels helped formulate new contexts and conversations that strengthened this work. I am thankful for the inspired contributions of many participants of workshop events and co-organized conferences I have been fortunate to host here at Princeton, including Dan Abbe, Michelle Cho, Carrie Cushman, Victor Fan, Arnika Fuhrmann, Yuriko Furuhata, Daniel Johnson, Ju-Hui Judy Han, Go Hirasawa, Rachel Hutchinson, Osamu Kanemura, Nick Kapur, Gyewon Kim,

Hiroko Komatsu, Petrus Liu, Tom Looser, Christine Marran, Yasu-fumi Nakamori, Thy Phu, Paul Roquet, Takuya Tsunoda, Tomiko Yoda, Mitsuhiro Yoshimoto, and Alex Zahlten.

The Japan Foundation made it possible to spend a year in Japan, generously hosted by Meiji University, thanks to the efforts of Shino Kuraishi, whose inspiring work has profoundly contributed to this study. In Tokyo I was fortunate to be able to spend many memorable hours with Chonghwa Lee, Osamu Kanemura, Hiroko Komatsu, Shino Kuraishi, Mikiko Hara, Yoko Sawada, and Aki Yasumi, all of whom have deeply impacted this work. Since the fieldwork stage of this study, Yoko Sawada has made it possible to conduct many essential aspects of this research, sharing her deep wisdom and the unparalleled Osiris archives with me. For almost a decade, Yoko's generosity and collaborative efforts have made manifold contributions to my work, including unforgettable meetings with Takuma Nakahira in 2009 and 2015.

Ross Yelsey, formerly of the Weatherhead East Asia Institute, guided this work toward publication, and Christine Dunbar of Columbia University Press has generously made an extraordinary effort to see this volume to print. I am particularly grateful to the anonymous readers who provided invaluable suggestions on the manuscript.

Over the years and through the streets of Loz Feliz, Hongo, Mar Vista, Cambridge, Charlotte, Princeton, and Tokyo, many friends and neighbors have made it all worthwhile. Many extended families provided generous encouragement and support over many years and on both coasts; Walter and Margorie Malishka, Peter, Elizabeth, and Ian Malishka, Tommy and Tootsie Malishka, Debbie and Robert Byrd, and of course Emma. I am forever thankful to my mother, father, and brother for the love of learning and myriad forms of inspiration and support they have shared with me. I am most thankful for my companions on these shared journeys; without my partner Sara's infinite wisdom, the humor, dancing, and beguilement of Lauretta and Mabel, and Kinako's nudges, none of this would be possible.

I have infinitely benefited from so many who have shared their innumerably diverse ways of knowing the world. This book is dedicated to the shared knowledge of how the world might be—and is always already—otherwise . . .

RESIDUAL FUTURES

Introduction

The questions informing this book arise from a rather simple observation and a somewhat complex methodological problem that follows from it. When we survey the histories of Japanese literary and visual media together, as opposed to in isolation, it is obvious that during the 1960s and 1970s many works produced in Japan were rife with depictions of "urban problems" (*toshi mondai*). At the time, this term indexed a wide range of phenomena in journalistic discourses, such as urban renewal and reconstruction, traffic, pollution, street protest, problems of urban-rural divide and difference (the depopulation of rural communities and the "discovery" of virtualized homelands, or *furusato*, as exemplified by the National Railways' Discover Japan campaign), and suburbanization (such as the ubiquitous figure of the *danchi* housing developments, increasingly lengthy rail commutes, and a rapid expansion of commodified and gendered consumer cultures).[1] Such an abundance of urban, suburban, and rural transformations within a broader context of intensive sociohistorical change offers scholars an important framework for grasping the vast set of forces shaping the horizons of Japanese literary and visual media in these decades. Moreover, the burgeoning of works crafted with nuanced perspectives on urban change was occasioned by intensive forms of questioning and exchange that spanned a wide range of media in ways that were influential on subsequent developments of literary and visual media practice.

The noticeable proliferation of urban phenomena in these decades leads to a compelling set of methodological challenges for studies of literary and visual media from Japan. How might we account for the emergence of a panoply of works that were preoccupied with the flux of the urban landscape? How can we define the localized contexts of works of different media while engaging with the expansive scope of the urban imaginaries they produced? In what ways might we enrich our understanding of each work's specific material and conceptual vocabularies by situating them within the broader set of critical discourses concerned with urban and media developments? How might we attend to the affinities among the geopolitical and aesthetic strategies of works born of discrete contexts and discursive domains? Along with these methodological questions, we might ask how the explicitly urban contours of works produced in these decades help us to establish transdisciplinary and transnational frameworks for reconsidering the histories of urban transformation through works of literary and visual media.[2] That is, specifically, how might we understand the flux of urban spaces and media ecologies traced in these chapters as constituent forms of a broader Cold War transformation of the planetary conditions of human and nonhuman experience? One of the central aims of this study is to not only make legible the specifically urban vocabularies of representative works of literary and visual media from Japan, but to also think through the shifting geopolitical and aesthetic limits and potentials expressed in the Cold War remaking of Japan.

To illustrate how these general questions might operate in this context, I'd like to introduce a snapshot of the bibliographic record of photographer and critic Nakahira Takuma (1937–2015), a central figure of this study.

We can discern a few significant features from this partial sample of the lengthy list of bibliographic entries meticulously compiled by Ishizuka Masahito on the occasion of the first retrospective exhibition of Nakahira's work in 2003. The first thing we notice is that, in addition to the entries of exhibitions and photobooks that we might expect from a photographer, there are also essay collections. Second, the overwhelming majority of entries are those of Nakahira's publications in print periodicals, with photography indicated by the squares and his critical writings indicated by the circles. Spanning the four decades from

展覧会・文献目録　　　　石塚雅人編

主要展覧会

**カタログが出版されている展覧会は、末尾 [ ] 内に示した。

・「第6回パリ青年ビエンナーレ」パリ市立近代美術館、1969年9〜11月（日本コミッショナー＝東野芳明）[カタログ]
・「第7回パリ青年ビエンナーレ」ヴァンセンヌ植物園、パリ、1971年9〜11月（日本コミッショナー＝岡田隆彦）[カタログ]
・「写真のための写真」シミズ画廊、東京・荻窪、1974年4〜5月
・「15人の写真家」東京国立近代美術館、1974年7〜9月 [カタログ]
・「Takuma Nakahira, Kazuo Mutoh, Kazuyoshi Oishi: travaux/débat/projection: l'avant-garde au Japon」ADDA画廊、マルセイユ、1976年11月（武藤一夫、大石一義との三人展）
・「11人の1965〜75―日本の写真は変えられたか」山口県立美術館、1989年1〜2月 [カタログ]
・個展「あばよX」FOTO DAIDO、東京・渋谷、1989年5月
・「東京国立近代美術館と写真1953-1995」東京国立近代美術館フィルムセンター展示室、1995年5〜7月 [カタログ]
・個展「日常　中平卓馬の現在」中京大学アートギャラリー・Cスクエア、名古屋、1997年6〜7月
・「琉球烈像――写真で見るオキナワ フォトネシア／光の記憶・時の災害　復帰30年の波島」那覇市民ギャラリー、2002年7月 [カタログ]

写真集・著作

・『まずたしからしさの世界をすてろ　写真と言語の思想』（共著、多木浩二、中平卓馬編）、田畑書店、1970年3月
・『来たるべき言葉のために』風土社、1970年11月
・『なぜ、植物図鑑か　中平卓馬映像論集』晶文社、1973年2月
・『決闘写真論』（共著、写真＝篠山紀信）、朝日新聞社、1977年9月、文庫版（朝日文庫）、1995年5月
・『新たなる凝視』晶文社、1983年1月
・『Adieu à X』河出書房新社、1989年3月
・『日本の写真家36　中平卓馬』岩波書店、1999年2月
・『中平卓馬の写真論』（リキエスタ）の会、2001年4月
・『The Japanese Box』（クリストフ・シフェルリ編）ドイツ、Steidl社、2001年10月、限定1500部（『プロヴォーク』第1〜3号、『来たるべき言葉のために』。森山大道『写真よさようなら』、荒木信雄『センチメンタルな旅』計6個の印刷物からの復刻版を木箱に収録、同封小冊子解説＝八角聡仁）
・『histeric Six　NAKAHIRA Takuma』Hysteric Glamour、2002年3月

発表作品・著作（逐次刊行物）

**■は写真掲載、●は著作を示す。
**誌名は『　』、記事名は「　」で示し、原則的に誌誌名、号数・出版年月日、記事名、その他事項の順に記した。

●『現代の眼』1963年8月号「考えさせられるいくつかの思いつき――寺山修司『現代の青春論』」（読書室）（筆名＝卓）
●『現代の眼』1963年9月号「わずかにのこった『革命者』の風説――谷川雁『影の越境をめぐって』」（読書室）（筆名＝卓）
●『現代の眼』1964年4月号「分析しつくすロジッタ――松本俊夫『映像の発見』」（読書室）（筆名＝卓）
■『現代の眼』1964年12月号「I am a king 最終回／パレード」（筆名＝袖木明）《他に写真＝内藤正敏、菅須賀功光、深瀬昌久、東松照明》
●『現代の眼』1965年2月号「無言劇」（クレジットなし）（写真＝森山大道）
●『日本読書新聞』1965年2月22日号「映像は論理である――住目される東松照明氏の紀行」
■『日本読書新聞』1966年1月1日号「顔 寺田隆彦氏」
■『日本読書新聞』1966年1月24日号「顔 寛満凱氏」
■『日本読書新聞』1966年2月7日号「顔 関公彦氏」
■『日本読書新聞』1966年2月21日号「顔 高木達夫氏」
■『日本読書新聞』1966年3月14日号「顔 渡辺浩子氏」
■『日本読書新聞』1966年3月21日号「顔 桑原史成氏」
■『日本読書新聞』1966年4月4日号「顔 小沢正氏」
■『日本読書新聞』1966年4月11日号「顔 入沢康夫氏」
■『日本読書新聞』1966年5月2日号「顔 クロイフ・カズ氏」
■『日本読書新聞』1966年5月30日号「顔 尾田亨氏」
■『日本読書新聞』1966年6月27日号「顔 渡辺一衛氏」
■『日本読書新聞』1966年7月18日号「顔 折原浩氏」
■『日本読書新聞』1966年8月8日号「顔 津野海太郎氏」
●『日本読書新聞』1966年8月22日号「視力の衰えた作家ゴダール――『立派な詐欺師』の演繹の意識と言葉」
■『日本読書新聞』1966年9月5日号「顔 宇野亜喜良氏」
■『日本読書新聞』1966年9月19日号「顔 関本白日氏」
■『アサヒグラフ』1966年9月23日号「街に戦場あり 2 放浪の馬への手振」（テキスト＝寺山修司）
■『アサヒグラフ』1966年10月7日号「街に戦場あり 4 親指無宿たち」（テキスト＝寺山修司）
■『日本読書新聞』1966年10月17日号「顔 今井祝雄氏」
■『アサヒグラフ』1966年10月21日号「街に戦場あり 6 エロダクション交響曲」（テキスト＝寺山修司）
■『アサヒグラフ』1966年10月28日号「街に戦場あり 7 喜劇・百万長者」（テキスト＝寺山修司）
■『日本読書新聞』1966年11月7日号「顔 金鋼泳氏」
■『アサヒグラフ』1966年11月11日号「街に戦場あり 9 新宿のロレンス」（テキスト＝寺山修司）
■『日本読書新聞』1966年11月14日号「顔 辻邦生氏」
■『アサヒグラフ』1966年11月25日号「街に戦場あり 11 友情阿けするものぞ」（テキスト＝寺山修司）
■●『現代の眼』1966年12月号「白い風景――国立下総療養所」
■『アサヒグラフ』1966年12月9日号「街に戦場あり 13 参兵の思想」（テキスト＝寺山修司）
■『アサヒグラフ』1966年12月30日号「街に戦場あり 16 銃（最終回）」（テキスト＝寺山修司）

FIGURE 0.1　Bibliography, *Nakahira Takuma Degree Zero-Yokohama*.

■『日本読書新聞』1967年1月30日号「顔 清水幾太」

■『日本読書新聞』1967年2月13日号「顔 秋浜悟史氏」

■『アサヒグラフ』1967年2月17日号「メートへのチャンス」（クレジット＝森山大道、中平卓馬）

●『日本読書新聞』1967年3月6日号「科学的発見としての写真と表現――ゲルンシャイム著 世界の写真史」

■『日本読書新聞』1967年3月24日号「青い空をかえせ！――大気をむしばむ "白いスモッグ"」（クレジット＝森山大道、中平卓馬）

■『現代の眼』1967年4月号「J・バエズひとり」

■『日本読書新聞』1967年4月3日号「顔 富内達氏」

■『アサヒグラフ』1967年4月7日号「医は美容なり――美容革命の戦士たち」（クレジット＝森山大道、中平卓馬）

■『日本読書新聞』1967年4月24日号「顔 桑原幹夫氏」

■『日本読書新聞』1967年5月29日号「顔 阿奈井文彦氏」

●『日本読書新聞』1967年6月5日号「カメラはペシミズムを背負って「欲望」（ミケランジェロ・アントニオーニ監督作品）」

■『日本読書新聞』1967年6月19日号「顔 中島岑夫氏」

■『日本読書新聞』1967年7月17日号「顔 白井健三郎氏」

■『日本読書新聞』1967年7月31日号「顔 金井美恵子氏」

■『現代の眼』1967年8月号「路上」

■『日本読書新聞』1967年9月11日号「顔 鈴木義則氏」

■『アサヒグラフ』1967年10月6日号「入笠山パムのたわむれ 長野県」

■『日本読書新聞』1967年10月16日号「顔 清水幾氏」

■『日本読書新聞』1967年11月27日号「顔 杉本昌純氏」

■『アサヒグラフ』1967年12月29日号「そこにハタハタがいるからだ（秋田県北浦海）」

●『フォト・クリティカ』創刊号（1967年12月）、「不動の視点の崩壊――ウィリアム・クライン〈ニューヨーク〉からの発想」

■●『アサヒグラフ』1968年1月12日号「イメージ・ニッポン '68 みんなバラバラ」

■『日本読書新聞』1968年1月15日号「顔 高藤豊氏」

■『現代の眼』1968年2月号「BIG AGE（2）夜」（テキスト、構成＝岡田隆彦）

■『アサヒグラフ』1968年2月9日号「暮しの中のコンピュータ――その夢と現実」

■『日本読書新聞』1968年2月12日号「顔 富田日出子氏」

●『日本読書新聞』1968年4月15日号「正気が見た狂気と死――細江英公写真展〈とてつもなく悲劇的な喜劇〉の破壊」

■『現代の眼』1968年6月号「BIG AGE（5）文明」（テキスト、構成＝岡田隆彦）

●『デザイン批評』1968年6号、7月刊「写真にとって表現とは何か？ 写真100年――日本人による写真表現の歴史展の意味するもの」

■『アサヒグラフ』1968年7月12日号「不信のとき 「現代」の心理分析」

■『アサヒグラフ』1968年7月26日号「目大の「解放区」」

■『アサヒグラフ』1968年9月20日号「守るも攻めるも目大の……――仮処分執行に抵抗する学生たち」

●『日本読書新聞』1968年9月30日号「写真は言葉を蘇生しうるか――"写真屍" の流行とその背後の問題」

■●『アサヒカメラ』1968年10月号「終電車」（日本の生態10）

■『現代の眼』1968年10月号「BIG AGE（9）夏の名残り〈新宿〉」（テキスト、構成＝岡田隆彦）

■『アサヒグラフ』1968年10月25日号「現代カブ人間考――イザナギ景気の勝員師と大衆」

■●『プロヴォーク』第1号（1968年11月）、多木浩二、岡田隆彦、高梨豊との同人誌

■『美術手帖 写真 いま、ここに――』1968年12月増刊号「街」

■『シネマ69』創刊号（1969年1月）、裏表紙

●『デザイン』1969年1月号「写真・一九六九 リアリティ復権」

■『文藝春秋 漫画読本』1969年1月号「〈ゲリラの眼1〉路上のセックス」

■●『プロヴォーク』第2号（1969年3月）、多木浩二、岡田隆彦、高梨豊、森山大道との同人誌

■●『アサヒカメラ』1969年3月号「熱狂」（日本美新見・3）

●『デザイン』1969年3月号「写真・一九六九 証拠物件」

■『朝日ジャーナル』1969年3月30日号「脱ぐ・勝つ・売る」

■『アサヒグラフ』1969年4月25日号「日本の中の国境――大村収容所の謎の中へ」

■『アサヒグラフ』1969年4月25日号「金嬉老は朝鮮人だったか」

●『デザイン』1969年4月号「フラグメンツ」〈他に写真＝森山大道「ボケ」〉（「〈対談〉写真という言葉をなくせ！」ページ内の写真ページ）

●『デザイン』1969年5月号「写真・一九六九 同時代的（コンテンポラリー）であるとは何か？（1）」（写真＝新倉孝雄「ヨコハマで見た＝ヨコハマのひと」）

●『デザイン』1969年6月号「写真・一九六九 同時代的（コンテンポラリー）であるとは何か？（2）」（写真＝北井一夫「三里塚」）

●『デザイン』1969年7月号「写真・一九六九 同時代的（コンテンポラリー）であるとは何か？（3）」（写真＝牛腸茂雄「who's who」）

■『プロヴォーク』第3号（1969年8月）、多木浩二、岡田隆彦、高梨豊、森山大道との同人誌

●『デザイン』1969年8月号「写真・一九六九 同時代的（コンテンポラリー）であるとは何か？（4）」

■『アサヒグラフ』1969年8月22日号「無名なものの自由と反戦のために！――大阪・熱気の中の "ハンパク"」

■『デザイン』1969年9月号「夜」

■●『朝日ジャーナル』1969年9月14日号「言葉を支える沈黙」（生と転生の潤飾・映像作品・その2）

■●『アサヒグラフ』1969年9月26日号「火の世界」（幻想と怪奇 その3）

■『ニュー・ミュージック・マガジン』1969年10月号「ニュー・ロック・リポート――オレたちにとってのロック」（テキスト＝西山正、油田ひとり）

■『ニュー・ミュージック・マガジン』1969年10月号「夜明けのサンパよう」（詩＝佐藤信）

■『現代の眼』1969年11月号「広場・反戦」

■『朝日ジャーナル』1969年11月2日号「TPO' 69 44 産業総和都市 川崎」

●『アサヒカメラ』1969年12月号「物の影の底にあるもの」（回転展望台・44年12月号）

●『デザイン』1969年12月号「写真・1969 エロスあるいは、エロスではないなにか 森山大道」（写真＝森山大道）

■『アサヒグラフ』1969年12月12日号「自己をかけて権力と対決――東大斗利・山根二郎弁護士」

■『朝日ジャーナル』1969年12月14日号「TPO' 69 50 フェリーボート」

■『アサヒグラフ』1969年12月19日号「バカまるだしヒーロー――香山富三郎の《男のやさしさ》」

●『日本読書新聞』1970年1月19日号「ドキュメンタリー映画 その今日的課題 「パルチザン前史」（土本典昭）と状況の童苦しさ」

■●『アサヒカメラ』1970年2月号「話題の写真をめぐって」（『アサヒグラフ』1969年12月19日号から転載）

FIGURE 0.1 *(continued)*

the mid-1960s to the time of the 2003 exhibition, and traversing a wide range of journalistic domains, Nakahira's diverse output is nearly impossible to contain within a single definitive genre or discursive context. I will explore a number of the diverse threads of Nakahira's photographic and critical practice in later chapters of this volume, but here I want to highlight how through such kaleidoscopic variations a consistent and intensive questioning of urban and media transformation emerges.

From his early collaboration with poet, playwright, and filmmaker Terayama Shūji (1935–1983) in the series "The Streets are a Battlefield" ("Machi ni senjo ari"), in *Asahi Graph*, to the wide range of disparate photographic works and critical essays with titles that included terms such as "city," "landscape," and "streets" ("toshi," "fūkei," "machi") between 1970 and 1977, on the paratextual level of these bibliographic traces we can discern a consistent, though changing, focus on urban topics. The question then becomes, what were the constituent features of Nakahira's urban inquiry? What can we learn from the diversity of discursive engagements that his work evidenced as the contours of this urban pursuit transformed over these decades? How might the changing parameters of Nakahira's questioning of urban materialities and media ecologies open new lines of inquiry that can respond to the general methodological questions I have proposed? How might such an inquiry unsettle or invite generative ways of troubling the boundaries and pathways of our given constellation of disciplinary formations?

But these are not questions that pertain only to Nakahira's photography and critical writings. In fact, when we examine Japan's literary and visual media together, we discover similarly persistent instances of urban inquiry among diverse discursive domains. The transverse dimensions of these inquiries—how they speak across and through the discursive formations that govern them separately—reveal decisive shifts in the urban conditions of cultural possibility of these decades.[3] This book explores the changed aesthetic and geopolitical vocabularies that select literary and visual media generated through dynamic forms of urban inquiry. In particular, I seek to read literary and visual media together to delineate their singular modes of urban inquiry across changing engagements with discursive forms of infrastructure, visuality, and landscape. As suggested by the bibliographic traces of Nakahira's ceaselessly changing strategies, such readings provoke us as contemporary readers to derive a critical understanding of prior media and moments of urban inquiry to reflect on the limitations and possibilities that inform contemporary urban social spaces and media technologies.

I want to provide further definition to the specificity of the changing vocabularies of urban inquiry we encounter by situating these works within an evolving worldwide Cold War context. The Cold War frames this study, allowing me to illuminate the shared, but profoundly uneven, geopolitical system of distributing the boundaries and pathways of power at play in these decades. I am interested in the differing ways literary and visual media disclosed the specifically urban forms of distribution through which the Cold War informed the contours of Japanese social space. Following ongoing reconsiderations of the geopolitical in studies of literary and visual media, I trace how infrastructure, visuality, and landscape constituted important sites in the urban transformation of the Japanese archipelago during the Cold War.[4] I am interested in works that revealed the changing relations of mediation and exchange among infrastructural forms, sensory capacities, and discursive practices produced amidst the rebuilding of Japanese social space. As we shall learn, the Cold War staging of the military-economic logic and logistics of the U.S.-Soviet contest for global hegemony was a crucial factor in Japan's urbanization. However, the curious forms of urban inquiry that we discover in reading literary and visual media together demonstrated that what constituted the geopolitical nature of urban transformation could not be reduced to the a priori discursive practices and instrumentalized logic/logistics of capitalist state power.

As a result, my readings explore the often noisy, illegible, opaque, fragmentary, and incomplete aesthetic vocabularies derived by literary and visual media to interrogate the emergent geopolitical contours they unearthed in Japan's Cold War urban "remaking." I use "remaking" here to index the assemblage of geopolitical forces at play in the material and discursive rebuilding of the archipelago's social spaces in accordance with a Cold War system of military-economic governance. "Remaking," moreover, is used to mark the changing aesthetic strategies of literary and visual media that were invested in deriving new horizons of possibility from the flux of urban materialities and social relations that accompanied this process. At once geopolitical and aesthetic, these residual vocabularies of practices were extracted from the crucible of dissolving social forms and emergent forces unleashed in Japan's Cold War remaking.[5] In this sense, they recall what Michel de Certeau described as the "microbe-like, singular and plural practices which an urbanistic system was supposed to administer or suppress, but which have outlived its decay."[6]

We thus discover new perspectives on the persistent implications of Japan's Cold War remaking, long after the end of the Cold War as the primary horizon of geopolitical determination, by reading this panoply of residual vocabularies together.[7] On the one hand, this approach situates the specific vantage points of literary and visual media from Japan within a worldwide experience of intensified urban change and expansive mediatization during the Cold War.[8] On the other hand, the specificities of the abundant urban vocabularies produced in Japan reveal the diversity of the interrelated forms of urban transformation worldwide at the heart of the Cold War and post—Cold War orders.

TRANSVERSE READINGS

To be clear, the urban ecologies I pursue here are not sought as substitutes or replacements of the expansions of biological and environmental science-based studies of the specific ecologies of urban environments or the ecologically inflected urbanist discourses that have emerged in recent decades. But rather, as part of a humanities-based inquiry into the transformations of urban and media systems that inform our worlds, this study explores the development of critical perspectives on the forces and flow at play in the evolutions of urban ecologies, as made sensible from the Cold War remaking of Japan. By reading a set of residual vocabularies of urban transformation within this context, the geopolitical and aesthetic dimensions of the Cold War's uneven and heterogeneous articulation gain new definition through the specificities of the works we encounter in these chapters.

In part, my approach seeks to expand the modalities of critical knowledge we work with based on the potent redistributions of geopolitical and aesthetic vocabularies we discover in reading literary and visual media together. Along with Rita Felski, whose work has done much to elaborate the limitations of criticism's dominant ways of reading *beyond* the text, a compulsion to seek out an inner or deeper significance of every work, this study seeks to contribute to expanded ways of engaging with the manifold readings *of* a text; or, as Felski puts it, "rather than looking behind the text—for its hidden causes, determining conditions, and noxious motives—we might place ourselves in front of the text, reflecting on what it unfurls, calls forth, makes possible."[9] This positioning (as an act of dispositioning and repositioning) of our critical reading in "front" of, rather than beyond, the text, is an invitation to consider the act of reading as something other than a procedure for conveying meaning from one position to another within a static set of fixed coordinates (author, text, context, and reader, for instance). Instead, we can undertake reading by attending to its operations among a distributive set of thresholds within a multidimensional constellation of discrete but variable space-times, working through a continuum of mediating relations in a given instance of reading and the sensory intensities it makes available as such. Reorienting our plane of critical focus *across* and *through* the shifting thresholds of a text to trace a fluid distribution of frames that organize our readings, we need not simply rely on a selection of fixed intervals (text-context, author-text, text-reader, reader-author), arbitrarily privileging one over another as the ultimate horizon of a text's meaning. While this is a rather abstract proposition at this point, my own readings will emphasize the ways the texts assembled here themselves modeled diverse and fluid strategies of reading and relating across and through the manifold strata of forces at play in their worlds.[10]

In this sense, these chapters participate in the expansion of critical modes of reading to better understand how literary and visual media generated new geopolitical and aesthetic vocabularies from the Cold War remaking of Japan. I want to understand how such novel vocabularies were themselves wrought from changing strategies of "reading" the flux of the material and affective infrastructures that accompanied Japan's integration within the United States' Cold War military-economic order. I mobilize these ways of reading to delineate how the Cold War and its "afterlives" continue to shape the boundaries and pathways of possibility for thinking critically (in the expanded senses Felski and others invite us to consider) about ongoing urban transformations.[11] From this attention to the critical role of reading *in* and *of* different media, I seek to develop an understanding of how literary and visual media *read* differently the geopolitical and aesthetic conditions of their respective media and moments. These differences allow us to elaborate the possibilities and limits encountered while reading *across* a range of media forms. In seeking ways of reading—and reading together—the specific vocabularies of literary and visual media, we can discern decisive changes in the ecological contours of the disparate strategies we encounter along the way. This volume seeks to contribute a nuanced look at a specific set of vocabularies as singular mappings of the limiting conditions and latent potentials of critical responses to the Cold War in Japan to the study of urban and media cultures. Just as the literary and visual media examined here sought to illuminate the changing geopolitical and aesthetic horizons of Japan's Cold War remaking as part of their refusal of capitalist state power, the modalities of knowing and becoming that these works reveal, moreover, deepen our understanding of the historical and contemporary struggles over the use and abuse of urban and media infrastructures.

The expanded strategies of "reading" found among these chapters invite us to consider how they engaged in the kinds of mapping that Alberto Toscano and Jeff Kinkle have argued constitute an important aesthetic problem for the global present; to discover "ways of representing the complex and dynamic relations intervening between the domains of production, consumption and distribution, and their strategic political mediations, ways of making the invisible visible."[12] However, such mappings are not simply seeking to produce a legible representation of an absent or otherwise inaccessible totality. As these chapters hope to demonstrate, the different readings produced a diagram of the sensible relations and forms of exchange sampled from the flux of urban transformation. On the most basic level, the readings produced by these texts can be regarded as participating in what Jacques Rancière describes as the act of dissensus at stake in the redrawing of the boundaries of the political. "Politics invents new forms of collective enunciation; it reframes the given by inventing new ways of making sense of the sensible, new configurations between the visible and the invisible, and between the audible and the inaudible, new distributions of space and time—in short, new bodily capacities."[13] Moreover, I am interested in disclosing the entangled mesh of boundaries and pathways that constituted new possibilities for reimagining the material and affective exchanges

among humans and nonhumans, as well as the ontological and epistemological thresholds of the worlds they shared; in other words, in delineating the ecological relations such texts traversed.

From the explosive expansions of its historical urban centers to
the intensive (dis/re)integration of its peripheries, Japan's urban transformation in these decades enveloped the entire archipelago.[14] In this
sense, we cannot limit our understanding of the urban to the cities
themselves. Instead, I seek to grasp the specific contours of mediation
and exchange produced among the different thresholds of the distributive systems from the most immediate layers of city life to those of
geographically remote margins. Regarding the urban as a continuum of
thresholds rather than as a static set of discrete places, these texts compel us to consider the distributive forces that patterned the everyday
rhythms and flows of the emergent urban orders produced by the Cold
War.[15] Hence, a crucial problem encountered in this study is the entanglement of the urban as an object of knowledge and subject of practice
itself. In asking how each text differently grappled with the urban across
and through these diverse strata, including the postcolonial conditions
of Okinawa's "reversion" to Japan, we gain a better understanding of the
range of diverse layers of transformation at play.

In the context of these decades, a discourse of landscape, or *fūkei-
ron*, emerged in the wake of late 1960s wave of radical student movement
to mark precisely the archipelagic scale of these urban transformations.
The reconceptualization of landscape emerged through a convergence
of film theory and practice forged in the making of the 1969 film *A.K.A.
Serial Killer* (*Ryakushō: renzoku shasatsuma*).[16] Seeking to overcome the
limitations of existing forms of documentary practice, the filmmaking
collective decided to record only the shifting vantage points brought
into view by retracing the itinerant movements of the film's subject.
In the process, the traveling team of critics and crew confronted an
expansive landscape wherever they went. "Whether in the center or the
countryside, the city or the periphery, in Tokyo or the 'homeland,'[*furusato*] there was only a homogenized landscape." The essay's author,
prominent film critic Matsuda Masao, critiqued a predominant binary
logic that sustained existing celebrations of either the urban center
or the rural periphery as loci for novel forms of political collectivity.[17]
At its most basic level, the term "landscape" named a radically expanded

geopolitical imaginary that spanned both poles of this predominant binary. "We must recognize that at the end of the 1960s the schematic opposition between 'Tokyo' and 'homeland,' presupposed when Tanigawa Gan composed 'Don't go to Tokyo, invent your homeland,' no longer has any currency. The rapid growth of Japanese monopoly capital blatantly makes clear its aim in the increasing homogenization of the Japanese archipelago as one gigantic city."[18]

In Yuriko Furuhata's exhaustive study of Japan's radical cinema of these decades, *Cinema of Actuality: Japanese Avant-Garde Filmmaking in the Season of Image Politics*, she reads the emergence of *fūkei-ron* evidenced through such films as *A.K.A. Serial Killer* as "a way to look beyond the documentary qualities of images of urban landscapes and to extract a particular diagram of power from them—that of governmental power, which operates through subtle, noncoercive, and economic forms of policing and managing the urban population."[19] These insights invite a changed approach to the expansive and extensive urban transformations wrought through the remaking of the Japanese archipelago. While landscape discourse indexed one crucial point of inflection of the geopolitical and aesthetic dimensions of urban change in these decades, the evolving urban vocabularies delineated in these chapters make sensible a vast constellation of urban ecologies traversed by a range of moments and media of critical inquiry.

CHAPTER SUMMARIES

In Chapter 1, I outline the definitive role played by vehicular mobility, and its correlate, traffic, in revealing the fraught infrastructure of Japan's Cold War remaking.[20] I engage the geopolitical dimensions of Japan's "traffic war" produced by the proliferation of automobiles and professional drivers with the infrastructural lens of experimental documentary filmmaker Tsuchimoto Noriaki's transportation-related public relations films produced on the eve of the 1964 Tokyo Olympics. This chapter explores Tsuchimoto's cinematic cross sections of Tokyo as a central relational core in the elaboration of administrable networks of transportation, communication, and exchange where the Cold War reimagining and revisioning of the archipelago's social spaces took root in the early 1960s. Engaging with critical interest in infrastructure's role as a geopolitical medium that immobilizes even as it accelerates, which as Paul Virilio famously noted, "the more speed increases, the faster freedom decreases," this exploration of Tsuchimoto's efforts to remake the PR film revealed an important geopolitical and aesthetic battleground in the Cold War reimagining and revisioning of Japan's rapidly urbanizing social spaces.[21] While Japan's integration within the United States' Cold War military-economic order provoked widespread protests from the late 1950s to the anti-U.S.-Japan Security Treaty demonstrations in 1960, the ambitions of Tokyo's Olympic Games reconstruction revealed how the geopolitical often takes root through the infrastructural as pervasive structuring forms. Making legible the geopolitical within the infrastructural, Tsuchimoto's work invests the explosion of the urban fabric heralded by Olympic reconstruction with an embedded locus of potent aesthetic affordances.

Chapter 2 takes up this embedded view to explore the singular forms of visuality of writer Abe Kōbō's literary inquiry into changing contours of urban society. We learn how Abe's 1967 novel, *The Ruined Map*, derived an acutely visual literary vocabulary from what, I argue, amounts to a topological diagraming of emergent infrastructural networks and abstracted spaces, such as large-scale public housing projects, expressways, and Shinjuku Station's renovated underground plaza (*hiroba*). These spaces, as Jordan Sand describes in his study of the political and discursive struggles over Japan's urban commons in the late 1960s, constituted a marked shift in the spatial horizons of possibility, as symbolized by the changed status of the *hiroba* into a space of transit.[22] Reading these changing contours topologically, the visuality of Abe's novel revealed the environmentalization of the sensible that accompanied the Cold War remaking of the archipelago, even as it located potential new forms of solidarity as part of Abe's ongoing urban inquiry.[23] With the sensibility of the social at stake, Abe's exploration of urban visuality opens a new horizon of inquiry into the geopolitical and aesthetic conditions of urban society.

Chapter 3 delineates photographer and critic Nakahira Takuma's pursuit of a photographic vocabulary of urban becoming, exploring his 1970 photobook *For a Language to Come* and his integral participation in an emergent discourse of landscape. Drawing attention to how networked forms of transportation, communication, and exchange gave rise to an increasingly homogenized material and sensory environment, Nakahira's writings and photography sought what he described as new vocabularies of thought from the gap between powerlessness and possibility that constituted the conditions of this landscape. Tracing the entangled trajectories of the radical discourse of landscape and Nakahira's photographic pursuit of a "language to come," we encounter a shared set of limiting conditions that necessitated a profoundly different vocabulary for grasping the geopolitical and aesthetic thresholds of the all-encompassing urban landscape.

Chapter 4 reveals Nakahira's pursuit of such a vocabulary, as further developed in his first essay collection, *Why an Illustrated Botanical Dictionary? Nakahira Takuma's Collected Writings on Visual Media* (1973), and the large-scale photographic installation, *Overflow* (1974). Reading the turbid materiality of his changed praxis of urban inquiry, this chapter explores Nakahira's efforts to theorize and make sensible, a fragmentary, living fabric of transverse relations antithetical to the totalized environments and smoothly integrated forms of infrastructure, visuality, and landscape that became operative in the "intermodal" logistics of the Cold War remaking of the archipelago.[24] The term "illustrated dictionary" came to delimit the parameters of Nakahira's striking redistribution of the thresholds of human and nonhuman worlds in both his writings and photography. By tracing the development and depletion of the "illustrated dictionary" form across a number of discursive contexts, we discover how Nakahira's urban praxis sought to question the place of photographic visuality within highly systematized sensory environments. As such, this chapter expands the scope of our inquiry to explore the specific forms of photographic visuality at play in the integrated systems of infrastructure, visuality, and landscape that became operational in the reconstruction of the geopolitical and aesthetic conditions of possibility in the early 1970s.

Chapter 5 gives further definition to the distributive thresholds embodied in the "reversion" of the administrative rights of Okinawa from the U.S. military to the Japanese government in 1972. From 1974 to 1976, Nakahira would travel to the islands of Okinawa, Amami, and Tokara to interrogate the role of photographic visuality in the redrawing of the boundaries and pathways of the Japanese archipelago. Attending to the changing contours of a "permanent revolution of the gaze" developed through Nakahira's post-reversion texts, we discover the deeply embedded fissures and contradictions subsumed within the Cold War remaking of the relations among these archipelagos. Nakahira's work starkly disclosed the thresholds of what becomes (im)possible in the dispossession and depletion that delineated the postcolonial conditions and shifting discursive elaborations of photographic visuality at play in Okinawa's reversion.

In Chapter 6, I outline definitive shifts in the discursive contours of the literary and visual media of urban transformation of the late 1970s, a moment illuminated by the changed trajectories in the work of the central figures explored in the prior chapters. Rather than delineating the endpoints of diverse strategies of reading urban change, this chapter elaborates a horizon of resonance shared among historical and contemporary urban image practices. From the entangled redistributions of the critical vocabularies of historical and contemporary urban praxis, I close with readings of the urban ecologies they model when read together in the present tense.

EXPANDED ECOLOGIES

In the interest of contributing to the expansion of the geopolitical and aesthetic vocabularies of urban change and disclosing the limiting conditions confronted therein, I want to provisionally assemble these readings as the constituent elements of an ecological inquiry. My use of the term "urban ecology" encompasses not only the material and imaginary conditions of limitation and possibility that span human and nonhuman coexistence, but also situates urban phenomena alongside frameworks such as "media ecology" that afford a dynamic understanding of the complex entanglements of materialities and sensory capacities. As Matthew Fuller notes, the term ecology "is one of the most expressive language currently has to indicate the massive and dynamic interrelation of processes and objects, beings and things, patterns and matter."[25] As the texts undertaken in this study demonstrate, urban infrastructure and media systems were crucial sites and stakes in Japan's Cold War remaking due to the ways they informed how people see, know, and relate in a changing world. For instance, describing the eruption of visual practices centered on Shinjuku in the late 1960s and early 1970s, Yukio

Lippit has noted how such works produced, "a specific mode of interrelational subjectivity," in which, "the resulting subject was not so much a *flaneur*-observer of the streets, but a participant in a dynamic process of becoming through encounters with the fragments of an abstracted, post-industrial landscape."[26] Like the performance of "interrelational" modalities of becoming, the ecological approach I elaborate across these chapters seeks to delineate the matrices of mediating relations and sensory intensities, which engaged with the multiple registers and scales of change at play in the urban transformations that shaped Japan's Cold War remaking.

This inquiry is, moreover, inspired by ecosophical and ecocritical forms of thought, as first articulated by Félix Guattari in his pivotal essay, "The Three Ecologies," in seeking to delineate the mediating relations and sensory intensities of Japan's Cold War remaking. Breaking from the dialectics of bureaucratic Marxism and dominant modes of psychoanalysis, Guattari's work sought to delimit the prospects of ethical-aesthetic modes of critical praxis for grasping complex and interrelated sociohistorical transformations. Guattari's ecological mode of inquiry affords a means of traversing the differences and shared mediating relations across/among discrete domains of transformation, such as the mental, the social, and the environmental.[27] In defining the parameters of a general ecology for which Guattari's inquiry was oriented, Erich Hörl has described how such ethical-aesthetic pursuits in the present necessitate "the collaboration of a multiplicity of human and nonhuman agents: it is something like the cipher of a new thinking of togetherness and of a great cooperation of entities and forces, which has begun to be significant for contemporary thought; hence it forces and drives a radically relational onto-epistemological renewal."[28] In contrast to the capture and control of everything that informs the history of capital's cybernetic environmentalization of the world (a history profoundly shaped by the Cold War, but not reducible to it), Hörl locates the contemporary horizons of a general ecology in the unfolding of relations among techno-ecologically comingled human and nonhuman becoming. In this context, by framing my readings as urban ecologies, I seek to make sensible an assemblage of mediating relations and sensory intensities made available by urban coformation of human and nonhuman becoming. Despite, or because of, the fact that the vocabularies and materialities of ontological and epistemological flux that pervade these readings were produced at an earlier stage of urban development, they remain vital for defining an ecological mode of inquiry through the frames of an urban milieu.

As one crucial mediating figure among the social and material relations of our techno-ecological conditions, the mundane infrastructural networks that proliferate among historical and contemporary urban transformations remain a useful starting point in delineating the geopolitical and aesthetic dimensions of Japan's Cold War remaking. Urban geographers have explored the dynamic forms of relation that infrastructure networks sustain, often highlighting how their simple material connective functions betray a vast constellation of entangled social relations. "Infrastructure networks provide the distribution grids and topological connections that link systems and practices of production with systems and practices of consumption. They unevenly bind spaces together across cities, regions, nations and international boundaries whilst helping also to define the material and social dynamics, and divisions, within and between urban spaces."[29] The vast continuum of scales and magnitudes that the dynamic mediating figures of infrastructural networks span is evocative of the potential they harbor for considerations of how literary and visual media generate novel mappings of the material and mental relations such networks inscribe within the contours of social space.

The urban ecologies materialized here, moreover, weave together a number of entangled discursive trajectories for locating emergent affinities and amalgams *through*—as well as transverse openings, and solidarities *across*—otherwise-discrete domains. The resultant composite vocabularies made available in these readings work to proliferate lines of inquiry and exchange among differing ways of understanding literary and visual media together with the urban ecologies they make sensible. The aim of framing these readings as contributions to an ecological mode of inquiry, however, is not merely to conflate the specificities of literary and visual media together as part of a unitary horizon of techno-ecological "connectedness." But rather, as Swati Chattopadhyay suggests in her illuminating rethinking of infrastructure at play in the neoliberal urbanization of India, my exploration of infrastructural figures and an ecological way of reading these is unsettling in the sense of attempting to, "use the current vocabulary otherwise, by moving it out of its familiar usage and contexts. The task of defamiliarization is meant to unhinge this vocabulary from its existing certitudes and generate new contexts of meaning, new historical possibilities."[30] Thus, my attempt at readings of ecologies includes the necessity to unsettle and "unhinge" the nested signifying economies that govern urban media as discursive geopolitical and aesthetic constructions.

Likewise, the vocabularies that emerge across these chapters sit awkwardly within the inherited genealogies of critical thought, each inhabiting a different position that is clearly critical of capitalist modernity and attendant forms of cultural modernism. Yet, even into the late 1970s, we find much of what these texts evidence is not exactly postmodern in the myriad ways we might expect them to be. Thinkers like Nakahira were clearly participating in the rendering of different modes of critical inquiry at odds with the resilient discursive undercurrents of modernism that were endemic to the convolutions of the Cold War's worldwide military-economic logistical order following the formal suspension of the Vietnam War in 1975. Yet, as we shall see in the latter half of this volume, Nakahira's response to the integrated urban and media systems of monopoly capital, as Nakahira described the definitive structuring force of the era, was not necessarily a rejection of the revolutionary meta-narratives of a leftist geopolitical imaginary, nor was it a descent into the ceaseless play of signs often derided by reductive stereotypes of postmodern cultural practice.

While a comparative mapping of the different intellectual itineraries of feminist, poststructuralist, and postmodern thinkers across similarly situated postimperial/postcolonial Cold War partner states such as Japan, France, and Germany would be beyond the scope of this introduction, it should suffice to suggest that a reexamination of the contemporaneous elaboration of critical urban and media discourses and their respective contexts situated differently within the geopolitical division of the world would afford genealogies somewhat different from those codified within the North American context.[31] What emerges from the specific vocabularies explored here is thus an expansion of the conditions of possibility for such a reexamination and an invitation for deeper forms of exchange across these genealogies of critical thought.

RESIDUAL FUTURES

As we set out to traverse the disparate media and moments of the urban ecologies examined in the chapters that follow, I'd like to close by inviting readers to consider how these media might be read as residual futures; that is, not only as traces left from the bygone past, but as pathways for reflecting on both the contemporary and the yet-to-come. As these chapters make legible, these media exposed—and continue to expose us to—deep resonances among historical and contemporary efforts to produce expanded critical vocabularies and novel perspectives on urban change through literary and visual media. And in reading these media together, we obtain ways to grasp decisive sociohistorical changes that were articulated through dynamic shifts in the regional and worldwide geopolitical orders of their day. Such perspectives are crucial for efforts to work against the violent depletion of futures that have come to define the geopolitical and aesthetic conditions of the post—Cold War world. Working through and across the Cold War's distributive thresholds, we discover ways of reading the shared limits that govern the collective horizons of possibility evidenced by the residual futures lining the present.

As Henri Lefebvre conceived the urban, it cannot be grasped "as an accomplished reality, situated behind the actual in time, but, on the contrary, as a horizon, an illuminating virtuality."[32] For Lefebvre, the urban was not only a sociohistorical reality inscribed with a polyphony of divergent material and discursive formations, but was a phenomenon that encompassed virtual and latent arrangements and practices displaced by capitalist state power. Similarly, Raymond Williams identified the residual and the emergent as potent resources for delineating nondominant "structures of feeling" in the present, as ways of imagining futures in a state of "pre-emergence, active and pressing but not yet fully articulated, rather than the evident emergence which could be more confidently named."[33] Just as the need to identify such residual futures remains an urgent task, this book further elaborates ways to read the literary and visual media of Japan's Cold War remaking as important vocabularies for questioning the contemporary horizons of urban transformation in Japan and worldwide.

That urban transformations should inform and shape human affective and sensory capacities (as well as the social and ethical conditions of possibility these inform) has long been a rich source of inquiry among a wide range of discourses. However, the ecologies traced here suggest another dimension to consider: the Cold War's most pervasive geopolitical manifestations were derived through the production of particular ways of sensing and becoming in the world, not just as the battle of one political ideology over another. Thus, along with the proliferation of nuclear weapons/energy/waste, the weaponization of networked information/surveillance technologies, and the military-industrial-knowledge complex, we would do well to include the development of urban infrastructural/logistic systems in a continued interrogation of the ecological devastation and expansive forms of violence wrought by the Cold War. At the same time, we need to attend to the production of novel subjectivities and relations with nonhumans that these urban ecologies afforded. One of the central aims of this volume is to demonstrate that as a diversified range of geopolitical and aesthetic vocabularies are made sensible and brought into intensified exchange with contemporary ecological and materialist humanities discourses, the critical thresholds of (im)possibility shared among diverse media and moments of radical critique become available for collective transformation.

CHAPTER ONE

Prelude to the Traffic War

Infrastructural Aesthetics of the Cold War

Paul Virilio theorized the development of the logistics of war as the general conditions of the politics of speed, which crossed a critical threshold of planetary extension during the decades of the Cold War. Along with potent speculative insights regarding the transformed conditions of political agency that resulted, Virilio delineates a transhistorical diagram of speed's dispossessive force through a figuration of infrastructure as the mediating structures where these developments unfold. "The blindness of the speed of means of communicating destruction is not a liberation from geopolitical servitude, but the extermination of space as the field of freedom of political action. We only need refer to the necessary controls and constraints of the railway, airway or highway infrastructures to see the fatal impulse: the more speed increases, the faster freedom decreases."[1] As the most mundane and yet constitutive framework of the patterns of circulation and mediation that inform our lives, infrastructure matters in profound ways. Furthermore, as Keller Easterling reminds us in *Extrastatecraft: The Power of Infrastructure Space*, "far from hidden, infrastructure is now the overt point of contact and access between us all—the rules governing the space of everyday life."[2] Infrastructures are at once constitutive as the material forms and circulatory protocols that bind the world together and yet defuse as the habituated patterning of the pathways and boundaries of communication, transportation, and exchange that mediate selves, others, and material things.

This study explores ways of seeing both of these aspects of the infrastructural from the perspective of the urban ecologies made sensible in works from the transformative decades of the 1960s and 1970s. As the infrastructural histories of the Japanese archipelago's remaking make clear, these decades inaugurated a period of extensive building of logistical and transportation networks, one that continued in fits and starts into the present day. Transportation historian Kakumoto Ryōhei has described the "miracle" of Japan's postwar "transportation revolution" (*kōtsū kakumei*). Undertaken from a technocratic perspective based on rationalization and efficiency, the contradictions effaced in his narratives are often telling of the blind spots governing the retrospective historical accounts of infrastructural developments. However, at minimum, Kakumoto's account reveals how a changing sense of "speed" and distance informed widespread adoption of automobiles in Japan, while overlooking the profound changes in social space induced by automobile networks of transportation.[3] "More important than the speed doubling of transportation technologies was the generalization of automobiles and the building of roads. . . . The automobile has given the people [*kokumin*] a wider sphere of activity. For the Japanese people's sense of distance, this was a great change, and people looked upon the Japanese archipelago with a new sensibility."[4]

Along with reconsiderations of the worldwide Cold War that accentuate the everyday itself as the locus of its most durable political transformations, like those theorized by Virilio four decades ago, we might expand our understanding of the infrastructure as part and parcel of the evolving contours of a geopolitical "battleground" that continues to inform our world in underexplored ways.[5] Asking how the emergent infrastructural structures and "new sensibility" these afforded can be regarded as a constitutive geopolitical as well as aesthetic "front" in Japan's Cold War remaking, I will set out to explore an early moment in the generalization of the automobile on the eve of the 1964 Tokyo Olympics. Tsuchimoto Noriaki's 1964 film, *On the Road: A Document*, was ostensibly made to promote traffic safety among drivers seeking driver licenses.[6] Yet, it was never seen in its intended format as a result of its rejection by the film's sponsor, the Metropolitan Police Traffic Bureau. Making its subject the "traffic war" (*kōtsū sensō*) rather than "traffic safety" may have had something to do with its rejection. However, while it failed to merely illustrate the dangers of driving, the film offers a compelling starting point for considering the entanglement of aesthetics and geopolitics at play in the Cold War remaking of Japan in the 1960s and 1970s.

First, I will outline the formal aspects and historical conditions of the film's production within the context of public relations documentary films in Japan at the time. The aim of this initial step is to delineate a specific set of historical and methodological contingencies and choices that shaped the film's production. These help to ground our understanding of the film's novel modes of thinking about the urban by accounting for the specific ways that such contingencies and choices informed the film's capacities to disclose the forces at play in Tokyo's Olympic remaking and serve as a critique of the conditions of documentary film itself. In so doing, I argue that the film's unexpectedly experimental visual style offers an important way of seeing the Cold War at play in Japan's most intensive phase of urbanization. At the same time, by detailing the contingencies and choices of the filmmaker, this chapter will illuminate the crucial stakes for literary and visual media in articulating novel geopolitical and aesthetic vocabularies. One of the hallmarks of the specific urban ecologies that emerged from Japan's Cold War remaking during the decades of the 1960s and 1970s can be identified as a struggle over the thresholds of aesthetic and geopolitical legibility. The problem of how to make sense of the drastic transformations in the material and affective contours of Japan's urbanizing social spaces was profoundly entangled with the problem of how to make sensible the changing conditions of possibility for a wide range of leftist movements and correlate discourses at the time.

In addition to the important place that Tsuchimoto's *On the Road: A Document* plays in Japanese documentary histories as a crucial site of experimentation with documentary aesthetics, the film furthermore offers important insights into the development of the documentary methodologies and stylistic choices that informed much of Tsuchimoto's later work. Renowned for his series of films engaging with the Minamata environmental-medical disaster, Tsuchimoto's work occupies a singular role in the histories of both documentary film and ecological criticism in Japan to this day. As I hope to demonstrate here, the experimental style of this earlier Tsuchimoto film not only tested the limits of PR documentary film aesthetics but also offers a vivid portrait of the material and affective "battleground" of the Cold War played out in the destruction and reconstruction of Japan's urban social spaces. As such, I will examine how the film's singular way of seeing materialized a central site and stake in the struggle to render sensible the geopolitical horizons of Japan's Cold War remaking inaugurated by the 1964 Tokyo Olympics.

Tsuchimoto got his start as a filmmaker in the Iwanami Film Production Studios. There he worked with director Hani Susumu as assistant director on the film *Bad Boys* (*Furyō Shōnen*) in 1961, and made his film directorial debut with *An Engineer's Assistant* (*Aru Kikan Joshi*) in 1963, just one year before *On the Road: A Document*.[7] After what Tsuchimoto describes as a "failed" attempt to produce a television documentary on the Minamata disaster in 1965, he would again return to Minamata in the midst of the student upheavals of the late 1960s to produce his "masterpiece," *Minamata: The Victims and Their World* (*Minamata: Kanja-san to sono sekai*, 1971). Thereafter, Tsuchimoto made no less than ten more films and authored four books related to Minamata disease and the medical, ecological, social, and other aspects of a disaster that, until recently, had remained unparalleled in Japan's long history of environmental disasters.[8] While Minamata became the filmmaker's lifework under conditions and in contexts quite different from those of *On the Road: A Document*, the contingencies and choices informing Tsuchimoto's 1964 traffic safety film revealed both complex forms of continuity and profound differences among the earlier PR films and later masterworks.

We discover, for instance, that the realities—however fragmentary and discontinuous—documented by Tsuchimoto's films were the sites and stakes in highly contentious struggles over the very possibility of their representation. And, as a result, the relations among filmmaker, documentary subject, and audience played a crucial role as the battleground where realities were made visible or otherwise sensible, despite the fact that (or precisely because) they were unseen or forcibly disavowed in the normalizing violence of the everyday. Thus, while the problems of environmental disaster in the Minamata films might appear orders of magnitude different from the problems of traffic and transportation safety found in the early films, each film invites us to consider a variety of important relationships among the materialities and affects shared by viewer and viewed. By inquiring into the relationships among

Tsuchimoto's documentary subjects, for instance, we can at the same time inquire into ways of relating among discontinuous moments and audiences mediated by these works. It is in this sense I seek to consider the way of seeing generated in Tsuchimoto's early film as a starting point for an ecological inquiry into the geopolitical and aesthetic conditions of possibility wrought in the infrastructural battleground of Japan's Cold War remaking.

TRAVERSING THE TRAFFIC WAR

On the Road: A Document begins with a title text, stating that the film portrays a "cross section" of the daily "traffic war" in Tokyo of 1964. According to the revised *Dictionary of Postwar History*, "traffic war" was a term born in the 1960s to describe the increasing number of traffic accident fatalities.[9] The number of traffic fatalities, particularly pedestrians being killed by drivers, rapidly began to rise from the late 1950s, exceeding 10,000 fatalities in 1959. The number continued to rise until fatalities peaked in 1970 at 16,765. However, despite the stark clarity of these statistical traces of the human implications of automobiles, the term *traffic war* is profoundly ambiguous. As the only form of narration in a work lacking a narrator, or any other narrative structure other than the scripted elements discussed below, this title performs a crucial role in establishing a determinative framework for integrating the discontinuous scenes and passages that constitute the film. Inflected with this reference to the specific time and place of Tokyo 1964, the film's stated aim of portraying a "cross section" of the "traffic war" establishes the viewer's orientation as someone examining or surveying a chart or diagram from the start. Like a mechanic reading cross sections of an engine to reveal how the individual pieces fit together, such a position offers the viewer a sense of mastery or ownership over the world portrayed. However, accompanying the words of the title text, the soundtrack quickly complicates the certainty of such a position with a sense of doubt or confusion evoked by the rhythmic oscillations of woodwinds and percussion, quickly followed by a fanfare of asynchronous trumpets and trilling flutes as the film's title appears. An ominous cacophony, or perhaps discordant polyphony, thus commences *On the Road: A Document*, with the cracked surfaces of streets gliding under the transparent letters

"On the Road" of the title screen. As viewers soon discover, in form and content, the film betrays the most obvious meanings of the illustrative function of a cross section. Rather than producing a diagram of its world, the film instead consists of a series of discontinuous vectors, and variable velocities, of movement caught on film. In a dynamic visual style that ceaselessly traverses a kaleidoscopic array of spatial-temporal distortions, such as tight zooms that collapse the field of view, or slow motion sequences that momentarily arrest the ceaseless flows of traffic, the film renders even the most everyday act of crossing the street into an epic life or death struggle. While viewers are informed that what they are seeing is the "traffic war" of Tokyo 1964—or perhaps Tokyo, 1964 as a "traffic war"—they are never given a coherent global perspective of how those terms are bound together. Instead, the viewers are brought into direct confrontation with a named but undefined set of relations among "traffic war," Tokyo, and 1964 as the film's documentary subject from the start.

The localized vantage point through which its portrait of the relations among these terms unfold is provided by taxi drivers. The film's detailed look at the daily struggles of a taxi driver to survive this "traffic war" discloses a tense and potentially dangerous context of urban transformation. At the same time, throughout the film we see fragmentary glimpses of Tokyo's reconstruction for the 1964 Olympic Games, as the taxi's itinerant commutes reveal many of the definitive Olympic construction projects. Through the film's cross section of the "traffic war," the dismantling and reconstruction of the city is more than a background, more than the mere historical context framing the subject of the film. Instead, the film evidences an incomplete urban subject in its becoming; it records an emergent assembly of forces at play in the reconstruction of Tokyo's streets, disclosing a raucous zone of encounter where the infrastructural horizons of urban transformation make contact with the viewer's sensory capacities.

On its most basic formal level, the film consists of sequences depicting different aspects of a central protagonist's life as a taxi driver. In some cases, sequences portray the protagonist as he interacts with a cast of coworkers, family members, police officers, and the strangers who hire his taxi. While the film draws on scripted elements and casts amateurs in scripted roles, many of these sequences merely depict the taxi, the streets, and the relentless flows of traffic. Often, the film's attention slips

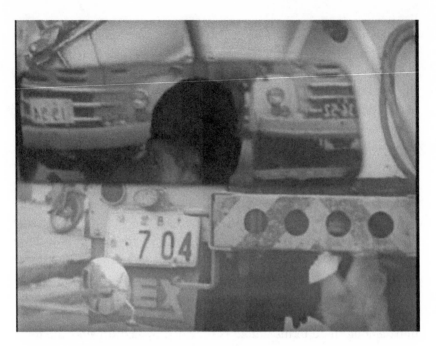

FIGURE 1.1 Tsuchimoto Noriaki, *On the Road: A Document*, 1964.

away from the human protagonist and extraneous aspects of urban life come into view. The illustrative function of a cross section is further frustrated by the nonnarrative structure that refuses to fix a coherent meaning or reading to what is depicted. The discrete slices of the taxi driver's life and fleeting glimpses of urban reconstruction are mediated together through a proliferation of visual styles and editorial methods. As much a cross section of urban destruction and reconstruction as it is a cataloging of experimental film techniques, the singular vision of the world presented in the film reveals the emergent infrastructural aesthetics of the traffic among human bodies and nonhuman materialities.

DECONSTRUCTING THE PR FILM, SEEING DECONSTRUCTION

Produced as a PR film, *On the Road* was originally commissioned by the Metropolitan Police Traffic Bureau to be shown when one's driver license was renewed. When we consider that the only conditions stipulated by the Traffic Bureau were, according to Tsuchimoto, "make it however you like, as long as the basic theme is traffic safety," we gain a sense of the unique constellation of possibilities and limitations of PR film during a pivotal moment in the history of documentary film in Japan.[10] According to Tsuchimoto, he and his filmmaking team sought to interrogate the larger social problems behind the "traffic war," rejecting the sponsor's notion of traffic safety.[11] At the same time, the film was the product of a moment that saw the breakdown of the codified practices of PR film, and part of an intensive moment in the theorization and formal innovation of documentary aesthetics in Japan. Thus, the film's experimental aesthetic method of making a cross section of the "traffic war" can be seen as part of the changing contours of documentary praxis at the time. As Japanese film historian Abé Mark Nornes notes in his seminal study, *Japanese Documentary Film: The Meiji Era Through Hiroshima*, the early 1960s were a pivotal era when a younger generation of filmmakers and critics sought to break from established conventions and production frameworks, marking an outpouring of theorization and novel modalities of documentary practice.

The 1950s was also the era in which the fields of public relations film and television drove spectacular growth in documentary production. The high-growth economy demanded moving images to create sellable reputations among consumers and to sell product, and the television networks hungered for programming. However, this exacerbated tensions within documentary that were strongly reminiscent of the 1930s. Public relations films required filmmakers who would toe the line in terms of style, and divergence through stylistic excess or apparent critique was disciplined. The tensions this created within the documentary and PR film community, which was still dominated by the Japanese Communist Party and left-leaning artists, came to a head on the eve of the Security Treaty renewal in the late 1950s. Led by such filmmakers as Matsumoto Toshio and Kuroki Kazuo, younger filmmakers brought the dominant style under severe critique and pointed to its roots in the wartime cinema. They wrote articles, published journals, held conferences, and forged a politicized, highly experimental documentary cinema.[12]

When illuminated by this rich historical context of intensive meth-odological and theoretical questioning of documentary form, the film's aesthetic fluidity and discordant portrait of urban transformation are no less extraordinary. Tsuchimoto himself later suggestively described the point of making the film precisely in terms of making the city sensible in a specific way. Collaborating with former colleagues from his days working at Iwanami Film Productions, the director and crew sought to "render the city as a space where thousands of people die like insects killed within a beautiful transparent glass bottle, completely unawares."[13] This collective decision to capture the violence of an invisible urban totality informs the film's portrayal of the relations among the taxi drivers and the "traffic war." As one critic points out, Tsuchimoto's depiction of the city as an "insect killing device" links the style and content of the film:

> On the Road: A Document was a work that most succeeded in achieving the synthesis of documentary and avant-garde methods that Matsumoto Toshio called for at the time. Although it was a PR film promoting traffic safety, Tsuchimoto depicted Tokyo on the eve of the Olympics like a hell painting. "We shot it so the cars would be terrifying. Traffic safety is not a problem with the driver; it is a problem with the city. I called it an insect killing device, like putting cyanide in a bottle, where insects come flying and die instantly, even though it just looks like clear air. That's how we wanted to capture the city."[14]

The trope of the insect-killing glass bottle that Tsuchimoto mobilized to describe the urban focal point of this film reveals his efforts to discover a means of capturing the changing dimensions of urban social space—dimensions that despite, or because of, their transparency go unseen and unrecognized as a profoundly violent mechanism. Moreover, Tsuchimoto and his crew sought to go beyond the instrumental views of the Police Traffic Bureau, which commissioned the film to promote traffic safety, of the dangers of traffic accidents. "We could in no way make a film that could immediately 'prevent' traffic accidents. Instead we wanted to get to the root of the problem. Perhaps there is something within our own everyday senses that makes us accomplices, numb to the ongoing situation of vehicular manslaughter (kōtsū satsujin). Instead, could we not make a film to rid us of exactly this numbness?"[15] In twisting and transfiguring the notion of "traffic safety" into that of "traffic war," the film expands upon the available documentary aesthetics to implicate the sensory capacities of its audience, dulled to the violence of automobile-related casualties and injuries that occurred every day. The film's disorienting and discomforting portrait of the "traffic war" demonstrates a profound struggle to make sensible the unseen mechanisms that govern urban subjects as they are habituated to an emergent infrastructural order.

In this sense, this work shared a focus on transportation and the unrecognized physical and psychological dimensions of the labor of transportation workers found in Tsuchimoto's prior PR work, *An Engineer's Assistant* (1963), demonstrating Tsuchimoto's continued interest in social problems that straddle the threshold between visibility and invisibility.[16] In *On the Road: A Document*, Tsuchimoto aligns the camera with the taxi driver's mobile vantage point by working with a self-managed cab company that had thrown out its managers during a labor dispute. In casting a set of limited characters using members of this company, as well as other amateurs, the film consists of a series of scenes scripted to varying degrees without extensive narrative exposition. Marshaling the unique set of resources made available by the Metropolitan Police and the participation of the autonomously self-managed taxi company, the film's conditions of production generate a locus of embedded contradictions. With this polarized set of concerns, to disclose the contours of the "traffic war" on the one hand, and the labor conditions of taxi drivers on the other, the filmmaker confronts the unseen realities of an urbanizing social space in the midst of being dismantled and reconstructed in the name of the Olympic spectacle. Regarded to this day as the crowning moment in Japan's "recovery" from the wrongs of the wartime past and the consummation of the bilateral military—economic framework between the United States and Japan, the 1964 Olympics continue to play a crucial role in the nationalized imaginaries within and beyond Japan. With this in mind, the depth of the contradictions made sensible through Tsuchimoto's film take on increasing importance in the contemporary moment. As these chapters will demonstrate, the infrastructural frameworks sustaining the myths of "recovery" at play then and now, fostered a range of potent geopolitical and aesthetic vocabularies for an ecological critique of capitalist state power.

As noted above, the sensory faculties of the audience became a central site and stake within Tsuchimoto's efforts to expand the available documentary aesthetics within the confines of the specific conditions of a PR film production. To depict the city as a "transparent fly-trap" and expose its violence, the film renders a way of seeing that displaces viewers' sensibilities habituated, anesthetized, and inured to the sweeping changes in their surroundings. However motivated in making the unseen mechanisms of urban reconstruction visible and sensible through the film medium, it is important to note the ways the documentary aesthetics of "enlightenment" seem to be operating differently here, as well as in most of Tsuchimoto's work. Despite the unprecedented scale and magnitude of the transformations under examination, the film generates what amounts to a disorienting survey of the constituent parts of an emergent infrastructural order wrought by Olympic reconstruction. Rather than a comprehensive analysis of this order from a removed distance that might afford a totalized view, the film instead collapsed the safe distance between the viewer and the streets to reveal a precariously unstable terrain that provocatively mediated both.[17]

We thus need to grasp how this dynamic topos took shape in the film and how it operates on the static relations between documentary subject and audience in the act of mediation it performs. I will here outline the specific ways the "cross section" of the "traffic war" engenders a fragmentary way of seeing urban transformation, and elicits a dynamic kind of topography even as it refuses a total comprehensive view. Tsuchimoto's film traverses the strange materialities of an urban terrain suspended between states of construction and destruction, immersed within the ebb and flow of the "traffic war," obtaining a vivid mosaic of the pathways and patterns of circulation wrought in Tokyo's Cold War remaking. *On the Road: A Document* is topographical in the strict sense of making legible the changing forms of the streets as the singular topos of an emergent infrastructural order.

SEEING SUBJECT, SEEN SUBJECT

The film's central organizing focal point is the conditions confronted by taxi drivers, both collectively and individually. This choice plays a crucial role in making available a distressing and dynamic way of rendering sensible the diverse forms of violence that proliferate through an unseen urban mechanism. The embedded view obtained by this focus on taxi drivers in *On the Road: A Document* follows a pattern that Tsuchimoto had carried out successfully in his prior film, *An Engineer's Assistant*, to incorporate views antithetical to the sponsor's interests within a PR film. In one telling sequence (18:46~24:00), the film's taxi driver vantage point is mobilized to disclose a fluidity of movement between the driver's interior and external reality that constituted the film's means of depicting the "glass insect killing device" from within.[18] Following the scene of the taxi driver protagonist's payment of a heavy fine for a speeding violation at the police traffic bureau (a fascinating look into the film's sponsors' headquarters, which records the massive scope of the economic exchanges involved in police regulation of traffic violations), he joined a group of fellow drivers at a nearby cafeteria-style eatery. After much discussion of the ludicrous penalties professional drivers have to pay and how their livelihoods are unfairly targeted by the police, one driver suddenly shows up with an x-ray of his stomach, which has been discovered to be herniated internally. The other drivers commiserate with the x-ray-wielding subject, evoking a shared sense of alarm among the drivers who fear they too might succumb to such abnormalities due to their line of work.[19]

The disquiet produced by the x-ray's technical vision, which materializes the unseen abnormalities within the driver's body, is brought into direct confrontation with the protagonist's own anxious gaze, whose look crystalizes the collective conditions of precarious labor specific to taxi drivers. A remarkable sequence of shots then ensues from this gaze. While the protagonist-driver anxiously looks at the x-ray, we briefly see his infant baby in an increasingly overexposed shot of the baby's innocent gaze. This is followed by a return to the close shot of the x-ray itself, where the abnormal protruding organ is inscribed on the film as a large transparent field within the dark recess of the body cavity of the afflicted driver. An ominous sonic pulse suddenly reverberates through the soundtrack, evoking the sound of a steam pylon driver from one of the ubiquitous construction sites that engulf the world of the driver. As the shot continues to linger on the empty transparency of the abnormal organ in the x-ray film, the machinic pulses of the audio layer seem to invade and unsettle the thresholds between internal and external worlds within the very core of the driver's body and mind.

Then, as if peering through the x-ray film into the innards of the city itself, the film cuts to a shot of a scene besieged with a mass of twisted steel fibers, a pile of cement reinforcement bars high atop a span of the unfinished expressway being built alongside Shibuya Station. From there, the camera pans dizzily upward, then sweeps downward to gaze upon the street below. Music commences, building tension as the camera begins to move backward, in parallel with the movement of the walking taxi driver as he negotiates the crosswalk below. In the foreground, the pointed reinforcement bars protrude from the edge of the cement slab, like barbs on a defensive wall. Then, as the driver passes under the traffic sentry tower in the bus terminal below, the camera comes to rest and pans back upward to Shibuya Station. In the next shot, the soundtrack's ominous pounding continues as the driver next emerges from a pedestrian walkway tunnel, approaching the camera as he passes along the mountainous rubble of a construction site, and the camera briefly moves backward again in parallel with his advance. Next, the vantage point shifts once more, and the camera looks out from the scaffolding under the expressway. It then dramatically pans directly downward to zoom in closely on the walking driver as he passes through the tangled flows of automobile and pedestrian traffic below the scaffolding. This pounding sequence comes to a close with three static shots of ongoing construction projects: a construction crane marked with the letters "safety first," a low-angle shot of the expressway from the station area, and the oblique cement surface of a newly constructed expressway on-ramp.[20]

TRAVERSALS

Through this sequence of shots, the camera shifts from the driver's anxious gaze at the protruding organ disclosed in the x-ray, through the disorienting and agile lines of sight described above, tracking the protagonist's movements as he negotiates ceaseless flows of human and automobile traffic, to weave together a tense field of intertwining gazes as the actualities of the emergent forms of the Olympic city, captured in the process of taking shape. The tangle of opposing gazes and the menacing soundscape that permeate this sequence of shots delineate a view of the emergent urban landscape as disquieting as the x-ray portrait. The visibility of urban reconstruction is explicitly brought into relation with the visibility of the x-ray penetrating the deepest layers of the driver's interiority. The dynamic series of shots accentuates how a changing terrain wrought through a proliferation of human and nonhuman gazes constitutes the battleground where the drivers must negotiate the challenges of increasing speeding fines and abnormal medical conditions. The central focal point on the protagonist exposes a riot of entangled gazes, situated as both seer and seen within a visible order that transgresses the boundaries among individual/collective, internal/external, and material/mental worlds. From this visible web of human and nonhuman gazes, the film makes sensible the forces of urban reconstruction that had become naturalized to the point of transparency, like the abnormal rupture of organs caught on the x-ray film itself. In making that very transparency visible, the film exposes an unseen net of material and mental relations that mediate discrete phenomena like the pathological eruption of internal organs recorded in the x-ray, the precarious conditions of taxi drivers as individuated and disorganized laborers, the overflowing rubble and debris of reconstruction, and the inescapable quagmire of traffic itself.

Recalling that the film sought to materialize the figure of an urban mechanism as a transparent glass bottle filled with deadly gas, this fraught entanglement of gazes seems to go beyond simple efforts to convey a message of traffic safety. How might the turbulent flux of visibilities to which urban inhabitants gradually become habituated be implicated in the film's figuration of the violence of such a mechanism? For one thing, the film's creative cinematic sequences, such as the one above, highlight how the film moves beyond the didactic function of illustrating preexisting meanings, such as the instrumental notions of traffic safety as problems of individual responsibility sustained by the Metropolitan Traffic Police who commissioned the film. For example, in this sequence the legibility of the drivers' working conditions and travails of the protagonist reveal the incoherence of existing labor politics before the pervasive conditions of exposure revealed in the film. The film records a modulated politics of labor through its attention to the specific conditions of the drivers in the film, as well as the drivers from the self-managed taxi company participating in the production of the film. In revealing how the plight of taxi drivers exceeded the existing framework of labor organization the film was not abandoning a leftist critique of the exploitation of labor, however. Rather, the film's detailed portrait of the protagonist's work and living situations dynamically remapped the exposed and precarious conditions of the drivers, as this sequence does, within a rapidly changing urban terrain. Confronting the limits of existing aesthetic and political vocabularies, the viewer is made witness to how this emergent landscape exploits the driver's labor differently than, say, a factory, a railway, or another institutional form of work. It works, in a sense, to expand, rather than to dismiss, leftist discourses of labor. The film invites the viewer to consider how the emergent urban constellation of hyper-visible relations of exposure made visible in the film might necessitate an expansion of the vocabularies mobilized to see, to know, or to relate with/in such a changed terrain.

In fact, if we were to situate this film in the context of Tsuchimoto's other early works, or, along with many of the other renowned "experimental" documentary filmmakers' works of the early 1960s, such as those of Hani Susumu (b. 1928), Kuroki Kazuo (1930–2006), and Matsumoto Toshio (1932–2017), we would find that each filmmaker was actively reworking the aesthetic vocabularies of existing leftist discourses, albeit in a variety of ways. Thus the aesthetic developments materialized through Tsuchimoto's film were part and parcel of a shared attempt to grasp the shifting geopolitical horizons of their moment.[21] Not only were the compelling aesthetic experimentations of the film part of broader efforts to render more complex forms of engagement with documentary subjects, or *taishō*, but also, at the same time, the disquieting visibility in Tsuchimoto's film sought to disclose the geopolitical horizons of Japan's urban reconstruction. Exposing— and exposed to—a visibility specifically derived through the driver's precarious position among traffic as both seer and seen, the film makes sensible an otherwise illegible terrain of transformations that exceeded existing aesthetic and (geo)political vocabularies. We must consider what this unsettling topography of the "traffic war" makes legible, and how its expansion of documentary aesthetics therein can be understood as an expansion of the geopolitical vocabularies of urban transformation as a result.

To better understand how such a topography operated, we need to explore how the film reveals a cross section of traffic elaborated in the flux of the myriad patterns of mobilization and immobilization unleashed in Tokyo's Olympic reconstruction. From this perspective, we find the cross section consists of different velocities of flow, juxtaposing and overlaying a variety of rhythms, rates, and routes that structure these flows. These are most obvious in the scenes of packed commuter trains and lines of cars waiting at the rail crossing, where an endless stream of trains passes, and a litany of ubiquitous police presences, situated among the resultant flows of traffic as the daily commuter rush unfolds. These shots accumulate a tense cacophony of stoppages, collisions, and tangles among the endless streams of traffic. Not unlike the contrapuntal movements of the "city symphony" films of the 1920s and 1930s, the serial juxtapositions of visual relations, flows, counterflows, and immobilizations condense together as a topography of the "traffic war."[22] Moving beyond the given meanings of traffic as an inevitable inconvenience of urbanization that necessitates expanded forms of policing, the film grasps the "traffic war" as a mediating topos overflowing the administrable logic that governs the flow of humans and things within an emergent infrastructural order. At the same time, among the overwhelming deluge of the "traffic war" depicted, patterns and rhythms suggestive of order do emerge. Yet, the police are shown to be utterly unable to serve as the "conductors" of the polyrhythmic Brownian motion of the emergent urban expanse that the film makes sensible.

For instance, in one telling sequence (24:01~27:17) the camera follows the taxi, driven by the protagonist, as it slowly inches through crowds like a fish swimming upstream, surrounded by the communing flows of students and workers, returning from or going to their designated places. The otherwise remote structuring forces that shape and pattern the changing distributions of dwelling, working, learning, and leisure of the urban everyday are here briefly made apparent in the taxi's movements against the city's diurnal human tides. Next, we hear the piercing whistles of a traffic officer attempting to tame the slow moving flows of bumper-to-bumper traffic consisting of trucks and cars on a major thoroughfare. A soundscape of traffic is interrupted by the hiss of the steel contacts of a bus or tram slinking along a predetermined path, as the camera shifts to a low-angle zoom shot, tightly framed to capture the deliberate steps of a boot-wearing traffic cop beneath the whirlwind of passing automobiles. In this sequence of shots, the taxi-as-focal-point serves as an avatar that traverses an uneven and incoherently expansive topography, one governed not by the regulatory functions of the police, but some other logic, only made discernible as a variation of rhythms, patterns, and conflicting flows of traffic.

But once immersed in this manner, the camera's gaze itself becomes seemingly motivated by this other logic. This logic of what might be described as the automobile-eye takes on new meaning in Karen Beckman's study of the ethical and theoretical affordances found among the affinities of cinema and automobiles, as seen through the event of the car crash. She notes how the fragmentary aesthetics of industry-sponsored automobile safety films mirrored an automobile-induced visuality of the drivers themselves by "adopting an increasingly kaleidoscopic, almost surrealist, aesthetic that fragments both the urban landscape and the drivers' subjectivities and bodies, eliciting in viewers the kind of fractured and multiplicitous vision that the analyst L. Piece Clark identified in 1907 as one of the pathological effects of driving."[23] As Beckman shows us, despite the didactic message of such safety films, the resultant synthetic attraction between the automobile and cinematic apparatus produces "bodies and modes of vision that are decentered, abstract, illegible, and polysemous." Here, Tsuchimoto's repurposed traffic safety film renders a compound cinema-traffic gaze, derived from the pulsating circulatory pathways of an illegible urban mechanism. The localized flows captured by the compound gaze index the patterned intervals and pulses of the changing city as a vast relational matrix made sensible in the fragmentation and erosion of the habituated thresholds between the visible and the unseen. Just as the film's production mobilized the resources of the traffic police and a self-managed taxi company to traverse the existing distinctions between fiction and documentary film, the film's topographic way of seeing traversed the distributed structures and patterns of an emergent urban reality, at once polyrhythmic and pathological. Immersed within the flux of traffic, the camera discloses a "kaleidoscopic" cross section of illegible patterns, forces, and flows. The cross section cuts across the normalizing sensory registers of experience to confront the ongoing transformations of urban reconstruction unfolding across the relations among interiority and exterior world, the human and the nonhuman, seer and seen. At times, the film's vantage point fluidly shifts across each of these paired terms to delineate a rather disorienting portrait of the changing relations among them.

For instance, the next sequence (27:18~29:45) begins with a scored musical soundtrack and a static shot of horizontal electrical wires, beyond which amorphous gas clouds pass in front of a steel smokestack, rising up vertically in the background. Inside the taxi, the driver is at work, filling in paperwork on a clipboard while slowly moving in traffic. The camera closes in upon the microcosm of the driver's world, recording a rapid succession of objects and gestures; his hand on the transmission, a baby shoe placed upon the dashboard, a handful of coins, the activation of the taxi meter, coins, the driver adjusting his wristwatch and changing the meter again. Weaving together these incidental fragments, the camera eye outlines the measurement of time and the quantitative traces of his labor. The camera next shifts its gaze outside the car onto the passing road surfaces, then pans outward to confront a massive construction project, looking upward into the underbelly of a great structure being erected above the road traveled by the taxi. The bare steel frames delineate a homogeneous linear form, abstracted from the streams of traffic below, looking like the imposing wreckage of an alien civilization. In the densely layered shot that follows, the camera looks through the lumbering frame of a steam shovel toward a line of helmeted road workers, laboring silently beside a loud stream of heavy traffic. Turning to capture the tortured road surface, we witness a worker wave a flag to release the pedestrians waiting to cross, and the camera pivots further downward. Then it too crosses the road, almost stumbling over the deep fissures and weblike cracks in the street that blur together in its forward motion. As strange backward sounds are heard in the soundtrack, the blurred surfaces dissolve into a view of the steel panels used in road construction shot from a moving car. With more unsettling backward sounds, the road's surface is then broken up into a raw gravel plane as the camera passes over wooden planks, which are the daytime coverings of streets undergoing massive underground infrastructural projects, such as the construction of subway and sewage lines. The camera comes to rest in a still shot of planks undulating under the tires of passing vehicles. In a closer shot, the camera closes in upon a nail that has been crushed back into the battered planks. As the scored music returns to the soundtrack, the camera reveals the scarred bark of a tree, producing a visual analogy with the wooden planks that cover the road surfaces, the protective surfaces of the city likened to that of a living organism, both subjected to the tortuous onslaught of machines tearing them apart.

Sequences such as these compel us to marvel at how in reworking the generic conventions of the PR film, the film also performs a kind of topographical inquiry into the geopolitical and aesthetic conditions of the "traffic war." In a sense, these fragmented gestures and material surfaces are accumulated together in a way of seeing that renders equivalent the invisible forces that drive the taxi driver's daily labor with the unseen forces informing urban reconstruction. With each sequence, different aspects of a fragmentary totality are materialized as unseen presences that haunt urban reconstruction. Here, for example, the encounter with the hulking form of the unbuilt overpass

FIGURE 1.2 Tsuchimoto Noriaki, *On the Road: A Document*, 1964.

(just as with the span of freeway under construction near Shibuya described above) dislodges the camera-eye from its embedded position with the driver.

Brought into equivalence through the camera's fluid gaze as unnamed material residues, they are rendered as bare presences, dispossessed of the valuations and meanings that were once attached to them. The destructive force of reconstruction is laid bare within this cross section of the "traffic war," rendered sensible by the mechanism of the camera, which indifferently records the wreckage, ruins, and the unbuilt monuments of an emergent Olympic Tokyo. The film works to defamiliarize the habituated flux of traffic from its status as both administrable datum of the police and iconic inconvenience of an ideologically constructed image of city life. Instead, the film exposes the viewer to the ebb and flow of human and material remnants unleashed from their moorings within prior orders of valuation and signification. However, the cross section outlined here is not necessarily plotted upon a stable geometric plane with a fixed set of coordinates. The traversals it charts are not linear trajectories of getting from one fixed location to another, nor are they figural translations of meanings from one a priori existing city to another. It is a topographical inquiry that self-reflexively exposes the unseen processes of dispossession at play in Japan's Cold War remaking. Becoming exposed therein, we find human and nonhuman domains are suspended together within the flux of destructive reconstruction.

Cutting across as it exposes, the film moreover uncovers the disintegration of existing distributions between center and periphery, delineating an incipient landscape of relations that traverse both the city and the countryside. In a subsequent sequence (30:40~37:41), the taxi driver traverses a quickly changing urban-rural continuum, ostensibly transporting a passenger from the densely packed boulevards of the Ginza, across overcrowded residential areas, and to the edges of the city as it spills out into the surrounding farmlands. The journey is anything but continuous, as a number of telling encounters punctuate and interrupt the taxi's traversal. Rife with scattered discontinuities and diversions, the drive nonetheless reveals an emergent terrain of changing relations between the urban center and its surroundings. As it moves across the distributed spaces of consumption, dwelling, and agriculture, the amalgamated camera-taxi gaze delineates a mediating topos where these were entangled differently among the daily flux of centripetal and centrifugal flows.

The sequence commences with the driver negotiating with prospective passengers in the alleys of Ginza, crowded with pedestrian shoppers. After rejecting one passenger for requesting too short a ride, he accepts another, sharply pointing to his watch as the passenger fills the back seat with his bags from a day of shopping. We watch the taxi fall into place among the lines of traffic jamming the main road in a broad, but densely cluttered, vista of one of Tokyo's central shopping districts. Briefly we see the driver watching children crossing in front of the taxi at a crosswalk, and the nonsensical signals of a traffic cop, controlling the crossing. Then, the camera shifts to an embodied view of the driver's gaze, glancing shakily at each of the clusters of signals and signs that indicate a dense proliferation of coded directives and prohibitions governing the main boulevard. But then, as the taxi comes to a stop at one of these lights, this gaze randomly scans the surrounding area. In this brief montage of discontinuous looks, we witness the pounding of a pile driver and the perimeter of a tall office building, and then quickly gaze upward to see a man precariously edging along a ledge and closing a window on the outside of another tall office building.[24] Next, framing the scanning eyes of the driver in the rearview mirror, the camera retreats within the taxi, taking up the passenger's point of view. Thus situated, we watch as the driver curses at—and miraculously avoids running into—a pedestrian who jumps back at the last second, then swerves around another man in the middle of the crosswalk, only to career around an oncoming car, wildly turning the steering wheel to return the taxi to the forward crawl of traffic, likened to the pace of snails. Here, the urban center unfolds as a highly coded, information-dense environment. The film delineates the acutely high risk of accidents here, and further makes apparent the potential depletion of the driver's capacity to assimilate all of the overflowing signs and messages. We watch his shifting gaze as it is saturated by potential signs, and he, like the viewers themselves, becomes increasingly unable to differentiate the critical thresholds among signals, noise, and chaos.

Finally breaking free of downtown traffic, the taxi accelerates as it crosses a long bridge heading out of town. An establishing shot briefly fixes the viewers' gazes on a static landscape across the river, where the densely packed roofs of a residential district are woven together with antennae and tall towers carrying power lines, before plunging viewers into the district's narrow streets, where we are confronted with layer upon layer of laundry hung out to dry. The taxi carefully passes through the densely packed main street of the residential neighborhood, and the camera makes a sweeping survey of the potential hazards (children, dogs, bikes, and pushcarts) before embedding itself in a low-angle view from the front of the taxi as it charges forward. As it playfully swerves around apron-clad housewives, some bearing both babies and bikes, we watch the vigilant eyes of the driver constantly assessing the dangers before the cab, as though playing a challenging game, glancing back, we now see *with* him; roller skates, and a baby playing with its feet as its diaper is changed, lingering as if to allow the audience to imagine the driver thinking of his own baby at home.[25] These details of the intimate domestic domain played out in the streets are interrupted as the taxi turns off the busy strip to follow after a pair of skating youths through a narrow alleyway, lined with older wooden homes. There, the camera-taxi's forward motion comes to an abrupt stop, confronting the looming form of a large stadium. A static reverse shot of the stadium where a piece of paper slowly floats around on the breeze in the empty parking lot marks the end of the taxi's passage through the residential area. This monolithic stadium, empty and distinctly at odds with the immediate surroundings, poses a telling contrast of worlds. In the taxi's passage among the diverse uses and multifunctional microcosm of the residential neighborhood's streets and alleys, an uncanny threshold is revealed in the barren, spectacular macroscopic expanse of the stadium's concrete walls and ramps.

The juxtaposition of lifeways and spaces captured here resonates with the seemingly random indices of the Olympic remaking that occasionally erupt in the film. Alien and empty, the stadium and its functional forms are irreconcilably other to the intimate neighborhood streets overflowing with life in its shadow.

But the film doesn't linger to mourn the "loss" of one use of space over another. Moving on, the taxi gains speed as it reaches the open highway through farmlands at the edge of the city. After an ambulance overtakes the cab, its passing sirens reverberating over a static scene of a farming couple working in their fields, the taxi has come to rest. The driver and passenger relieve themselves at the side of the road, as if

FIGURE 1.3 Tsuchimoto Noriaki, *On the Road: A Document*, 1964.

marking an invisible boundary between worlds, a undeclared frontier in the sprawling urban expanse, on the verge of overtaking all preexisting modes of dwelling. Tight zoom shots linger on the farmers' bodies as they slowly till the soil; looking beyond their bent forms, the passing of traffic can be seen in the distant background, concluding the taxi driver's journey to the city's edge. Though each region encountered along the way is bound within a discrete landscape, the taxi's traversal of a continuum that encompasses them all traces a changing distribution of spatial-temporal intervals among them. The center and periphery, though discrete, are collapsed together as mere quantities of time and degrees of coded information in the taxi's traversal of these landscapes. From the road they look different, but are also related and mediated together through the compound gazes of the driver and camera-taxi as they traverse this integrated landscape of differentiated lifeworlds. The film portrays an emergent topography, made legible in the erosion of a city's given contours, and sensible through its distributions and rhythms as the traffic among worlds in flux.

I have attempted to read with the grain of the film's topographic capacities to render the geopolitics of an emergent urban order sensible within the infrastructural aesthetics of traffic, charting the differentials, flux, and forces at play in the destructive reconstruction of Tokyo on the eve of the 1964 Olympics. Within the frame of this reading, the decisive features of this film can be enumerated in their ability to draw our attention to the interrelated mental and material forces encompassing a topos of kinetic intensities, variable temporalities, and fragmenting spaces. Along with this singular topos, the film traces the precarious conditions of taxi drivers and pedestrians alike. Set in motion through specific vantage points afforded the taxi driver and camera-taxi gaze, the filmic cross section elaborates various disintegrating surfaces, open fissures, and excavations of the changing urban terrain. Moreover, in Tsuchimoto's efforts to produce dynamic and fluid forms of relation with its subject, or *taishō*, as the basis of an expanded documentary aesthetic, there was no attempt to force a definitively legible narrative or otherwise static framework upon the traffic of human and nonhuman urban residues that the film unearthed. By exploring the shifting relations among documentary subject and viewer, inside and outside, fiction and nonfiction, Tsuchimoto and his collaborators evidenced how novel forms of exposure, encounter, and exchange could be located within the flux among disintegrating social relations and social spaces disclosed in the gyres of reconstruction. In what amounts to a fortuitous conjuncture between Tsuchimoto's documentary praxis and the specific contours of urban reconstruction on the eve of the Olympics, we are able to glimpse the complex entanglement of contending forces informing what this book seeks to elaborate as the urban ecologies of Japan's Cold War remaking.

In one of the few reviews of the film published at the time of its limited screening, architect Isozaki Arata described the film as a protest against the contemporary state of the city, an act of dissent so acute that Isozaki felt compelled to reexamine his take on urban transportation.[26] Historicizing the city as having many characteristics belonging to the premodern and early modern eras, Isozaki noted that what made it contemporary were the machines that inundated the city. "The film discloses the spatial-temporal requirements that must be maintained for the taxi-machine to be able to assimilate the city's energy. And while this machine lacks the capacity to derive its own preventative measures, it occupies the spaces where humans are in motion. Thus, within the contemporary city, whether it is New York, Paris or Tokyo, all these machines must co-exist with humans."[27] The contradictions of the contemporary city—the contradictions that render New York, Paris, and Tokyo contemporaneous—are here revealed in the struggles of the driver as machinic operator, forced to negotiate the streets of an urban landscape wholly incapable of sustaining the coexistence of human and machine (a result compounded by the city's Olympic reconstruction, which came too late and was too little to absorb the ongoing inundation of automobiles).

This, for Isozaki, was the compelling result of the choice of the filmmakers "to record the contemporary city through the eyes of the driver whose very livelihood depends on nervously controlling this machine, and thus [operating] the paralyzed state of the city in a transitional phase."[28] The film's intense encounters with the limitations and dangers of the contemporary city were further evidenced in the anecdotal fact that three of the film's crew members were hit by cars during the making of the film itself. Moreover, for Isozaki, this portrait of the driver's exhaustive struggles to avoid accidents cannot elicit the catharsis of sports, where the pushing through of physical and mental limitations could afford new pleasures, even, or especially, when played with a machine. As Yuriko Furuhata has shown, in the early 1960s Isozaki was interested in the cybernetic human—machine interface as a lens for grasping how the urban environment was not constituted by architectural objects but by flows of information and communication signals. Moreover, for Isozaki this was a historical shift in how such spaces could be grasped, as Furuhata notes: "Lacking grid patterns and landmark structures, the urban space of the contemporary city is no longer representable through spatial coordinates. Instead of landmarks and grids, the city is grasped relationally, that is, by gauging constantly shifting 'relations between objects.'"[29]

The confrontations fostered by this tense clash of worlds, conceptualized here by Isozaki as one between machine and human, further informed the film's topographic cross sections of the conflicts between an existing urban order and an emergent one. The brute kinetic forces portrayed by the film not only raised questions about the limits to human control but also revealed the highly uneven distribution of risks and profits secured in the reconstruction of the city. In so doing, the film captured both the limitations and possibilities of the infrastructural aesthetics of the streets, grasped as a fluid topos of irreconcilable coexistences undergoing reconstruction.[30] The film at once confronted the stultification of senses naturalized in the everyday flows and disclosed a mediating topos capable of forging novel ways of seeing, knowing, and thus relating among the changing patterns, cycles, and circulations that informed the emergent urban expanse. Though Tsuchimoto would lament the painful and confusing nature of the myriad stylistic experiments undertaken in rendering this cross section of the "traffic war," the pursuit of an embedded place or locus of mediation for bringing out the contradictions of a situation clearly informed many of his later independent documentaries.[31] Moreover, as an expansion of documentary aesthetics to engage the thresholds of the sensible, the filmic topos discloses manifold dynamic relations among the materialities and sensibilities of urban subjects, both then and now.

The film's novel forms of relation and mediation were rooted in an attempt to provoke the perceptual capacities of urbanized subjects, which served as an important site and stake in its cross section of the "traffic war." In this sense, we might consider how the film's efforts to recast documentary aesthetics revealed how both infrastructural forms and sensory capacities played a crucial role in the Olympic remaking of Tokyo. If the filmic topos was that of the "traffic war," then we must take seriously the geopolitics of urban reconstruction as a "war" fought at the level of the streets and the sensory capacities of urban dwellers. We must, in other words, see the filmic topos as a cross section of the geopolitical horizons of the "battleground" of Olympic reconstruction. In so doing, we obtain a sense of how the conditions of geopolitical and aesthetic possibility that informed Japan's Cold War reconstruction were heralded by the Tokyo Olympics of 1964.

TRAFFIC WARS, COLD WARS

As I have already mentioned above, the 1964 Tokyo Olympics embody a crucial locus of transformations in narratives of Japan's postwar history from wartime to recovery. By all accounts, more than competitive sporting events themselves, the Olympic spectacle afforded an opportunity for invested interests to promote a specific vision of Japan's past, present, and future trajectories of becoming on both domestic and international stages.[32] Such narratives demonstrate how the 1964 games made clear Japan's place within the U.S.-led Cold War geopolitical project, and recast, reimagined, and remade the material and imaginary contours of the Japanese nation-state, emerging from the shadows of the former Japanese empire. Independent of whether these historical narratives were critical of such changes or not, the narrative effects of "recovery" and "miraculous growth" seem to repel any other reading of the Olympic spectacle.[33]

However, if the Tokyo Olympics marked the reinvention of Japan's image in both domestic and international eyes, the topos described by Tsuchimoto's film produces a different reading of this event horizon in two interesting ways. On one hand, the "traffic war" depicted by the film cannot be easily untangled from the aftermath of the historic public outpourings of political contestation produced during the widespread struggles against the ratification of the 1960 United States-Japan Mutual Security Treaty.[34] On the other hand, Tsuchimoto's filmic cross section of the Olympic reconstruction of Tokyo affords an expansion of a critical understanding of the geopolitical itself, rendered here from diverse and discrete-yet-interrelated "fronts" of the Cold War's manifold "wars."[35] Thus, the "traffic war" traced in Tsuchimoto's film contributed to an expanded understanding of the geopolitical at play in the Cold War. Providing an embedded view of the "war" taking place on the streets and through the sensory capacities of urban dwellers, the film makes sense of the vast magnitude of the changes heralded by the Olympics, and the lived realities of the Cold War that extended far beyond the scope of military—economic cooperation. We discover, for instance, that the foundations of the emergent infrastructural order are profoundly uncertain and rife with indeterminate new perspectives and potential forms of relation. We encounter a vibrant topos of flux overflowing in a cacophony of unruly materialities, coursing with the residues and rhythms of untold urban ecologies that deplete the smooth teleologies of "recovery." Moreover, the film suggests the magnitudes of material and affective (im)mobilization that govern and control the geopolitical trajectory of Japan's future, as made sensible from the "battleground" of infrastructural forms and sensory capacities. As such, the film introduces the conditions of possibility for an ecological inquiry into the Cold War remaking of Japan, and offers an opening for the dynamic elaboration of a wide range of vibrant geopolitical and aesthetics vocabularies of urban transformation. In the chapters that follow, I trace the manifold and mobile dimensions of the urban ecologies wrought by literary and visual media through the displacements of generative loci of questions and relational potentials, like those revealed in this film, as they shift and evolve across disparate media and moments.

CHAPTER TWO

Disappearance

Topological Visuality in Abe Kōbō's Urban Literature

In the essay, "For a Literature of Space," the renowned Japanese literary scholar Maeda Ai (1931–1987) argues it is nothing less than a new language of the city that Abe Kōbō (1924–1993) has produced in his 1967 novel, *The Ruined Map*.[1] Framing Abe's novel as a foundational work of "urban fiction" (*toshi shōsetsu*) in the Japanese literary context, Maeda's essay further situates Abe as occupying a singular position in literary history of writing the urban in Japan.[2] Taking my cue from Maeda's reading, I will outline the ways we might begin to grasp the "new language of the city" found in the novel as constituent parts of Abe's theorization of urban society. This chapter will explore the ways *The Ruined Map* produced such a language in the process of considering urban transformation, and in particular, a transformation that was ongoing during the moment of its production. I argue that *The Ruined Map* derived a mode of reading and thinking about the urban as part and parcel of Abe's attempt to remake the literary practice of writing the city. The novel contributed to Japan's rich history of urban writing, and it also attempted to illuminate the complex forms of continuity and discontinuity that ushered in Japan's urban transformation of the 1960s.

Recent scholarship on Abe's writing has explored how his work demonstrated an unwavering attempt to question and expand the given contours of modern literary practice.[3] Abe's literary works evidence a distinct capacity for perpetually shifting their generic forms over time, evolving across poetic genres, reportage, science fiction, short story, novel, radio play, theater, cinematic screenplay, and much more in the first three decades of his career as a writer. As this scholarship demonstrates, this ever-shifting traversal of genres reflected instantiations of the limitations and possibilities Abe felt each form possessed in relation to a consistent mode of inquiring into the transformative contours of Japanese society. In this context, Abe's work continues to present an indispensable lens for us to consider how these trajectories of generic form and urbanizing social space intertwined in fascinating ways in the novel *The Ruined Map*.[4]

At the heart of the work is the figure of a private detective who serves as the privileged vantage point for the reader in an often-disorienting traversal of an urban terrain undergoing reconstruction. Through the detective's ever-restless pursuit of a missing person, Abe's novel invites the reader to trace the emerging contours of Japan's transforming social spaces. As such, the work evidences a topological inquiry into the continuity and change of the urban remaking of the Japanese archipelago. My reasons for delineating the topological contours of this work are twofold: First, the demonstration of a mode of reading that centered on the reader rather than the protagonist/author was an important part of Maeda's claim that Abe's work contributed a new language of the city. Maeda himself introduced the value of reading Japanese literature topologically in a later essay that served as the introduction to his landmark essay collection *Literature in Urban Space* (*Toshi kūkan no naka no bungaku*). In part, this was a significant stake in what scholar Komori Yōichi describes as Maeda's critique of the centralizing perspective of protagonist as authorial subject.[5] The fact that Abe's "new language" was topological was an important resource or model for Maeda's own critical efforts to further develop a topological way of reading both the urban spaces within texts and the texts of urban spaces. Topology here in this critical endeavor afforded the critic, and by extension, the reader in general, a means of opening a text to other ways of reading, specifically readings other than those that condensed through the centralizing perspective of the protagonist, and by extension the authorial subject.[6] So within the literary-critical horizons of reading Abe's novel, it becomes important to understand how such a topological reading is modeled by the text, and what attributes Maeda identified with the operation of its "new language."

Second, I would like to explore how the text's topological figuration, in addition to serving as a resource for expanding the contours of literary criticism, makes legible the urban transformations of Japan's Cold War remaking. I argue that Abe's topological fiction mobilizes both novel sites (*topoi*) within the urbanized terrain and the emergence of a visual environment derived through a logic of abstraction to trace the forces at play in this transformation. Through the topological inquiry delineated by the text, we encounter a proliferation of the logic and logistics of capitalist state power, potent new forms of violence and exploitation on a transformed scale, and troubling continuities with prior modes of power at play in the remaking of the urban fabric. This, I contend, further demonstrates the ways that an interrogation of the continuities and discontinuities of urban transformation offer an important resource for Abe's ongoing efforts to rework literary practice.[7] More than just a demonstration of his unbridled authorial creativity, Abe's work is a lifelong pursuit of expanded modes of writing and reading—modes of relating with others and the changing world—that dynamically adapted to a transforming landscape of power. Here, I outline the topological inquiry into an incomplete urban transformation operative in Abe's novel. Like many of the practices discussed in this book, *The Ruined Map* fosters an important resource for a critical theoretical understanding of urban change by challenging the naturalized and habituated perspectives that deplete and stultify our sensory capacities. In tracing the specificities of the topological inquiry produced by this novel, I seek to disclose the aesthetic challenges the work poses for its reader, as well as to highlight how the work translated the incompleteness of the urban into a politics of reading the urban in the process.

SEEING THROUGH THE FAILING GAZE

In Abe's prior novels *The Woman in the Dunes* and *The Face of Another*, and the subsequent work *The Box Man*, the theme of disappearance takes center stage as a means of examining the urban contours of Japanese society, community, and individual identity.[8] The social phenomenon of *ningen jōhatsu*, or people who vanish into thin air, was a central thematic framework for Abe's most celebrated novels. With *The Ruined Map*, Abe narrates the process of "becoming disappeared" from a vantage point embedded among a milieu of profound social and material transformations that unfolded after the 1964 Tokyo Olympic Games. As we shall see, the novel's story of disappearance discloses more than the protagonist's metamorphosis—one that is at times comedic, satirical, and intentionally disorienting. Derived from an ever-moving gaze situated in transit among the new material forms that embodied the Cold War remaking of Tokyo's social spaces, the novel mobilizes the subject of disappearance—and with it the disappearance of the subject—to reveal a logic of abstraction that proliferates across an emergent landscape populated by novel topoi, such as the large-scale housing developments (*danchi*), the freeway, the subway, and the labyrinthine alleys of Shinjuku.[9] In *The Ruined Map*'s topological inquiry, the reader is exposed to expanded forms of violence and exploitation within the emerging contours of urban Japan. At the same time, the writing that discloses these expanded forces also models a mode of reading through the blind spots within the logics governing the emergent terrain. Thus, to discover what a new language of the city might express not only for literary history but for a critique of the expanded forms of violence and exploitation that proliferated through Japan's Cold War remaking, we must attend to the politics of this way of reading the urban through an understanding of how the writing operates topologically.

The plot is deceptive in its clarity: a detective who is hired by a woman and her brother to track down the woman's missing husband, pursues all leads to dead ends and then the detective himself "disappears" in the end. Unlike the ambivalence of *The Woman in the Dunes*, and its conclusion in particular, which has engendered perpetual speculation and interpretation of the text's determinate meaning, the seeming simplicity of *The Ruined Map* may be the reason for the lack of critical attention to the profoundly transformative efforts Abe undertook in this work.[10] Taking Maeda Ai's critical reading as our starting point, I will first introduce the powerful implications of the novel's deceptive simplicity. Maeda notes that throughout the urban terrain traversed by the detective, each element has lost its connection with the other. Nonetheless, what unifies and preserves this as a coherent landscape is the structure of perspective latent in the expert gaze so crucial to the protagonist's work as a private detective; this city is a totality abounding in signs that the detective *must* be able to decipher. Yet, as his gaze increasingly fails him, his "map" of coherent signification is dismantled, and with it, what Maeda calls the feedback loop regulating the circuit of exchange between information and action falls apart, leaving only a map full of blank holes that exceed the detective's expert gaze. "Each element constituting the landscape, despite his perception of them as distinct images, images that should indicate meaning and metaphor, is cleanly erased and the correspondence that reconciles the protagonist and the landscape is completely severed since only the outer surface is disclosed."[11] It is at this point that the detective himself becomes a missing person, taking on the role of someone who has lost his memory, and "disappearing" from his formal life as a detective. With the breakdown of the protagonist's gaze, the readers themselves must piece together a new provisional map of their own to reassemble the disparate fragments chanced upon within the protagonist's vantage point. In part, this disorienting perspective arises, as Maeda suggests, from the protagonist's inability to adhere to the classical system of codified temporal and spatial coordinate axes specific to literary fiction.[12]

This salient evaluation is where we should be to realize that the most important dynamics of the novel and the methodological innovations Maeda extols are those that are mediated by the protagonist's perspective. By returning to our interest in the mode of reading that this vantage point renders, we can better explore the question of the relationship between methodological innovations and the transforming social spaces they depict. Although the visual register of experience takes on heightened importance in this work (arguably true for much of Abe's work), the crucial features of the particular vista of the protagonist have as much to do with what is unseen at the limits of the detective's gaze and what forces interrupt the ordering functions securing his fixed map of correspondence between expert seer and seen landscape. The dynamic sources for the new language of the city that Maeda locates in this work are in fact derived through the breakdown of the detective's expert gaze as he traverses the emergent networks of capitalist state power at play in this moment of accentuate urban transformation. Throughout *The Ruined Map*, we discover the blind spots in the detective's gaze, not only what he cannot see, but what he sees and cannot "read," drawing the reader's attention to the latent fissures, ruptures, and continuities with prior assemblies of power shaping and shaped by the Cold War remaking of Japan. Thus, with the detective as our unreliable guide across this fraught landscape, readers are charged with assembling a coherent text from the scattered forms and fragments that inform the novel's emergent terrain.

ENVIRONMENTS OF ABSTRACTION

From the outset of *The Ruined Map* we come face-to-face with the imposing figure of the *danchi*, the large-scale housing development where the detective's client lives. The disorienting sequence of vistas that opens this novel delineate the starting point of the detective's search for his client's missing husband. In these pages we are confronted with three views, an oblique street surface seen from the detective's small car struggling to scale the sloping approach to the hilltop development, a small open area of the development's bus terminal, and a wide panorama of the plateau where the uniform dwellings stand. The reverse-telescoping and expanding projections of the professionally observant detective's gaze guide the reader into the heart of the alien urban world of this novel, as the detective emerges upon a wide expanse atop the hill.

> It was if I were looking at some patterned infinity: the four storied buildings, identical in height, each floor with six doors, were lined up in rows of six to the right and left. Only the fronts of the buildings, facing the road, were painted white, and the color stood out against the darkish green of the sides, emphasizing even more the geometric character of the view. With the roadway as an axis, the housing development extended in two great wings, somewhat greater in width than in depth. Perhaps it was for the lighting, but as the buildings were laid out in staggered lines, on both sides one's view met only white walls supporting a milk-white dome of sky.[13]

Like a description of an abstract minimalist painting wrought of pale white tones and dark green margins, this topos is first encountered as a wholly visual spectacle. Narrated by a disembodied gaze as it encounters the figure of the *danchi* development, the text describes the geometric details and the ordered distribution of linear patterns and lighting that give it form. Thus, exposed to a topos produced in the reduction of dwelling to the visuality of rationalized and functional needs, the gaze and its object reveal the *danchi's* logic of abstraction. Some of the most prominent figures defining the emergent landscape of post-Olympic urban Japan were the large-scale housing developments that were constructed with increasing frequency and magnitude from the late 1950s to the 1980s. In part, the developments were constructed to ease the critical housing situation for the ceaseless inundation of new urban populations, but they also dramatically transformed the most intimate domestic spaces defining everyday life.[14] The *danchi's* logic of abstraction evidenced here at the outset was not just a formal aspect of the functionalist architectural priorities of public housing projects. As a topos abstracted from the existing sociohistorical coordinates that governed the real, the *danchi* here embodied an ontologically other place isolated from the immediate surroundings, out of place and out of time from the world around it.[15]

Those familiar with Abe's fiction will recognize this topos among many others that have been similarly abstracted, such as the shacklike hovel at the bottom of the sandpit in *The Woman in the Dunes* and the boxes employed by the protagonist(s) of *The Box Man*. Moreover, like each of the central sites examined in the novel, the topos itself does not fit neatly on existing cartographic projections of Tokyo's actual built environment, but instead indexes a generalized figure derived by the formal elements and abstracted functional logic of "real" places. All of the topoi examined by *The Ruined Map* are at once abstractions of actual places in the expanding urban landscape, while equal effort is made to provide sufficient detail to both index analogous sites as well as synthesize generalized features. The novel's topologic abstraction is moreover rendered in the proliferation of toponymic subtractions that mark the important sites in the novel, such as "S-station" and "F-city." Thus, the textual production of this topological figuration of urban transformation materializes and makes legible a logic of abstraction operative in the remaking of Japanese social spaces. Within the novel's topological inquiry, it matters less *where* a place is in its absolute cartographic spatial representation, than *how* these topoi are related and mediated together. To be "read" together as components of a topological figure, that is, as a concrete virtuality abstracted from lived space-time, the novel makes perceptible the sensory artifacts of urban transformation, naturalized and just beyond the threshold of perception in the patterned flux of the everyday. Here, the topos of the new *danchi* settlement serves as a vital node among the other topoi that inform the unfolding of the narrative. It thus serves as the origin point that the detective repeatedly returns to and departs from in his flight through the emergent landscape, embodying the zero degree of the novel's topologic writing of urban transformation.[16]

Among these uniform units of urban dwelling, myriad details are accumulated by the private detective's gaze, providing a foundation for organizing the mass of latent signals that the detective must piece together in a coherent totality to discover the "truth" about his client's husband's disappearance. Through a method of perpetual substitution, whereby the detective projects himself into the missing husband's position, the detective "reads" and orders the evidentiary traces through perpetual speculations and often delusional theorizations anchored to the frame of the *danchi* apartment of his client. However, in situating his inquiry by standing in the missing person's shoes, both literally and figuratively, the flood of material objects and empirical facts that come into view exceeds the detective's pursuit of coherence. At the limits of his ordering gaze, the visible and invisible dimensions of the profoundly transformed city unfold. In seeking to ascertain the whereabouts of the client's husband, the detective pursues a picture of what he was disappearing from, and by standing in his footsteps at the point of "origin" in his plot of fragmentary clues, a powerful bond emerges between the substituting and substituted identities.[17] That is to say, there is a structural bond established at the narrative's point of origin, or "node." And it is from this node that the story unfolds as the protagonist attempts to overcome the distance between his position and that of the missing husband. Through the pursuit that brings the detective ever closer to the missing husband, orienting the detective's search like a magnetic pole guiding the needle of a compass, a cascade of repetitions, substitutions, and discontinuities comes to mark the novel's distinctive language and form.[18] As I will discuss later in the chapter, the interior space of the client's apartment is where the detective effectively becomes the disappearing husband, briefly pairing with the client in an ironic twist of the heteronormative reproductive function already established as the *danchi's* symbolic DNA. However, the narrative as a whole concludes as the detective flees from the *danchi* point of origin and joins the husband in the condition of disappearance. Structured as such, the origin point of the *danchi* links together the strands and segments of the detective's traversals to orient and plot a map of the "clues" and fragments that are the novel's topological inquiry into the emergent urban landscape. As a "patterned infinity," this container proves to be a robust and flexible foundation for assembling a diversity of novel perspectives on Japan's urban remaking.

With the *danchi* as the detective's starting point, his perpetual movements reveal a central dimension of the "map full of holes" that the detective vainly attempts to navigate to "solve" the husband's disappearance. The spatial-temporal displacements from this point of origin materialize and give shape to the detective's mapping of the emergent terrain informing the husband's disappearance. As the detective's detailed descriptions make apparent, the "human filing cabinet" of the *danchi* indexes a novel set of social and historical conditions at play in the construction of housing estates, erected at increasing distance from urban centers as an outcome of the limitations confronted by the central and municipal governments.[19] For the hordes of commuting workers living in the *danchi*, the novel modernity of their rationalized homes came at the cost of ever-increasing commute times as urban population growth reached new heights in the late 1960s. Observing the landscape from this crucial node where the changing spatial-temporal relations among public and private life were most acute, the novel charts the distributive forces at play in urban transformation.

In one scene, the protagonist detective stands in the last known location of the missing husband, and just as he begins to imagine the final moment before going "missing," Abe's detective reveals an image of the city as a massive rhythmical pump defined by powerful flows and cycles. "The first beat of the city's heart is a signal; within a five minute period hundreds of filing cabinets are unlocked at one click and swarms of different but indistinguishable workers, like a wall of water released from the floodgates of a dam, suddenly throng the streets . . . a time of living."[20] Traffic, as we encountered it in the previous chapter, indexes the homogenizing flux of everyday flows that naturalized the distributive forces of an emergent urban order. Anthropomorphized here as the lifeblood of this order, the rhythms of the city's circulatory systems are made momentarily visible in the detective's displacement from them. Always situated outside the highly patterned flows of commuters by the vantage point of a private detective—who must pursue traces and clues left by the missing husband across the city to ostensibly "solve" the case at hand—the contours of an expansive urban totality arise in the displacement and traversal between the detective's and missing husband's points of view. It is the displacement from the normative everyday flows of the city that permits the detective to pass through the managed topos of the *danchi* with an indifferent gaze, accumulating fragmentary clues from the landscape. Along with the detective, the readers are afforded a margin of distance to examine these for themselves, in part because of their further displacement from the ceaseless flow of details rendered by the detective's traversals from place to place. These structural displacements among the missing husband, detective, the landscape, and the reader are crucial to the topological mediations that inform the text and its politics of reading the urban.

In moving through this abstract topos, the detective brings into relation that which has been displaced, distributed, or otherwise disavowed from the amalgam of entangled topoi of abstraction. "I walked slowly ahead, halted, turned on my heel, and walked back again over the rough asphalt sidewalk. With normal strides, it was thirty-two paces from the corner of building number three. When I looked up, the row of street lights, artificial eyes that had forgotten how to blink, seemed to be waiting for a festival procession that would never come. The pale, rectangular lights reflected in the windows had long since abandoned such festivals."[21] Abstracted from the ritual forms of "festival" rooted in the reproduction of the agricultural community, the *danchi* topos affords another kind of community among the visible relations of the text. The detective reenacts the last thirty-two steps taken by the husband before he "boldly and irreversibly stepped across a chasm, turning his back to the world," and this topos mediates the distance between the two characters. The act of performing this mediating enumeration of shared steps affords a poetic observation of the nightscape in an analogical language that draws parallels between the detective's expert gaze and the lights' "artificial eyes that had forgotten how to blink." At the same time, the chasm between the detective and the husband is materialized as the threshold between the visible and invisible, as the difference between one who had escaped the hypervisibility of the *danchi* topos, and one who is fully subsumed in the visuality of those "artificial eyes." Moreover, through the textual production of this mediation, the gaze of the reader is evoked as the observer of the detective's observations, operating analogically to render the chiasmic differentials between the husband and detective, and the detective and reader, into a coherent experience of "reading" the topos that mediates them all. With the *danchi* as the foundational topos where these mediations are linked together in this manner, the detective's movements, out of phase and displaced from the everyday flows, elaborate a topological tracing of the emergent forms of urban becoming. These traces in turn induce the reader's participation in "reading" both the transformative and incapacitating dimensions wrought by the specific contours of urban change assembled by the text.

READING INCOMPLETENESS

To understand how *The Ruined Map*'s politics of "reading" the ongoing urban transformation operate, we must further make sense of the novel's many "surplus" passages, often lengthy descriptions of seemingly unrelated details. These take two discrete forms in the text. For the most part, the reader is subject to the free associations and observations of the central protagonists in the body of the novel. In addition, the body of the novel is punctuated by the report compiled by the detective. These entries include dates and times (starting with February 12 at 9:40 a.m. and concluding with February 14 at 6:30 a.m.); abbreviated notes on the detective's findings, rationalizations, and expenses; an extended interview with a taxi driver; and two maps. Although the entries are compiled for a report, ostensibly for the detective's employers, they are no more "objective" than the main text, and later we discover the detective's having fabricated at least the final entry in the report itself. In addition to drawing the reader's attention to the unreliability of the protagonist, the entries insert an additional degree of self-reflexivity to the acts of writing and observation that inform the detective's narration of his own disappearance. Moreover, the heterogeneous status of the entries as pieces of a report subsumed within the narrative accentuate the reader's privileged role in the production of the text itself. Situated outside the text, the reader completes the work in the act of "reading" the totality of fragments and observations made by the protagonist to assemble together a coherent narrative. In this way, the narrative structure's self-reflexive employment of the position of the reader is crucial to the topological inquiry it produces. To better understand how this topologic reading operates, I will first explore the role of the seemingly superfluous and excessive attention to the boundaries of urban growth found in the novel.

Trailing the missing husband's dealings with a propane gas supplier, the detective is drawn to the edges of the city. There the detective undertakes a detailed study of the dynamic impact of urban expansion and the overlapping strata of social spaces undergoing reconstruction and reorganization with urban change. While contributing little to the narrative of the search for the missing husband, the detective's journey to "F-city" in the following report entry materializes a mapping of the shifting distribution of municipal boundaries and transportation pathways that defined the emergent patterns of Tokyo's remaking.

> The whole west side, separated by the street, is the third ward of F-city. In F-Village which appears on my map (published in a previous year) there is no such division into wards, and the relative position of the streets appears to be quite different. When I inquired I found that they had decided to build near here an interchange for the turnpike at present under construction, that there was a lively buying and selling of land and subdividing into house lots, that the municipal cooperative movement was bearing fruit and was being extended to the present F-city. Come to think of it, the rushing about of heavy trucks filled with excavated soil was conspicuous.[22]

With a crudely sketched map of the area inserted into the text itself, this setting serves as a snapshot of forces of the urban to come as it undergoes both municipal consolidation and integration into the incomplete expressway network. At the time, the construction of Japan's expressway system had set in motion changes that extended far beyond the narrow path of asphalt: it heralded a vast new scale of circulation and exchange that redrew the boundaries of Japanese social space. The text registers these changing contours through the rumble of the ceaseless flow of heavy trucks laden with excavated soil that echoes throughout the older village. The roughly traced map and the detective's further observations capture the overlapping layers of discrete moments in the history of urban transformation. As made evident in the disconnect described here, there remained a discrepancy between the newly delineated ward boundaries and the earlier strata of mixed agriculture and small-scale industrial or sericulture households found in the Musashi Plain region of western Tokyo. With the planned construction of a highway interchange, worlds apart collided in the remaking of outlying zones on the frontline of Japan's Cold War urbanization. Exploring a topos that holds a prominent place in Japan's literary modernity, the specific weave of new and old that defined the Musashi Plain is here subjected to the text's topological aesthetic, one that sought to render the geopolitics of urban remaking visible.[23]

> Mixed among the tile-roofed stores, the farmhouses stood out conspicuously with their lattice doors and high-pitched roofs—apparently the farmers had raised silkworms. In the spacious yards were small passenger cars, bought by the sale of mulberry fields. The same as everywhere else, the electrical appliance shops were unreasonably brilliant. There were even barrel makers, whose shops seemed on the verge of collapse. Generally the shops seemed affluent, still keeping some touch of the old days. However, the paucity of street lights suggested the fate of the old town, which was being left behind and forgotten.[24]

Certain trends marked a shift away from the prior mixture of agricultural and light industrial sources of wealth; people selling land in order to purchase cars with the proceeds and the propane gas merchant's new prosperity both heralded a total transformation in the property relations, orientations, and rhythms defining the social space at the margins of urban expansion. On one hand, we can simply describe this as the result of the Fordist economic restructuring and its accompanying petrochemical dependencies ushered in with the bilateral United States—Japan mutual security framework. Freed from the tedious labor of agriculture and sericulture, these once-prosperous communities could share in the novel mobility and consumer habits of city dwellers.²⁵ Rather than investigating the missing husband's disappearance in any meaningful way, the detective here seems more interested in an ethnographic study of the impact of the freeway interchange's construction on local property relations. How might we situate this strange attention to the details of these processes within the novel's topological inquiry into urban transformation? Like the generalized figure of the *danchi* at the novel's outset, the site F-city is an abstraction extracted from the specific features of the actual terrain of western Tokyo.²⁶

Within this figure of the fluid relations abstracted from the landscape, the detective notes the fleeting nature of the growth-dependent prosperity that undergirds this once-peripheral community, revealing a transitional moment in the local energy market. He describes how the local fuel suppliers that arrived to supply the new patterns of settlement would be overtaken by city gas after a certain point of development, a profoundly limited business cycle: "born of the city's growth and of that growth they would die—a paradoxical business."²⁷ This provides the detective with an excessively detailed context for pursuing his subsequent investigations of the propane supplier for whom the missing husband worked, linking the husband's prospects with this peculiar cycle. At the same time, the detective draws the reader's attention to a profound shift away from a landed property relation (which, as a product of imperial modernity, was by no means "traditional," and had already gone through many transfigurations during the wartime and Occupation land reforms), toward a Fordist economy of consumer goods and real estate exchanges that were spurred on by the generalization of the automobile and its attendant social forms. Although these shifting property relations are but one aspect of a broader transformation within the landscape, they reveal in a concrete manner a way of "reading" the localized forms of the defuse and unintelligible forces at play in the remaking of place. The detective's movements do not comply with the logic of narrative development, but they do adhere to the outlines of a topologic inquiry into the shifting contours of an emergent urban landscape. Each fragmentary site or scene captured by the detective's gaze makes available a way of "reading together" a topology of the complex forces at play as well as potential forms of becoming that undergirded Japan's Cold War urbanization.

At these margins *The Ruined Map* undertakes a surprisingly robust inquiry into the conditions of construction workers in what serves as a microcosm of the assembly of interests working in concert to produce the expansion of the urban landscape. In the newly designated second ward, a large-scale *danchi* housing project is under construction, and upon this site converge the most frictional forces of the expanding landscape. As one local worker mentions to the detective, the construction advances the city's explosive reach into the margins, suggesting, "once the working men's temporary flats were finished in the second ward, the city kind of began to come out here."[28] When construction laborers began taking up makeshift dwellings on the housing development construction site, an informal economy of "recreation" emerged; this took the form of prostitution and drinking stalls furnished within converted microbuses. Managed by the brother of the detective's client, this mini-black-market economy of mobile and fleeting pleasures that wells up from the shadows on the periphery of the construction site demonstrates the powerful tensions that accompanied the reconstruction of Japan's urban landscapes.

The detective further provides a detailed map of the changing terrain, depicting a panorama overlooking the work site and the riverside pleasure quarters, revealing both sides of a closed circuit of exploitation. The "brother" brings the detective to the scene after their chance meeting at the local propane distributor, facilitating the detective's insider peek at the exploitive economy of reconstruction unfolding on the riverbed.

> Red lanterns dangled saucily in the wind, and on the side of the broad, dry riverbed several little buses, their gloomy, pale mouths open, were scattered here and there in a semicircle, irregularly spaced and facing in different directions.
>
> But it was the view of the opposite side of the river, separated by the bank, that caught my attention. Until now it had not been visible, being concealed by the levee around the pear orchard, but a broad expanse of naked terrain clear of fields, houses, and woods was brilliantly illuminated from three sides, like a stage, by great

projectors three feet in diameter. About a hundred yards to the left a field office and a number of mess buildings, like blocks of light, were brimming with animation; it was as bustling as a miniature city. Bulldozers and power shovels were biting into the front of the hill. Patterned stripes cut by the caterpillar trucks ran in and out among them. A dump road connected the main road with the work site. Suddenly the sound of a siren howled across the river bed, and the roar of motors and machinery that had reverberated through the black sky slipped into silence. Three trucks rushing from the lodging to the work site, for the third change of shifts, seemingly overflowing with male workers. Perking up, he says, "this is when the commotion really gets started," and we entered the river bed.[29]

The powerful contrast between the large-scale mobilization of workers and machinery to literally eat away the terrain—they hollow out the hills and contours of one terrain to make room for another—and the temporary informal pleasure space that has sprouted up in tune with the patterns of growth belies a vast remaking of subjects and social space that exceeded all formal organizational networks and boundaries. That is to say, the vast magnitude of forces at play in reconstruction are condensed here like a "scale model of the city," bursting with dislocated urban-immigrant laborers, heavy trucks, and a topography of human exploitation that exceeds the everyday limits of time and space.

Approaching from an indifferent outsider's perspective, the detective comes face-to-face with the intensifying asymmetries and contradictions at play in the reconstruction of the Japanese archipelago, seemingly by chance. Attracted to the riverbed pleasure district to piece together a rudimentary portrait of the "brother" (and the various programs he operates for his particular unit within a vast syndicate organization), the detective is suddenly drawn into a vortex of violence that erupts from this liminal zone at the edges of the expanding city. There, the detective confronts the circulation of laboring bodies that pour into the cities from the countryside, disclosing the emergent forms of exploitation that fueled Japan's growth. In fact, through the detective we "hear" the voice of a laborer who is himself considered among the "missing" by his local government; a laborer who, like those resistive bodies in motion around him, explosively rose up against the joint management-syndicate regulated system of wages and credit that the informal riverside mobile pleasure quarter depends upon.

> Between shouts of "Saké! Saké!" the man in the padded kimono sobbed in a choked voice.—"You! I'm on the list of missing persons for investigation. Ha, ha. My wife's put in a request at the town hall for an all-out search."—"Never mind," said the smaller one, a friendly, balding man, patting his sobbing comrade on the back, "if you start worrying about that, there'll never be an end to it."—"Saké!" shouted the man in the padded kimono, still grumbling. "What's a missing person? I'll send a letter. If they knew I was working that'd be the end of the welfare checks. That's what I told my wife. Try and put up with it for two years and not say anything. Be patient, and just imagine your husband's dead. You can scratch along on welfare." The larger fellow spoke in a quiet voice that carried surprisingly: "Don't worry, it's not your wife's fault. It's the interference from the city government. Interference from the government wanting to cut off your welfare checks. The head of the gang came with the search papers and threatened her. Look at this. Shall I contact city hall, or will you write a letter yourself? Don't worry, we're witnesses that you're here. Look, you've got hands and feet; it's a big laugh, you being missing. You are right here, aren't you?"—"Right, I am. Ah ha!"—"You're right here," chimed the big fellow and the small one from either side.—"Saké, damn it! Still, do I have to write a letter? It's a plot in the government office. Never mind. I'm so sad. I can't play my favorite pinball any more. I'm missing. I get drunk all the time."[30]

This worker's dialogue in the original text goes uninflected with quotations, thus posing an interesting collapse between the detective's vantage point as an indifferent "outsider" and the immanent voices of the exploited workers bound within the syndicate's relentless circuit of labor and pleasure.[31] Moreover, the direct enumeration of beneficiaries to the workers' immiseration is made all the more apparent in the protagonist's inability to assimilate this fact into his compulsive abstractions and speculations. As a fictionalized case, one that remains telling of the persistent labor shortages that haunted and continue to haunt

Japan's construction industry, the novel reveals how the subcontracted "syndicate" in charge of procurement has refined its apparatus of labor extraction to an advanced degree. Not only are workers exploited for their labor, their wages are reacquired through temporary pleasure districts like the riverbed "city," entangling them in debts beyond any means of repayment. Moreover, workers like the one speaking here go "missing," extracted from their hometowns for temporary and insecure forms of employment, and kept in place by threat of ceasing the welfare support for their dependents obtained by being "missing." Thus, here in a fictional narrative we discover an attempt to inquire into the foundational units of the extraordinary mobilization of resources and materials that produced the remaking of the Japanese archipelago. The exploitive economy of insecure labor and the forcible "disappearance" of sovereign working subjects therein, saturate the expansion of the urban terrain. Though mere fictions, their voices "speak" to the reader here in a way distinct from the voice of the detective obsessed with his pursuit of a missing person; he is blind to those missing before his very eyes, a blindness dramatized for the reader of the novel.

In a related way, the brother's exploitive syndicate should be read as more than a thinly veiled fictionalization of an actually existing yakuza criminal organization. More than merely fictionalized versions of "real" places, groups, or events, the syndicate adheres to the same logic of abstraction as the *danchi* or "S-station"; these are all localized manifestations of the exploitation and violence that permeates the language of the novel. The relationship between fiction and reality is after all at the heart of the topological inquiry produced by the text. The text's translation-through-abstraction of such a topos is the very ground for the novel's topology, a language derived to make legible the deforming continuities and discontinuities among the relational forms and the forces informing these transformations. For instance, when the brother casually mentions transporting laborers to work on the front lines of Vietnam as a source of income to cover the detective's expenses, he unwittingly reveals the extent of his syndicate's economy of labor procurement.[32] Of the many ways the most potent geopolitical dimensions of Japan's Cold War remaking are subtly woven into the fabric of the text, the passing reference to the syndicate's labor procurements for the U.S. war in Southeast Asia evidences the novel's consistent efforts to expand the reader's capacities to read a multitude of topoi within a constellation of changing relations. Beyond merely reductively echoing the antiwar slogans of the day, or somehow casting doubt on the brother's moral constitution, the exploitive syndicate's extensive operations are part of the novel's topological inquiry that seeks to manifest for readers the magnitude of the transformations of urbanizing Japan.

The detective spends a great deal of time and effort attending to the minutia of the cycles of boom and bust, advancing economies of exploitation, and diverse forms of violence that inform the syndicate's operations. It is through these details that the text locates a focal point embedded within this fluid constellation of forces to reveal changes and continuities with prior modalities of power, such as the industrial and agricultural forms of collective belonging.

The detective's traversals not only disclose the dimensions of the syndicate, elaborating on meticulous details of its operations across several sites within the emergent landscape, but also fix the reader's attention on the badge worn by the brother and syndicate members. The abstract symbol, described variously as an s-shaped or lightning-shaped mark, repeatedly captures the attention of the detective. Like much of the material evidence captured in the detective's expert gaze, the badge does not trigger any solid meaning or message within his dissolving matrix of signification. But as a focal point for the readers' gaze, presented to them again and again through the inadequacy of the detective's gaze, the badge marks both a boundary and a pathway within the textual topology. On the one hand, the abstracted symbol functions as a node within the textual network of signifying material signs, such as the matches from the café and the maps included in the detective's reports. These are linked together in the detective's failure to "read" them, and made available to the reader as pathways for constructing legible connections among the deluge of details afforded by the detective's pursuits. On the other hand, the badge marks the boundary of membership within the syndicate, the artificial and abstracted signifier of fidelity among its bearers; however, it also testifies to the ease with which such membership can be obtained. For instance, once the brother is dead, the detective is given the brother's badge and toy gun, revealing a logic of substitutability at the heart of the syndicate's facile form of pseudo-collectivity. This mark then draws attention to precisely the structural forms responsible for the social compulsion to belonging that Abe's writings confronted again and again.

Thus, the violence that erupts within the riverbed microcosm of urban transformation further reveals the geopolitical contours of the text's topological inquiry. As a key moment within the text's exploration of the vast networks of exploiter-exploited relationships that proliferate and adapt to the urban changes at hand, this violence is made legible despite, or because of, the detective's inability to "read," or recognize it. Despite his being brought directly into the thick of this inescapable web of exploitation and his witnessing the desperation of the intoxicated workers, the detective remains unmoved by the tensions that give all signs of a violent storm unfolding around him. Instead, he remains fixed on the hope of uncovering the truth about the "brother," a character the detective trusts the least throughout the novel.

> Yet I couldn't take it all seriously. Even if something were brew-
> ing, it would doubtless be at most some unpleasant words or a
> demonstration. A demonstration would mean, in other words, that
> the brother had enemies. The most important thing now was to
> get some clue as to who the enemy was. Every loop is traced with
> a beginning and an end. . . . every maze has an entrance and an
> exit. . . . And since it doesn't matter anyway let's make a grand
> spectacular time out of it.[33]

Misrecognizing the reality of the situation as an opportunity to resolve the mazelike riddle surrounding the "brother," reality nonetheless bursts through the detective's narrow field of view, and refracting his indifferent gaze, he is forced to confront an unnamable violence that goes far beyond his a priori assessment of the situation. In the gap between his vision and the visible, we discover the distortion between his view that "every loop is traced with a beginning and an end. . . . every maze has an entrance and an exit," and the view offered by the text of the closed circuit of exploited-exploiter where every exit is forcibly made equivalent to an entrance to an ever-tightening labyrinth of exploitation. With the breakdown of the detective's vision, and engulfed in the outbreak of violence, the reader is forced to confront the brutality of this distortion itself along with the heinous acts of physical violence, rape, and robbery that ensue. To underscore the importance of grasping the text's depletion of the detective's vision, it is necessary to understand the model for this extraordinary outbreak of worker revolt.

Throughout the 1960s and 1970s, riots and violent confrontations by day laborers erupted in Japan's *yoseba*, the concentrated zones of temporary lodging and labor procurement such as Sanya of Tokyo, Kotobuki-cho of Yokohama, and Nishinari of Osaka. Although the yakuza play a dominant role in exploiting the day laborer markets, the *yoseba* are an important topos for understanding the expanded economies of exploitation that undergirded Japan's "miraculous" growth. As we discover in Edward Fowler's introduction to the vivid lifeworld of Sanya, more than a mere repository of marginalized victims to be exploited as a reserve army of an unemployed underclass, the *yoseba* materialized a contradictory force field where myriad trajectories of escape, exploitation, and disappearance are precariously lived out by diverse individuals.[34] Without recourse to institutionalized labor organizations, the eruptions of violence within Japan's *yoseba* revealed in unmasked form the forces of coercion and control normalized and rendered invisible in the emerging urbanized everyday. In the early 1960s one prominent population among the *yoseba* were coal miners displaced by the closure of mines, among others displaced by economic restructuring fueled by policies seeking to deepen Japan's integration within the U.S. geopolitical order.[35] As heterotopic sites within the homogenizing terrain, the *yoseba* remain telling foci for understanding the vast informal and formal economies of informing the conditions of precarious labor in Japan.[36]

In the novel, we find the *yoseba* abstracted and transfigured into the "miniature city" on the riverbed. It becomes legible as a topos through the sudden upwelling of violence, revealing the radical fluidity, contingency, and indeterminacy that informed the exploited-exploiter relation found at the margins of the expanding urban landscape. Reading through the depletion of the detective's myopic blindness to the operation of the vast network of exploited-exploiter relationships governing Japan's reconstruction, the transfigured *yoseba* topos is laid bare by the text. Though fictional, its logic adheres to the actualities of *yoseba*. It is not a representation of a *yoseba* but a topological transformation of *yoseba;* one whose contours are derived from a portable form, resulting from exploits in the gaps in the juridical frameworks of commerce and traffic law, as well a periodic state due to the economics of urban development. The "excessive" irrelevance of the topos to the central plot of the novel further renders the profound violence and deepening fissures subsumed within the remaking of the urban landscape readily perceivable as a topological figure. The ritual-like violence inflicted upon the brother is but one of the limited forms that these fissures could have taken, as "natural" as the release of excessive pressure from a closed steam system. In the end of the scene, the detective narrowly escapes, his safety secured in part by the sacrificial bodies of the two female pleasure workers and the brother who is killed during this violent outbreak.[37] However, he is not unscathed. This chance encounter marks the start of a rapid deterioration of the detective's own mental map of reality, commencing—or perhaps concluding—his gradual envelopment and "disappearance" within the "bounded infinity" of an urban totality.

CAPTURING FLIGHT

Though the detective is unable to recognize his transformation, as the avatar of the reader, he continues to reveal in vivid detail an urban topos in emergence. As we have seen thus far, rather than a static and immediately given place, the traversals of the detective trace this emergence as a continuum of states (completeness-incompleteness), cycles (boom-bust), and flows (expansion-contraction). Through the limits of the detective's expert gaze, the reader realizes that the distribution of city and countryside is no longer determined by fixed spatial-temporal coordinates, and within the textual topology these areas emerge as differently related topoi among an expanding urban landscape. Here, it becomes important to understand how the emergence of the urban as an expansive totality of differentially entangled topoi is mediated by the sensations and sensibilities of the protagonist, and made legible to the reader in turn. By provocatively inciting the sensory capacities of the reader through the language of the text, *The Ruined Map* allows readers to witness the breakdown of the detective's ordering gaze that once defined and gave shape to the city and his place within it. Once this gaze has been decomposed, a constellation of relational forms within the flux urban transformation seeps in through the blind spots of his gaze, gradually revealing the spatial-temporal vectors of the change at hand. Readers must ascertain for themselves the orientations and values of the transformations rendered through the lines of flight drawn by the text; and with these the readers must complete diagrams for both the detective's substitution with the missing husband, as well as the emergence of the urban totality as a topology of interrelated forms.

We find traces of such vectors in the detective's circulations through the expressway system. After the death of the brother the detective's traversals of the expressway are described as "inexplicable." The detective's desire to link the brother with the husband's disappearance has reached a dead end, and the brother's death marks the end of the brother's financial support of the detective's case; thus, his role as detective is effectively terminated as a result. Yet, in his flight from this conclusive fact, the detective delineates the vectors leading toward his substitution with the disappeared husband, further accentuated by a peculiar experience of temporality.

> The dry pavement of the freeway seemed both black and white at the same time. I was doing nearly seventy miles an hour, about five over the limit. The motor sputtered, making a sound like a piece of wire thrust into the blades of a fan; the tires screeched like adhesive tape being torn away. I was immersed to my very core in noise, but I heard nothing; it was as if I were in a great silence. All I could see was the concrete road running straight to the sky. No, it was not a road, it was a band of flowing time. I was not seeing but only feeling time.[38]

As the detective becomes aware of his own desire for escape, the experience of acceleration and movement induces an embodied perception of time itself, or a kind of immanent apperception of the self as pure temporality, beyond any given human measure or space-time coordinate axis. "I was a point of tenseness. I had the sensation of suddenly awakening on a calendarless [sic] day at a place that appeared on no map. You are free to call this sufficiency flight [escape] if you wish."[39] Yet his path of escape is by nature circumscribed, for the tollbooths on the closed network of the expressway mark off predetermined intervals that inhibit the unobstructed continuance of his awakening to "pure time."

"But if this pure time was an awakening, then the sequel to the dream at once blocked the way. The toll gate. A long dream sequence after a short artificial awakening. Immediately I made a U-turn and entered the line of cars going toward the city."[40]

As critic Nakano Kazunori argues, the desire for escape consistently evidenced by the detective is not merely escape from a historical collective sociality (*kyōdōtai*) as a remnant of Japan's feudal past, but rather a desire to escape the contractual forms of human relationships that define urban modernity.[41] Furthermore, Nakano cites this scene to demonstrate the detective's desire for an experience of temporality beyond the passive subjectivity produced by modernity's contractual relations. Nakano's reading of this work as a critique of the passive subjectivity of contractual human relationships resonates here with the forms of circumscribed circulation that once secured the detective's increasingly unreliable map of social reality. The experience of "pure time" discovered in his flight on the expressway is by nature profoundly limited, not only by the toll gates but by the nature of the expressway system as a closed network. It is "pure" because its duration has been closed off from any sustained continuity.

Yet, despite its restricted form, the detective's experience of another form of time—a "pure time" discovered within the closed network of the expressway—marks the unraveling of his coherent map of social reality with greater acceleration. "Perhaps the husband's silhouette had come into view. In some corner of the superimposed town landscapes there were empty black holes. Shadows of the nonexistent husband, he was not alone; there was a limitless number of different hims. *The "him" within me, the "him" within her, the "him" within him.* Apparently in my mind some great change was beginning to take place."[42] The detective's map becomes populated with an infinite number of "hims," "others" within both oneself and the others—thus reflecting a profoundly split subject where both self and other are impossible abstractions in the face of the intertwined relational structures governing subjectivity. The once-blank areas become inhabited by a society of disappeared who exist beyond the limits of his coherent gaze, a society the detective now desires to join.

As we learn from the detective's subsequent discussion with his client, the husband too shared this experience of pure time on the expressway. After describing this event and the disquieting desire for perpetual escape the expressway had induced, she offers a telling detail of her husband.

> "It's strange, isn't it. My husband seemed to use the freeway a lot too. Of course, in his case it was to test the cars he had repaired. He said he used to go round and round on the freeway so much that he got tipsy. That was in the evenings when the iron roofs of the buildings still shone red in the sun. Though the underparts were already darkened."
>
> "Perhaps what I was saying was just that."
>
> "He said that as he went up and down the freeway a hundred times, a thousand times, the exits gradually diminished in number, and that in the end he felt locked in."
>
> "When you're driving, you never want to think of stopping. You want the moment to go on forever just as it is. But when it's over, you shudder at a state like that, with no end. There's a big difference between driving and thinking about driving."[43]

Although the notion of "driving" in this exchange is tense with overtones lost on the detective, it joins the detective and husband within a form of circumscribed movement for movement's sake, that is to say, a disquieting experience of time captured within a closed system of transportation. Through the husband's repetition of movement, he increasingly feels he will become trapped within the closed loop of the expressway, without escape. These movements offer a material form homologous to the contractual human relations that subordinate and render passive the "subject" of urban modernity according to Nakano. Furthermore, the parallax produced between the detective's desire for perpetual movement and the magnitude of obligations that bind and restrict him reveals a disquietude shared with the missing husband. This shared sensation of enclosure, materialized as a social rather than individual experience of inexplicable disquiet, ultimately lays the foundation for the detective's metamorphosis into a member of the community of the disappeared. What would form the actually existing metropolitan expressway system was only in the early stages of inception at the time of the text's production, with incomplete spans and segments of the system under construction since the time of the Tokyo Olympics. The discontinuities and incompleteness of this world, wrought as a mediating virtuality elaborated from these fragmented pieces, pose a problem to the reader. This peculiar form of spatial-temporal displacement of suspended flight and enclosure delineates the fluid ground of relations that embody the emergence of the urban as a totality inhabited by those who have gone missing. Where do these lines of flight intersect? And what topological figure do they produce for the reader? Once again, the reader must wrestle with the sensory details that govern one's reading of the orientations and values attributed to the "escape" to the urban wrought by the text.

THE CAMELLIA ANOMALY

A small matchbox found in the missing husband's jacket, the detective's only real "clue" from the outset of *The Ruined Map*, leads him to the Camellia coffee house at the base of the slope leading to the client's housing development. In all his comings and goings, the detective's pursuit repeatedly leads him to discover one dead end after another, except for the Camellia, which takes on increasing gravity as a persistent question mark within the ever-shifting contours of the detective's map. After the eruption of violence that leads to the brother's death at the riverbed, the detective slowly unravels a possible trajectory of the missing husband as he too assumes a similar path of escape.[44] The ultimate substitution between missing husband and detective is produced by the detective's deepening engagement with the café. The transformative dynamics of driving first revealed in the detective's spatial-temporal displacement on the freeway become linked to the anonymous pool of freelancing professional drivers that clandestinely operate at the Camellia. Furthermore, the plot of the missing husband concludes in the detective's reproduction of his disappearance vis-à-vis his run-in with the Camellia. But more importantly for the reader, the café delimits an anomalous threshold that utterly depletes the detective's ordering gaze. Thus, within the text's topological inquiry, it embodies an anomalous boundary beyond which the vague contours of another form of collective becoming emerges. Thus, the Camellia delimits a blind field beyond the reach of the knowable domain to which his gaze pertains through the blind spots in his expert vision. As a result, the Camellia performs a crucial function in the realization of the textual topology for the reader.

The café serves as a locus of autonomous, anonymous, and flexible forms of labor that exploit the urban's emergent forms of expanded mobility and patterned circulation to secure a degree of independence from contractual labor. The reader learns much about the drivers who gather at the café in the detective's interview with a taxi driver who purchased a car from the missing husband, included in the text as part of the detective's ongoing report. Of particular interest is the information the interviewee provides about the freelance nature of the drivers' work and the role of anonymity in mediating the collective's relations among drivers and clients.[45] Here, many of the same dynamics we found in Tsuchimoto's portrait of taxi drivers discussed in the prior chapter are found among the details of the laborers who converge at the Camellia. But here, the dynamics of driving, the autonomous forms of labor the automobile makes possible, and the changing social space they convey are all brought to bear upon the detective's trajectory. Transformative violence provokes his metamorphosis into one of the "disappeared," as one who has escaped.

The detective arrives at the Camellia just before dawn the day after he has resigned from his job as a detective. There, he finds the usually empty neighborhood café alive with an unexpected congregation of people.

> I could only assume someone was watching me. Outside it was all white, and although colors had not yet returned to objects, it was already light enough to distinguish clearly the shapes of things, and drivers were beginning to turn off their headlights. Yet the inside of the shop was still lighter, and through the loose weave of the Camellia's black curtains I could clearly make out the interior. The shop, which had always been so deserted and forlorn that it made me ill at ease, was now a confusion of closely packed black figures.
>
> It was impossible to discern exactly what was going on. Two or three men standing at the front turned and looked at me with hostile eyes; the next instant I was seized by the collar by hands extended from the corner near the door, while an arm violently beat on my

head, which unexpectedly began to reel. . . . Someone opened the car door and two others, supporting me on both sides, thrust me in. My legs were folded in under the dashboard and the door was violently closed. They were experts. Unfortunately I was unable after all to see the faces of the men who had manhandled me. . . . There were almost no passers-by yet, but the window of the Camellia had already become a black mirror, and the surroundings had taken on color with the onset of morning. Then the quiet and deserted street was suddenly swarming with people. I could not let a face like mine be seen. I rolled up a Kleenex and plugged my nose. Aware of the eyes that were surely peering out at me from the window of the Camellia, I started the car and slowly pulled away.[46]

Like a black box whose contents cannot be absorbed by the gaze, the Camellia is described as a highly visual environment that the detective's gaze cannot consume or control. Being repelled from his quest for knowledge, the former detective is physically and mentally cast out from the interior of the Camellia. The café and the anonymous collectivity it sustains not only confront his expert gaze as a black mirror, but also inflict him with a form of violence, depleting his visually mediated mapping of reality and propelling him toward his final substitution with the missing husband. His ultimate metamorphosis is a product of this violence that repels the detective's own gaze, but further projects him toward the community of the disappeared beyond the reader's own gaze as well. The text description of this violence is qualitatively different from the description of the spontaneous revenge conducted upon the brother at the riverbed. In one of the many perverse symmetries that govern this story, it was the detective's car and the sacrificial bodies of the sex workers that allowed him to narrowly escape from the crude rage of the exploited workers on the riverbed, and it was to his car that the anonymous collective at the Camellia returned the detective after pounding him, as if to guide him on his way toward his own "liberation." Two scenes of very different kinds of violence link to two very different forms of labor, and index two different trajectories of escape. However, within the text's topological inquiry, the Camellia embodies a crucial site as both boundary and pathway among the different topoi elaborated by the detective's movements.

The anomalous threshold of the Camellia, acting as both node and boundary, moreover permits the collectivity of anonymous drivers to independently contract themselves to meet the more flexible demands of the expanded urban totality. The drivers subject themselves to these flexible demands, contingently transporting clients without knowing the origin and destination of the ride, and exploit the administrable lines of flight of the patterned infinity of the emergent constellation of urban mobility. Paradoxically, by relinquishing contractual forms of labor and the competitive struggle they engender, the anonymous collective of drivers has obtained a kind of invisibility within the networked topoi of the emergent landscape, repelling the legibility afforded an ordering gaze like that of the detective's. The detective's flight toward inhabiting the terrain shared by these anonymous and ostensibly autonomous drivers is rendered a possibility only through the violence that erases the compulsion to a visual ordering and orienting of his world. In direct contrast to the brutality of the violence that erupts at the riverbed and persistently haunts the detective's struggle to come to terms with the brother's death, the reader experiences the detective's beating nearly anesthetically. Described as a "painless" and "expert" process, this peculiar form of collective violence affects the detective's sensory capacities more than his physical well-being.

Given the role of violence and visuality that condense around these two different forms of labor, the Camellia and the riverbed embody two crucial focal points within the topological inquiry of the text. They compel the reader to extrapolate an expanded sensory engagement with the text as the basis for rendering a coherent "reading" of the transforming constellation of forces informing both. Reading across the intensive and extensive forms of exploitation as well as potentials for individual and collective autonomy afforded by these forces, readers obtain a reinvigorated sense of how the transformative contours of the urban revealed by the text are mediated by visuality and violence. As both threshold and pathway in the textual economies of both visuality and violence, the Camellia-riverbed relational topoi make available an understanding of the continuities and discontinuities of urban transformation. In this sense, the text's topological inquiry affords an expansion of the modernist leftist political imaginary by inviting the reader to read across these topoi and grasp the forms of visuality and violence that differently pertain to each. For contemporary readers, the text's attention to the increasing demands for flexible and precarious forms of labor afforded by urban change has become acutely prescient.[47] However, at the time of the text's production, the horizons of the emergent urban totality were neither inevitable nor transparent to either the author or the reader. This is how the text operates topologically; as an inquiry into these transformations, it necessitates an expansion of readers' senses, inviting them to "read," and therefore to think, urban change with the language of violence and visuality produced in much of Abe's most influential fiction.

THRESHOLDS OF AN URBAN LANGUAGE

Thus repelled from the inner workings of the Camellia's anonymous collective, the detective takes refuge in a cocoonlike state, sinking into the bed of the missing husband's wife, where days pass in a liminal zone between his waking mind and unconscious mind. There in his passage of metamorphosis, while the transformation catalyzed by the violence of the Camellia drivers is rendered complete, the indeterminacy of the shared gazes opens up a vast void from which emerges the spectacular form of the urban totality itself:

> She sat down at the foot of the bed, staring at me intently from some place I could not see. Was she really looking at me? I wondered. Or, like the guest she had had to coffee, was I being made to join the phantoms who played the foil to her monologues with herself?
>
> For whom does it beat . . . this enormous heart of the city that goes on pulsating, not knowing for whom? I changed my position and looked for her, but she was no place to be seen. If that were the case, where in heaven's name was I, looked at by that nonexistent her?[48]

The text produces a critical destabilization of the relation between seer and seen through which the world emerges. The uncertainty of the woman's gaze cast upon the detective from a blind spot within his own gaze produces a deep gulf between the given relations that secure their subject positions. Within this zone where their gazes fall short of any static coherence between seer and seen, the image of the pulsing flows of an urban expanse as a vast cardiovascular system confronts and exceeds their anchored vantage points.[49] With a fleeting reference to Edgar Allan Poe's "The Tell-Tale Heart," an ethical question is being raised here. Through the detective's pursuit of the missing husband as a pursuit self-mediated by the pursuit of the woman, the irreconcilability of gazes between seer and seen opens a fissure in the static relations of sociality. Precisely from this fissure the trope of the urban totality as a vast pump asserts itself again as an uncanny social form, dislocated from existing spatial-temporal coordinates.

All of the novels in Abe's "disappearance" series feature a gendered pair that functions as the minimal unit of the forms of sociality under question. In this case however, the figure of the urban totality that emerges from the breakdown of visual relations between the gendered pair affords a deeply unstable telescoping of power relations from the most intimate gendered power differentials—the heteronormative desires and inequalities mediated by the detective's gaze in this case—to the most abstract social relations mediated by the urban itself. It does not fully render the meaning or magnitude of the urban as a coherent totality but rather discloses the permeation of the social by the urban, as the mediating ground of the social. Suffused with an endless series of dualistic pairs ranging from male and female, seer and seen, virtual and actual, abstract and concrete, fictional and real, and so on, the text repeatedly compels the reader to discover how this urban ground consists of the perpetual flux of relational forms rather than the fixed and determinant meanings associated with either pole of these pairs.

The instability of this ground embryonically harbors an open set of fluid relationships as a result. As the detective slides out from his cocoon and takes flight into the world defined by these relations, freed from the ordering gaze and hierarchies of meaning they sustain, his exit into the anonymous urban beyond presents the reader with a problem. The reader must question whether the detective has obtained a novel form of autonomy within the constellation of forces induced by the pumping motion of the expansive urban totality. Has the detective undergone a metamorphosis that traces a trajectory toward a novel form of urban sociality? Based on what we have outlined in our reading of the topological inquiry of the text, the answer to these questions does not depend on whether he has escaped or just descended into self-delusion, nor does it depend upon what he has escaped from necessarily.[50] Rather, it depends upon what possibilities a topological "reading" of the text can foster. As a means of emphasizing an active role for the reader in completing such a topological reading, the text need not point to a singular outcome of the detective's transformation.

In the final pages of the novel, a dead cat flattened in the road spontaneously diverts the flows of traffic, disclosing the unfree contours of the vehicles. Looking on, the detective smiles thinking of a name to give to this uncanny corpse. The text itself is situated in a similar fashion between the reader and a topological inquiry into urban change, one that seeks to expand the sensibilities and capacities of the reader. Nameless, the distorted figure of the cat invites readers to grasp for themselves a novel language that can describe the constellation of forces delineated in the text's topological inquiry. As a result, the novel transfigures the constituent relations among writer, reader, and text that inform modernist literary praxis, opening them up to indeterminate "readings." The text evidences Abe's investments in deriving a language of the urban to effect a liberation toward the novel forms of urban sociality he found to be antithetical to the pseudo-collectivities and residual forms of belonging he considered responsible for the so-called alienation and solitude typically associated with cities.[51] This was, moreover, an important aspect of the "new language of the city" that Maeda Ai attributes to Abe's writings, as I mentioned at the outset of this chapter.

However, the reader's capacity to "complete" the topological figure produced by the text remains the critical link in the operation of this "new language." Even as Abe's fiction interrogates the givens of modernist literary practice and expands the affective and political vocabularies of leftist writing and thought in the process, the text moreover reveals the limits of "reading" topologically. Although the topology it traces reveals a fluid constellation of forces and forms at play in Japan's urban transformation, it requires a fixed distance among the changing world, the dynamic text, and the active reader. When drawn as abstract figures, topologies require the fictional mathematical projection of their spatial-temporal dimensions within a plane discrete from the viewer who realizes their form. This limiting condition of topological figures is also what makes them so compelling for producing novel ways of understanding the relational forms of continuities and discontinuities within dynamic transformations. They reveal ways of understanding the relationships between the transformed figures that would otherwise be understood only as either continuous or discontinuous processes of change.[52]

Here, Abe's text demonstrates that the distortions of Japan's social spaces take place through specific relational forms of violence and visuality. These are derived at once by relations of "sameness" with the forms of belonging and exploitation that Abe identified with residual agricultural and industrial conditions that occluded urban becoming. Also, relations of "difference" found in the expansion of modernist leftist political imagery in literary thought and practice foster novel ways of "reading" of the immanent urban conditions of possibility. As such, Abe's topological writing translated the relational forms of "sameness" and "difference" into a new language of the city for the reader as part of his efforts to expand the urban vocabularies of the modernist left. As I have argued in this chapter, the text sought to expand the capacities of readers to realize the roles of violence and visuality within urban transformation. At the heart of its urban topology, and therefore of its novel language, was an effort to make it possible to sense the intensifying forms of precarity that inhered within the emergent landscape. While it did not actively seek to dismantle them, the text made available a vocabulary for grasping the limiting conditions and possibilities of urban change itself. This is perhaps the source of Félix Guattari's singular praise of *The Ruined Map* for its "admirable oneiric explorations," and in particular, Abe's identification of Japan's heterotopic communities of day laborers such as Sanya as "less representative of an absolute misery than an irrevocable refusal of the existing order."[53]

CHAPTER THREE

Landscape Vocabularies

For a Language to Come and the Geopolitics of Reading

As we have seen thus far, provocative reconsiderations of place (topos) were a central site and stake in the geopolitical and aesthetic conditions of possibility for engaging with Japan's urban transformation in the 1960s. Figured topographically or topologically, the urban afforded novel modes of visual and sensory aesthetics as the basis for expanding the geopolitical vocabularies available at the time. With these, new modalities for "reading" the emergent urban landscape relied primarily on the existing distributions among "author," "work," and "viewer/reader," even as they attempted to self-reflexively activate the latter's capacities in producing a different arrangement among these relations. Within the flux of urban reconstruction, this corresponded to the remaking of prior distributions of space (city/country, worldwide/nation, center/periphery, and so on) and time (past, present, and future, wartime/recovery, work/leisure, and so on). As Japan entered the 1970s, however, we discover how the works thinking through the remnants of intensive urban flux participated in an intensive questioning of the shifting relations among urban and media ecologies. The work of critic and photographer Nakahira Takuma (1938–2015) offers a crucial point of entry within the entanglement of media and urban forms of thought and practice that emerged from the breakdown of static conceptual architectures of language, landscape, and environment during the late 1960s and early 1970s.

In Japan, Nakahira, along with Moriyama Daidō (b. 1938), is legendary for establishing an iconic grainy, blurry, and out-of-focus (*are-bure-boke*) photographic "style," and for cofounding *Provoke*, the influential, experimental-photography magazine synonymous with this style. Nakahira was also a prolific thinker on the medium. He deftly traversed the boundaries between theory and practice during the 1960s and 1970s in his critical writings on photography, art, film, journalism, radical politics, television, and tourism. However, his work in its full scope became recognized only with the 2003 retrospective *Nakahira Takuma: Degree Zero-Yokohama*, curated by Kuraishi Shino at the Yokohama Museum of Art.[1]

Even a cursory glance at the many recent publications and republications of his writings and photography will reveal a decisively consistent texture to the decades-long evolutions in Nakahira's works. Among the dizzying aesthetic and conceptual turns and returns, we discover a relentless interrogation of Japan's urban landscapes and media systems. It is fitting, then, that the streets run wildly throughout Nakahira's writings and photography. Nakahira persisted in drawing attention to the uncanny remnants, residues, and irreconcilable differences that flooded the streets, which are the overdetermined places of circulation, exchange, and encounter that symbolize urban modernity. The entangled urban and media contours of Nakahira's work were critical to his pursuit of a radical photographic theory and practice. His work evidences a potent use for such fragments, torn from the breakdown and exhaustion of the systematizing and codified structures of language, landscape, and environment. Deconstructed and depleted in the magnetically charged flux where gazes, bodies, and material things collide, the world is nonetheless made present, exposed, and dispossessed, as are we, the viewers who must make sense of it all. In this chapter, I will explore the possibility of "reading" such residues that Nakahira presented at a crucial moment in the evolution of his writing and photography. Despite, or perhaps because of, its paradoxical illegibility within cultural histories of the late 1960s and the 1970s—characterized by a partial reception that persists in celebrating the "iconic" photographic "style" of Nakahira's early period, while simultaneously disavowing his criticism that informed a much longer trajectory of critical theory and practice—Nakahira's work captures an enduring set of geopolitical and aesthetic problems that constituted the conditions of possibility and limitation found among a broad range of cultural practices.

Here I will chart the evolution of Nakahira's critical photographic vocabulary from his magazine work in the late 1960s to his first collection, *For a Language to Come* (1970). This will serve as the foundation for exploring the diversification of Nakahira's theoretical writings and photographic praxis in and around 1973's *Why an Illustrated Botanical Dictionary? Nakahira Takuma's Collected Writings on Visual Media* in the chapter 4. Thus, these two collections will establish two nodes of inquiry for separate but profoundly interrelated chapters. In *For a Language to Come*, Nakahira's most "iconic" early photography is paired with a selection of critical essays. *Why an Illustrated Botanical Dictionary? Nakahira Takuma's Collected Writings on Visual Media* features Nakahira's critical writings on an expansive range of topics concerning not only photography, but also cinema, art, and media. Crucial for the inquiry undertaken here is the need to understand how these two collections do not constitute two discrete modes of practice, one photographic, one textual. Instead, the collections work together in important ways to reveal a shared concern with the entanglement of urban spaces and media contexts. On the one hand, the later essay collection's opening essay, for which the volume is named, "Why an Illustrated Botanical Dictionary?," repudiates Nakahira's own approach to photography taken in the first volume, setting the tone for the second volume's intensive interrogations of the workings of power and environments of visual media. On the other hand, striking continuities if not continuous developments of the questions posed by the essays appear in both volumes. To better understand the crucial differences and transformations that inform these two collections and to illustrate the latter's critique of Nakahira's own photography, already being assimilated into the commodified visual culture of the day as an iconoclastic "style" in its time, I will explore the shifting questions of language, landscape, and environment posed by each book. As different but interrelated focal points of theoretical and practical inquiry, each of these terms delimited enduring knots of entangled problems informed by the changing contours of urban and media power. In unraveling these changing sets of questions across his work, we discover a crux of geopolitical and aesthetic problems that delineated a lasting change in the theoretical and practical scope of critically informed cultural practices for decades to come.

ESCAPE FROM EXPRESSION

I would like to first briefly sketch the background that informed Nakahira's emergence as a photographer and critic. After graduating from Tokyo University of Foreign Studies, Nakahira worked as an editor for *Contemporary Eye*, a monthly cultural affairs magazine. Among the pages devoted to timely left-wing geopolitical and socioeconomic analyses of such topics as the affective foundations of postwar Japanese democracy and the collapse of the "ie" family system, we can discern a formative set of interests from Nakahira's contribution of review essays on major critical essay collections by Terayama Shūji (1935–1983), Tanigawa Gan (1923–1995), and Matsumoto Toshio (1932–2017).[2] From 1964 Nakahira worked with Tōmatsu Shōmei (1930–2012) on a photographic series entitled "I am King," where Nakahira published his first photographs under the pseudonym Yugi Akira.[3] At the same time that he was in charge of the photography pages, Nakahira was also editing Terayama's serialized novel *Ah, Wilderness (Aa, kōya)*.[4] With Tōmatsu's encouragement, Nakahira became a full-time photographer while collaborating with Moriyama Daidō on a series of photographs that accompanied Terayama's "picture essay," *The Streets Are a Battleground*, first serialized in the illustrated magazine *Asahi Graph* in 1966. As a celebration of Tokyo as a utopia of horse-racing tracks, boxing rings, pachinko parlors, strip shows, crowded trains, and pop singers, the photographs of Nakahira and Moriyama captured the sites and settings of Terayama's "antiestablishment" vision of nomadic urban existence.[5]

In 1965 Tōmatsu invited Nakahira to participate in the preparation for the exhibition *A Century of Photography: The History of Japanese Photographic Expression*, the first major historical survey of photography in Japan. Recent scholarship on this exhibition has revealed a number of important aspects of Nakahira's participation and the role it played in his work.[6] Of particular relevance for this study was Nakahira's encounter with critic Taki Kōji (1928–2011), who would play a significant role in developing the exhibition's conceptual framework. As the exhibition title suggests, rather than the nation or a preestablished narrative of national history serving as the organizing principle, it was the ambiguous term "expression" that structured the exhibition. Moreover, as scholar Tsuchiya Seiichi has noted, the exhibition coincided with the one-hundredth anniversary of the Meiji Restoration, which served as a rallying cry for diverse conservative causes at the time that seized the opportunity for a revisionist celebration of imperial authority. In that context, the exhibition's unique structure and scope had a significant and lasting impact on the reception of photography in general in Japan because, as Tsuchiya notes, "the purpose was neither simply an historical retrospective nor an affirmation of national identity. It was to build on an historical perspective, to lay an historic foundation on which photographers could take their own stand."[7]

While surveying Japan's photographic history, gathering and looking at more than 500,000 photographs from all over the archipelago, Nakahira and Taki would come to emphasize the concept of "record" in their critique of "expression" as the engine of photography's development to be gained from historical perspective. From the flood of anonymous photographic "records/documents" that they encountered, Nakahira and Taki both identified photographic technology's capacity to undermine the established hierarchies of artistic representation. As Gyewon Kim has detailed in her look at how the exhibition's historical perspective, and colonial photographic "documents" in particular, shaped subsequent photographic practices, Nakahira and Taki found the contingencies of the photographic process to be an important source for a sustained critique of "expression" itself. Within the historical perspective afforded by the exhibition, these "records" and "documents" proved to be a crucial resource for those seeking an understanding of photography that did not participate in the perpetual celebration of photographers as modern "artists" in a revisionist recuperation of national identity. These anonymous remnants of photographic history, as Kim poignantly notes, "uncovered how the modern conception of representation is bound to fail, since the object captured by the camera already transcends the individual will and the subjective consciousness of the artist."[8] Such perspectives help contextualize the fact that it was in the midst of their collaborative explorations of photographic history in preparation for this exhibition, that Taki and Nakahira undertook the production of the coterie journal, *Provoke: Provocative Materials for Thought.*[9]

Nakahira and Taki produced three issues of *Provoke* between 1968 and 1969 together with poet Okada Tadahiko (1939–1997), photographer

Takanashi Yutaka (b. 1935), and Moriyama Daidō in the second and third issues. Despite the journal's small run and limited circulation, the three issues of *Provoke* continue to elicit attention as an accentuated point of inflection in the art historiography of photography in Japan, as a recent series of international exhibitions and scholarship have soundly demonstrated.[10] As a result of these recent reappraisals, it has become clear, for instance, that it was not the pursuit of a new photographic "style" that inspired these thinkers to take up photography as a critical tool against "expression," one of capitalist modernity's foundational myths. Moreover, we have a clearer picture of how Nakahira's unprecedentedly rapid rise to prominence as both photographer and critic was solidified with *Provoke* (and a subsequent 1970 collection of material that initially appeared in *Provoke*, entitled *First, Abandon the World of Pseudo-Certainty: Thoughts on Photography and Language*). It has also become commonplace to note that a majority of his most iconic photographs recorded disquieting scenes of everyday city life. Nakahira's photography in *Provoke* was replete with grainy nocturnal views of illuminated streets, sidewalks, passageways, and modes of transportation including subways, trains, ferries, and automobiles. Within these fleeting glimpses of city life we encounter the undulating outlines of uncanny material objects and forms: soporific human figures, plants sealed within glass windows, and fish enclosed in aquariums. Thus, the fact that Nakahira's work was at times grainy, blurry, and out of focus, was not simply an assertion of an authorial intent to forge a new photographic style. This encounter between a flux of urban and aesthetic forms constitutes a crucial dimension of Nakahira's thought and practice, yet this fact has remained illegible in most accounts.

Here I will explore how Nakahira evidenced an urgent effort to capture a radically transforming world, and how the photography that resulted was merely the by-product of his provocations between the camera and the fluid contours of an urban subject. So how might we engage the urban contours of Nakahira's work within a larger constellation of geopolitical and aesthetic problems? The answer lies, in part, in questioning, as Nakahira relentlessly continued to do until his death, the seemingly indispensable notion of "expression" that defined photography as "art" and the photographer as an "artist," an ideological construct that continues to shape the reception of Nakahira's work. Furthermore,

Nakahira's work draws renewed attention to the urban forms and media contexts of Japan's Cold War remaking and raises different kinds of questions about the prospects for image practices therein. These are unsettling questions that invite us to problematize a number of assumptions governing the reception of the critical modalities of thought and practice at play in Nakahira's work.

Even in the process of taking up the camera, Nakahira was already engaged with a set of theoretical and practical questions that arose in traversal of editorial, poetic, critical, cinematic, and photographic practices. Together with Taki, who would become a long-time collaborator and coconspirator, Nakahira was interested in the decentering of representational aesthetics made possible through photography afforded a provocative horizon for engaging with a broad set of geopolitical and sociohistorical transformations that they (and others) found within Japan's Cold War remaking. Although we might note the influential roles of both Tōmatsu and Terayama in inspiring Nakahira to take up a camera, the contours of the geopolitical and aesthetic problems we discover throughout the trajectory of his photography and writings in many ways depart from those associated with these progenitive figures. As this chapter will demonstrate, Nakahira's work evidences a protracted exploration of the productive tensions and differences among literature, cinema, and photography as media for critical thought. Accordingly, we must triangulate Nakahira's work within the evolutions in thematic concerns and multiple media that characterized not only the works of prominent figures such as these, but also within the strikingly expanded contours of critical thought that ushered in the 1970s. Thus, if we divorce Nakahira's photography from his critical writings, or from the complex milieu of transformations and limitations surrounding his work, we lose sight of the novel forms of exchange among literary and visual media, and the shared questions of language, landscape, and environment that sustained and shaped cultural practice for decades to come.

PROVOCATIVE ACCUMULATIONS FOR THOUGHT

One of the defining characteristics of *For a Language to Come*, was the way it redeployed writings and photographs from Nakahira's diverse output from roughly 1964 to 1970. In addition to the material that appeared in the journal *Provoke*, the collection drew on essays and photographs that first appeared in a range of print media. Considering how each journal had a different audience and the status of photography within its pages was quite diverse, the photobook format not only consolidated and condensed his work but also decontextualized and flattened out the differences among the most common outlets for Nakahira's work at the time, such as *Contemporary Eye, Japan Reader's Newspaper, Asahi Graph, Asahi Journal, Asahi Camera,* and *Design.* While the translation from print periodical to photobook has in fact long been one of the primary formats of publication for photography, the differential between them is revealing in specific ways here. Many of the essays were first composed for a specific journal's readership, often within specific columns or serialized formats. For instance, one of the main essays included in *For a Language to Come,* "What is it to be Contemporary?," was first serialized in *Design* as "Photography, 1969, What is it to be Contemporary?" from May to August 1969.[11] The photographs also varied between those that appeared in a variety of journals under different names, and those that were produced for a specific series within the journal. If we briefly examine one example of this latter kind of publication, we can identify some important aspects of how Nakahira approached each format, and what transformations were rendered in the translation into a single volume.

Included as part ten of an ongoing series entitled, "Ecologies of Japan" ("*Nihon no seitai*") in the photography magazine *Asahi Camera,* 1969's "Last train" ("*shūdensha*") consists of five photographs and two passages of short text. In the concluding text Nakahira describes the process by which he came to conceptualize the work for this specific series, attempting to capture that particular slice of life "a la carte" found on the last train from Tokyo to his home in Zushi, Kanagawa, about an hour away.[12] The five photographs conveyed a grainy, out-of-focus sketch of the last train's distinct atmosphere, starting with an indifferent view of the train car ceiling hung with advertisements, seen from the vantage point of a passenger gazing upward, as if to situate the viewer within the space. In the nearly empty train car we find human figures slumped over in intoxicated slumber, captioned with a description of the peculiar emergence of a kind of intimacy among the bodies, sounds, and sensations of the jostling train as people come into their own after the long day's struggle. A photograph of a hauntingly indistinct figure enclosed within the train doors, hands pressed against the glass, where the outlines of the word "class" ("tō/nado") are inscribed, takes on an uncannily facelike appearance due to its proximity to where the absent face should be. Adjacent to this, a memorable photograph of a passenger tightly clutching his bandaged head, the vestige of some injury that fills the nearly empty car with a distinct sense of dread, suggests an unseen violence from which he has just barely escaped.[13]

In the included text, Nakahira notes that he shot all the photographs intentionally with the same slightly longer exposure, allowing the photographs to be blurred and shaken by the movements of the train. "I have difficultly believing the accepted idea that photographs should not be blurry or out of focus. First of all, when forming an image of things with only human eyes, each individual thing and each individual image are shaken and blurred together. Is it not our imagination that unifies them and fixes them into a stable image?"[14] We discover here in a basic form the transparent logic of Nakahira's photography. Through the mediation of the camera, situated between the photographer and singular phenomena materialized in the world before him, in this case the distinct specificities encountered on a last train, an entanglement is produced by dissolving the distances that separate both sides of the camera.

Nakahira fixed a slightly longer shutter speed to expose more of the material and sensory contours of the world at hand, drawing out both visible and nonvisible details from "the last train." Although this allows the train's vibrations to register on the film as blur, just as it would on any train, not just the last train, this technical selection eroded the coherence of the resultant image, mediated by the imagination of the viewer, in this case the general idea of "the last train" and also the material thing imaged, mediated by the camera, thus disclosing the singular atmosphere of each scene. They are made to dissolve together, drawing the viewer out into the world and drawing out the contours of the world itself. That is, both "sides" are exposed and displaced from their distributed or otherwise static states of being, and entangled within a mutual process of becoming through the camera. This performs a stark contrast to the ideological definition of the camera as a means for the unmediated capture of an "objective" reality existing in itself by a self-possessing "subject." Seeing with the machinic eyes of the camera, Nakahira's photographic "records" fix the fleeting traces of an encounter upon the photochemical substrate of the film as residues of the momentary dissolve among world and selves. But how might we begin to make sense of such residues?

Much of the significance that can be gleaned from these photographic remnants is informed by the immediate context of where and how they are encountered. In this case, as parts of an established series in a photography magazine, the readings of these residues are framed by both the text and context of "the last train," an installment in the "Ecologies of Japan" series. Albeit rather poorly, they can nonetheless be read according to these frames as illustrating a "slice of life" portrait of changing Japan, the exhaustion and injury of capitalist modernity seen "a la carte." The fact remains, however, that despite being selected, captioned, and narrated as such, these photographic records can also wrestle free of these limiting frames, oozing forth as the nameless heterogeneous residual minutia of an arrested flux between self and world. This is where the possibility of photography constituting a source for inciting novel forms of language seeps into the picture for Nakahira.

> The photographer presents the relations between themselves and the world, cut out within a square frame. These have been presented for themselves at the same time, for others. Those who have been presented with these relationships, again make selections and sort them out for themselves. This cycle of selection is perhaps how communication between people is formed. I consider photography to be a part of this milieu. The photography I have described as "provocative materials for thought" is of this order. Thus, photography can never become a completed work, and it is senseless to strain to make them as such with this or that kind of technique. They are utterly fragmentary materials that sometimes connect the processes of living one's own life with the lives of others. Thus, photography is always critical—in crisis—always incomplete.[15]

This definition of the critical possibility of photography depends upon the contingency of the viewers traversing the "fatal leap" between a photograph's incomplete form and their own lived experiences.[16] That critical potential, as in a state of crisis, is lodged within the processes of mediation and fleeting connection that constitute the communicative act, here described as a cycle of selections. We might further note that at least two discrete orders of selection govern the prospects of such a mediating encounter; first those of the photographer (including the taking of photographs, the processing of photochemical properties in the development of the negatives and printing of photographs, and the editorial or curatorial selections as print media or exhibited objects), then those of the viewer (including the myriad conscious and unconscious selections that govern the viewers' encounters with the material, including the impact of different formats these encounters take, as print, exhibition, or otherwise). At minimum, it was only upon the breakdown of "expression" (again, here in the limited sense of enacting the closed circuit of a priori meaning exchanged from "artist" to viewer via the "artwork") that photographic materials could sustain the possibilities of the critical communicative encounter that Nakahira described. Always incomplete and in crisis, photography was a profoundly fraught possibility.

Nakahira confronted the potential and limitations of photography once released from "expression" in another important essay, "Has Photography Been Able to Provoke Language?" ("Shashin wa kotoba o chōhatsu shietaka"), included in both *For a Language to Come* and *Why an Illustrated Botanical Dictionary?*[17] The essay further illustrates how the relationship between language and photography played a crucial role in the material compiled in *For a Language to Come*. Following the end of *Provoke*, the essay rhetorically asks whether the short-lived journal had succeeded in provoking anything. In so doing, Nakahira clarifies what kind of language he hoped to incite. Inspired by Roland Barthes, who described words as the "absolute objects" of poetic language, Nakahira named the contours of a lived language "that towers before us in the here and now, discarding relationships with a totality. By merely existing or just by being able to be uttered, they are words, like isolated 'objects' filled with madness that can shake a person. They cannot be the continuous, accessible language that presupposes communication with others. This kind of 'exploding language' is a language that has been fiercely lived here and now by a single person."[18] The fact that Barthes's thought constituted a significant foundation for Nakahira's work should not come as a surprise given the extent of the contemporary translations of Barthes's works into Japanese and geopolitical horizons at the time that fostered profound resonances between their respective intellectual contexts. However, it is crucial to recognize that Nakahira was invested in a critique of the codified circuits of meaning and "expression," seeking to forge novel forms of encounter between lived language and visual forms through the mediation of photography. In extolling the incomplete nature of his work, Nakahira was not simply disavowing the possibility of meaning. Rather, by drawing attention to the limits of both language and photography, he set out to produce an amalgam of entangled processes, forging critical forms of relation and mediation where legible systems of meaning break down.

> It is not reality itself but a secondary reality that has been transformed and made subjective by my confrontation with it. That is what an image is. To repeat myself, a photographer photographing a single tree cannot live without relation to the word "tree." While obsessing over the word "tree" like a compulsive thought, as the photographer fixes their gaze on a tree in the real world through the camera's finder, that word suddenly crumbles away, and they become a part of its reproduction as a new tree (it is in the strict sense of the word, "actual" [*genjitsu*: literally "expressed fact"]).
>
> That said, what about someone looking at an image of a single tree? They cannot expect to have the same experience as the photographer's encounter, of course. A single photograph cannot claim to have that kind of persuasive nature (the very word is rooted in continuity). A single photograph of a tree merely opens up to each individual viewer for their own recitation, just as the photographer who cited that tree from reality and amplified that word within themselves. In the end, whether the language of each person looking at the tree within a single photograph is expanded or not depends on the depth of its connection with the language of the person looking. Indeed, the intensity of an image is tightly connected to intensity of language.[19]

The essay presents the crux of limits and possibilities that informed *For a Language to Come*, composed of work assembled from a variety of media and moments itself. In the example of the single photograph of a tree, two qualitatively different moments of crisis arise, critical instants where the processes of amplification or expansion of language are at stake, when an existing word suddenly crumbles away, and is confronted with its reproduction as an "absolute" object. First, there is the moment of the photographer's initial "citation" from reality, the "secondary reality" of the photographic image, produced through the series of acts from shooting, developing, and printing. This primary moment is highly mediated and segmented by profoundly different processes, and different orders of intervention over the resultant image, each posing considerable difficulty to the facile notions of either a "direct" recording of reality, or a transparent "expression" of an authorial vision. Secondly, there is the moment of the viewers' "recitation" of the tree within the single photograph, mediated by the viewers' own lived language and subject to the conditions that inform their encounter with the photograph, itself existing as a material thing in the world after all. Therefore, *For a Language to Come* must be understood as a kind of experiment in self-reflexively mobilizing both moments. It presented a model for expanding and intensifying the lived languages of its readers, crucial participants who in fact materialize the incomplete work through indeterminate readings and reproductions afforded by the incomplete photographic residues rendered open to their eyes. It is in this sense that the "language to come" was not the teleological presupposition of meanings transferred from the photographs to the passive viewers, but rather the possibility of expanding and amplifying lived languages through the reading of the residues accumulated and organized as a printed text. While this squarely situates Nakahira's photobook within the trajectory of activating readers and viewers explored in this volume, it is perhaps worthwhile to trace how such active readings are modeled differently by the singular photographic-theoretical parameters of the work.

FOR A DECENTERING TEXTUALITY

As a printed text, the book in general, and the photobook in this case in particular, bear with their form a number of habituated codes, conscious and unconscious choices, that structure the readers' experience of the text. These codes are sociohistorically constructed and evolved over time with the proliferation of print technologies. Setting aside the fetishization of photobooks that has accompanied the assimilation of photography within institutional art practices in general, and their status as commodities within the relatively recent historical emergence of market speculation and valuation of photography in particular, there remains profound ambivalence to photography's currency as a printed media. Here, it will suffice to suggest that the differences among print journals from which the book was derived, and the way the photographs were assembled as a book, mattered. In this case, as "secondary realities," the photographic materials were read differently based in part on these differences in form and the codes accompanying their respective formats. For instance, the series "last train," as I touched upon before, is read differently in the context of the journal than the photograph from the series as it appears in book form. However, given the critical notion of photography outlined in his essays, Nakahira's reassembly of these materials afforded a method of accentuating the limits of the codified experience of reading photography, and the photobook in particular. How might we read *For a Language to Come* as a "text" organized critically, constituted in crisis from the material differences among image and lived language, self and world, theory and practice? Here, I will briefly trace the visual logic modeled by the text, attending to how it stages the breakdown of codified ways of reading photography, and how it opens up both world and subject to their mutual entanglement and exposure within the processes of photochemical capture and mediation.

The very format of the book presents itself to the reader in a somewhat bare form. Its photographs are assembled unpaginated and printed full-bleed, with the rather large dimensions of 11.8 × 8.2 inches. As a result, it is possible to traverse the photographs in an indeterminate number of sequences or selections. The photographs are followed by thirty pages of printed text, marked simply as a "supplement" (fu/附).[20] The supplementary status of the printed essays moreover brackets them from the reading of the photography; although a reader can easily turn from essay to photographic sections, the text as a whole is segmented by these two sections. Moreover, near the midpoint of the photographic section, the orientation of the photographs turns, so that the reader must rotate the book clockwise ninety degrees to view the stacked images for eight pages before turning back to the prior orientation. Even if one skips over this section without turning the book, the serial organization of the photographs is interrupted by this middle passage. The decentered form of this text is thus manifested in the format itself; the photographs are presented uncoded, lacking any narrative, hierarchical, structural, or contextual cues as how to organize them. Many of these images originally included brief captions such as place names or short descriptions when they first appeared in print journals, but here they have been assembled without any such references. This is not to suggest, however, that without such codes the text is meaningless.[21] It is precisely as an assemblage of denuded photographic remnants that the viewer must read the text, nothing more, nothing less.

So how might such a reading unfold, and what becomes legible through a text presented in such a form? We must attend to what is exposed among these residues and also to how they operate as exposures of selves and worlds. How do the fleeting photochemical traces of Nakahira's encounters make legible a model for seeing and considering the urban flux that saturated the text? We might begin by simply enumerating the contents of the photographs. Generically speaking, we find elements of street photography, portraiture, landscape, and even photomontage, all indiscriminately mixed together. Moreover, we find only humanmade environments, almost exclusively scenes, things, and bodies found in an urban setting. In a consistent dimension, the photographs engage with the urban through a visually organized delineation of infrastructural spaces of transportation, communication, and exchange. To our provisional listing of existent modalities of mapping urban flux, we can include something that more closely resembles a photographic sonogram than topography or topology. Rather than works of portraiture or typology of heterogeneous new spatial forms and sites, the images appear to be the results of an echolocation-like photographic transcription of the myriad facets of a vast urban apparatus.

As to what emerges from this photographic diagram, we can easily identify the unexceptional materialities of expansive infrastructural forms, such as trains, subways, freeways, cars, ships, ferries, televisions, public phones, and power lines. We discover construction sites, leisure districts, *danchi* housing developments, industrial complexes, seashores and seascapes, canals, movie theaters, storefronts, newspaper stands, and numerous aquariums. Human figures occasionally inhabit these scenes in such forms as illustrations, passengers, pedestrians, mannequins, naked bodies, and children. "Natural" forms are much rarer, but we can find cats, a stray dog, fish (alive and dead), and plants (real and fake). Among these settings, scenes, and subjects we further encounter print matter, signs, posters, advertisements, and incidents of both images and words. In addition to these immediately identifiable elements, the photobook can be read as an excess of photographic materiality itself, a self-reflexive proliferation of surfaces, shadows, flames, fluorescent lights, reflections, and of course the nameless excretions, effusions, and residues.

But more than *what* we encounter in these photographs, the text foregrounds a reading of the urban located in *how* we are exposed to the worlds of these photographs. Not only are we confronted with noisy, grainy, blurry, and shaken ways of seeing, but the text consists of a dizzy variation among the fields of view, viewing angles, convex and concave perspectives, layered spaces, and optical resolutions. As a text, it foregrounds the limits of its own legibility, and as a result it compels the reader's gaze to consume the heterogeneous excess of residues otherwise. For instance, the granular optics that engulf the photographs in varying degrees foster a nuanced array of textured resolutions, differential ratios of optical signal to noise that variously dissolve or amass the contours of the photographed world within a photochemical substrate. Ambivalent, and at times intentionally obscuring, the text dramatizes the breakdown of the photographic medium's fidelity to the promise of the technical reproducibility of the world. Sifting through oscillations between granulated intensities of noise and the limpid play of light and shadow, readers can nonetheless grasp the emulsifying processes of a photographic text wrought from the mutual exposure of seeing subject and seen world. As an assemblage of residues—composite traces of gestures and light—the text incites a delirious unraveling of the distances and intervals that govern the habituated distributions among material worlds, selves, and others. Not only does the text give form to, and render sensible, the flux of a vast urban landscape, indexing a discrete aspect or perspective through each of its photographic utterances, it provokes a crisis in the very language we possess to articulate a legible reading of the urban as such. The world and the language that orders our grasp of it, are mutually consumed and depleted by the text, hence the likeness of the text to states of madness, erotic desire, or catastrophe.²² But these are not the only possibilities for reading the residues of a world denatured in this way.

In one of Nakahira's early essays we find a clearly resonant delineation of mobile optics that resembles what is found in *For a Language to Come*. Problematizing the reception of William Klein's *New York* photobook as illustrating the a priori images of an artist, Nakahira described a critical form of fluidity made sensible through his photography.

> Rather than a single gaze oriented towards the world, it was a complex or multiplex gaze that afforded seeing the movement of one's own position [as a viewer] together with the limitlessly changing contours of the world. It would perhaps be more accurate to say that the order of these fluid perspectives had already been absorbed by his [Klein's] gaze. Rather than the world as a statically completed space, the world has been transformed, becoming a flowing, transfiguring, and endlessly mutating nebula that changes shape with each shifting vantage point.²³

The earlier essay's description of the fluidity of the world and changing points of view indexes the unsettled contours of language the later text sought to provoke. Rather than the static product of a reconciliation of the world with an authorial image, Nakahira mobilized the liquid form of photographic mediation that he first distilled in his reading of *New York* in the fluid assemblage of *For a Language to Come's* molten photographic text. Wrought from the meltdown of immobilized relations between worlds and selves, the text compels the reader to "swim" within a discontinuous array of shifting points of view. Along with the fragmentation of a continuous or uninterrupted field of view throughout, the "mutating nebula" of the text consists of both liquid contents (residues, seas, and effluent gasses) and fluidly formed images (blurred, shaken, reflections, and granulated). At the same time, as an assemblage of the photographic residues of the molten collapse of static relations, the text performs a fluid model of critical reading—reading in crisis—afforded by its liquid visual logic. It thus amplifies, and accentuates, rather than resolves the critical form of relating, or crisis, that Nakahira sought in the photographic mediation of world and language.

Following Nakahira's cue, recall that through the "secondary realities" assembled by the text, readers neither access the "objective reality" of the world, nor retreat into the "subjective reality" of the photographer. Instead, our grasp of the discrete interval between these fixed points becomes unsettled in the entanglements produced by the text, and reproduced in our readings of the dissolve of worlds and subjects. So amplified, the critical photographic text exposes its reader to a troubled form of relation with it, threatening to engulf the safe distance that separates the reader within the same "flowing, transfiguring, and endlessly mutating nebula that changes shape with each shifting vantage point." Moved with/in the fluid materiality of a photographic text informed by the crisis that erupts with the breakdown of language, the reader becomes immersed within the ontological incompleteness of a drifting constellation of assembled residues. Without discovering a vocabulary able to articulate a way out of this crisis, the reader's own position threatens to dissolve into the silence of the churning flux encountered therein. That, I would argue, constituted the embeddedness of the language "to come."

FIGURE 3.1 Nakahira Takuma, *For a Language to Come*, 1970.

Rather than gesturing to any sense of the "futurity" of a "new" language located beyond the text, the photobook instead sought to open up the relation between text and reader to an immanent form of crisis itself.

THE REVOLT AGAINST LANDSCAPE

Yet, as a decentering accumulation of photographs so wrought through with incompleteness and indeterminateness as to be rendered invisible and illegible to the ordering structures of language and the power that circulates through them, there were no guarantees that the critical amplification processes incited by such a text would succeed. Like the torn discontinuities of words indexed by the absolute objects of Barthes's poetic language, the results of this process were beholden to the reader. Although the reader is exposed to their "madness," any text can easily be re-enclosed within the very structures obviated by the critical forms of mediation and relation they elicit. In fact, it was not only a matter of the gambled and uncertain nature of the process of provocation outlined here that inscribed its own undoing within the text. The profound limitations confronting this pursuit were some of the significant conceptual points of departure that framed *For a Language to Come* as the reorganization and reorientation of Nakahira's photography and critical writings up to that point. Reading the fluid incompleteness of this photographic text assembled from the urban landscape was a means for making the limits of our critical vocabulary legible.

At once aesthetic and geopolitical, the flux of the urban landscape that informed the text marked an important shift in the conceptualization of power at the time. It must be said that the immediate geopolitical valence of the ontological incompleteness of such a text pales in comparison to the escalations of spectacularized political violence, which erupted at the end of the 1960s across Japan and worldwide. Although they were historically coeval, they were not commensurate politically.[24] Yet, part of the compelling nature of reading *For a Language to Come* is derived from how it staged both the amplification of a crisis of language and the powerlessness of the text itself. It did not seek to illustrate preexisting meanings of any kind, including political ones. Nor did it attempt to merely aesthetically manifest a set of political solutions to the assaults of state power. Even without turning to the supplementary essays, which explicitly named the text's conflicted forms as part of an assault on the "landscape," any reading will confront a peculiar condition of provocation and powerlessness.

The landscape that Nakahira confronted in *For a Language to Come* was nothing short of the myriad historical transformations converging around 1970, setting the tone for Nakahira's work into the 1970s.[25] One of the key discursive vectors shaping this pivotal work emerged in Nakahira's first direct confrontation with the site of the landscape in the essay "Rebellion Against the Landscape."[26] As Yuriko Furuhata reveals in her groundbreaking study of Japan's radical cinematic praxis in the late 1960s and early 1970s, the term "landscape" was an important keyword as it "offered a way to radically reimagine state power at a time when images of police violence and militant protests were saturating the mass media and limiting the political imagination of the public."[27] This essay defined one aspect of Nakahira's participation in the so-called discourse on landscape (*fūkei-ron*), which originated in a critical mode of film discourse and practice (discussed below). The essay also produced a specific vantage point derived from Nakahira's own confrontation with the larger horizon of historical transformations converging around 1970 to demarcate a critical discursive and methodological site of inquiry that would propel him toward a much deeper engagement with urban forms after *For a Language to Come*. While we will examine the critical exchanges and afterlives of this pivotal reconceptualization of the landscape, or *fūkei-ron*, in brief below, here I will examine the way the notion of landscape emerged as a definitive horizon for reading Nakahira's textual assemblage.

In a passage from the introductory part of the essay, Nakahira reveals the nexus of critical discourses, transformative events, and spaces that converged upon the term "landscape" and how Nakahira's engagement with these reframes much of the photographic work assembled in *For a Language to Come*.

> The prominent film critic Matsuda Masao once wrote that Nagay-
> ama Norio, the so-called "serial shooting devil," wandered about
> from place to place in order to slash apart the uniformly sealed-up
> landscape sustained by power itself. A landscape which unfolded
> before his eyes wherever he was, which he discovered within himself

with the sound of a gunshot. For me too, the world only appears before my eyes as a solid landscape, lustrous like plastic. While this certainly assaults my body and my senses, I could also say that it is precisely for this reason that I continue to take photographs. In fact, a city cannot exist without this landscape. No, on the contrary, the city is somehow a landscape itself. People often comment on the violence and disorder of cities, particularly Tokyo, but this is nothing more than a frame-up by journalists and social scientists. Although murders and traffic accidents occur in the city every night and industrial complexes spew forth poisonous gasses that shorten the lives of thousands of citizens, like mere celebrations of natural selection, these descriptions are preestablished harmonies that misrecognize the real nature of the city. Beyond being somewhat chaotic, somewhat toxic, the actual city continues to exist today as a transparent landscape, enduring without a single scratch. Each night the city wipes clean all impurities, acquiring a nearly flawless kind of beauty. It becomes an impregnable fortress, lacking even a single weakness.[28]

Nakahira here described the landscape as the real form of the city itself, an "impregnable fortress" that confronted his gaze and provoked a smoldering desire to somehow deform its smooth lustrous surface. This provocative confrontation between the city as landscape and Nakahira's gaze offers a key to understanding how this essay resituated the body of urban forms captured in Nakahira's photography. As I outlined above, Nakahira's photographs disclosed an expansive network of communication, transportation, and exchange, revealing the exhaustion of existing language(s) of the city as the privileged structure of meanings that mediate the relations among self, world, and other. The essay further deconstructed existing journalistic vocabularies of the city, which were not only powerless as critiques, but were also actively complicit in misrecognizing an emergent landscape through which state power increasingly sustained itself. Thus, the term "landscape" indexed both the crisis of language and pursuit of a novel vocabulary capable of capturing the changing scope and scale of power that was revealed through these confrontations with powerlessness. As we shall discover, while critic Matsuda Masao (b. 1933) took the violent forces revealed in the Nagayama "incident" as his starting point, Nakahira set out from the confrontation with the lustrous surfaces of an urban expanse, the very perspective afforded by *For a Language to Come's* assemblage of photographic residues. From the vantage of a "reader" of a photographic text, the violence of the expanding landscape was not the chaotic, disorienting, and destructive effects of industrial modernity—that is to say, not just these—but rather, the imperviousness of its surface, sealed off from any critique that could produce a disruptive break in its secured, orderly functioning. Even as it accentuated the heightened sense of crisis that erupts between the text and the reader, the word "landscape" was the indelible trace of the reader's powerlessness before the ceaseless restoration of the given order. It thus provisionally named a kind of ontological violence that utterly defused the explosive charge wrought by the decentering flux of the text.

In this sense, Nakahira's use of the term "landscape" emerged from the powerlessness of the photographic text, as an endemic result of its intervention. The defining fluidity of these photographs was derived through the melting down of the distance between the camera's embodied gaze and the city streets, recorded as streaks and molten traces of a "lived language" onto film. However, that critical gap between these residues being assembled together as a text, then again rendered coherent by the reader's "lived language," informed this provisional definition of the word "landscape." The contradictions described by Nakahira reflect a deepening awareness of the futility of his own approach to the urban contours of power, and with it, the concept marked a profound shift in the terrain of possibility and limitation for media practices that sought to contest the escalating violence sustained therein. Furthermore, Nakahira's essay recognized that the critical gaps opened by his photographic deconstruction had only momentarily rendered legible the expansive geopolitical forces at play in the shifting terrain of Japan's Cold War urbanization.[29] Through the cracks of the text's intoxicating blurring of established boundaries and dramatic dissolution of fixed distances between fluid bodies and streets, the accumulated residues indexed their own subsumption within this fraught, emergent landscape.

The heightened consciousness of the changing contours of power further informed Nakahira's descriptions of student protests in this and other essays included with *For a Language to Come*.[30] In his writings at this time, Nakahira persistently confronted the role of print and photojournalism in directly aiding the police, despite the ostensible claims of political sympathies with the students found among activist journalists associated with the mainstream leftist media. Nakahira was thus engaged in a self-critical confrontation with the assumptions of photojournalism in the face of a dramatic qualitative shift in the media's role, a change that had been manifested in stark form during the spectacular police violence of the nationwide assault on the Zenkyōtō student movement and other citizens movements on the eve of the 1970 renewal of the United States-Japan Mutual Security Treaty.[31] Thus, the interrogation of photographic media within a moment characterized by the escalation of state violence can be recognized in Nakahira's reading of the Kanda liberated district.[32] Nakahira's engagement with the student occupations disclosed the fact that what was at stake in these protests was not merely the opposition between student and state power, or even the ideological differences among them, but profound changes in how power proliferated within the transforming fabric of urbanized social space. Nakahira provocatively compared the conceptual artist Christo's wrapping up of pieces of the environment with the students' campus blockades.

What they both share is the fact that whether it was the city or the university campus, they confronted their surrounding environments and the world around them as hostile landscapes. And as a result, they both blockaded and wrapped up these landscapes in order to cut into them and blast them apart.

The desperate struggles of separate individuals to personally possess for themselves the public, historical city—and that which sustains it, power itself—are the actual substance of urban rebellion when such efforts are materialized. Returning to the Kanda liberated district, it was definitely not a free space that had achieved liberation on its own. As proof of this, their liberated district was temporary and localized; because from the beginning it emerged in tense relations with the external landscape that enveloped them. They barely put a single little crack in the absolutely dominating landscape. Yet by means of that crack, the structure of the world had been manifested all the more clearly. Wrapped up by Christo, the shoreline had been manifested as the shoreline, the city as the city. And at the same time, the students exposed the true form of the university by blockading and sealing off their campuses.[33]

Though Nakahira was not equating the artist's performative act of wrapping with the students' political acts of occupying, he was able to discover homologous logics among them from the standpoint of reading the resultant appropriations. Moreover, it does not take much effort to read the resonance of Nakahira's own work with the logic he describes. Just as in *For a Language to Come*, these interruptive assaults brought into view the vast asymmetries of power securing their subjects' relation to the landscape despite—or more importantly, because of—the drastically futile and circumscribed form these appropriations would take. Furthermore, they confronted changing dimensions of power that were otherwise illegible or invisible without the expanded modes of engagement born in the appropriations of these fleetingly liberated spaces. In this reading, we can include the crack that Nakahira's photographic text inflicted, and thus grasp how the critical form of relation it produced also vividly manifested the structure of the world. These methods of assault succeeded in demonstrating their own futility, which in turn revealed the full scope of the powerful and diverse forms of violence, that secured the ordered functioning of the urban landscape as well as language.

THE LIMITS OF READING

In taking the vantage point of a reader of the limitations of his own photographic texts in these essays, Nakahira delineated another means of confronting what had been revealed, provisionally naming this as a landscape shared by a range of practices. In fact, such a reading allows us to discover how landscape marked a shifting conceptualization of power that extended far beyond the spectacularized police violence waged against activists, and reconsider the explosion of cultural (or perhaps countercultural) practices that diversely mobilized their own futility and powerlessness, and at the same time, disclosed a vastly expanded terrain of both limitation and possibility from the late 1960s, 1970s, and beyond. The critical exchanges among diverse media practitioners and critics afforded by this reconceptualization of landscape have already been touched upon in the introduction to this volume. However, it should suffice here to briefly elaborate a few distinguishing aspects of the milieu illuminated by Nakahira's work in the early 1970s. In his readings of landscape Nakahira identifies the fleeting and ultimately futile interruption of the static ordering of relationships, which secured meaning, significance, and power. The fraught nature of these practices can easily be condemned by those accustomed to a transparently instrumentalized understanding of the world. Unable to produce legible markings of their effects, nor lasting traces of tangible results, and incapable of yielding demands, these practices at times evade the logical mesh of coherent discourse that operates within these ordered relations. But precisely in the way described by Nakahira's reading, such fleeting, insignificant cracks, and the illegible accumulations of fragmentary and residual forms of critical knowledge they materialized, were invaluable media for ascertaining novel and transformative orientations of thought and practice within a fluid constellation of power.

Operating critically within the entanglements of language and landscape that sustained a specific environment of power, the often-incoherent and seemingly nonsensical forms of such practices were informed by the disintegrative flux they located therein. That is to say, the illegibility of these practices indexed their irreconcilable differences with the illustration of given meanings that became complicit with power through the "expression" of static images or concepts, unable to grasp the shifting contours of power at play in the transformed relations among world, self, and other. As Taki Kōji would describe the different nature of these relations at play in Nakahira's photobook, *For a Language to Come* was not a provocation external to the event of language, but a critical form of mediation embedded within the resultant landscape. "To actually entrust one's body to the world, being within it and within this landscape, to awaken to this landscape, confronted with the impulse to become a part of this landscape, these do not necessarily render a logical understanding of the event itself."[34] In this sense, the difficulties evidenced in the "legibility" of such texts were the product of their Sisyphean efforts to dissolve the ordered and distributed distances among self, world, other, and in so doing, to discover within this dissolve an emergent constellation of power, and yet, to resist becoming reabsorbed and reinscribed within the expanding landscape saturated by the forces at play therein. Taking Taki's lead, we could simply describe Nakahira's critical pursuit of language embedded within a landscape in flux as but one instance of what might be described as a certain romanticism of the capacities of images to elicit language. Yet, while acknowledging the somewhat naïve desire to "resuscitate" language from its fossilized orderings and dispositions informed by power, the embeddedness of this locus of mediation compels us to consider the shifting contours of power that informed the critical relations disclosed by Nakahira's photographic text from within the confrontation with landscape. That is, rather than dismiss the distinctly different kinds of legibility wrought by this critical form of mediation as "nonsense," we must engage with the geopolitics of this landscape, as both a sociohistorically discrete moment of urban transformation, as well as an enduring problem lodged within every reading of such works. And in so doing, we confront the landscape as a threshold of limitations and possibilities that indexed the emergence of an entangled urban-media environment that reintegrate(d) these aesthetic strategies within a coherent order. The fraught reception of Nakahira's photographic works, then as now, discloses the continued operation of an environment that is at once geopolitical and aesthetic, sustained by the very flux of power and violence that such practices had in fact sought to derive critical vocabularies to work against.

The safe containment of Nakahira's photographic assault on codified meanings and attempts to dismantle the ongoing immobilization of fluid relationships embodied in *Provoke* pointed to its facile assimilation within a social world whose very dimensions were in flux. The blurred and shaken images of the urban landscape born in Nakahira's mobile gaze began appearing in advertisements, and most troubling for Nakahira, these kinds of images began appearing in the National Railways' Discover Japan (*Disukabā Japan*) campaign.[35] Discover Japan initiated a new mode of mass tourism through the extension and intensification of commodified travel by means of which, as Nakahira's description of the campaign noted, "the 'Japan' 'discovered' and the 'Japanese who discover' are tightly bound up in the mechanism of Japanese capital and all the more exploited as a result."[36] Nakahira was compelled to reassess the social function of photography within these conditions, whereby his fluid photographic encounter with an urban expanse could also serve as a mere image style for a new regime of tourism penetrating the remote reaches of the Japanese archipelago.[37]

Thus, Nakahira's confrontation with the landscape materialized a dizzying sense of parallax unleashed from the intensely changed contours of social space within which the highly charged act of "discovery" corresponded to the integration of the seeing subject within a vast network of enclosure that spanned domains of travel, transportation, and communication, extending from the city to the farthest reaches of the archipelago. Against the campaign to "discover" Japan, the discovery of the instrumentalized perceptions of integrated subjects forced Nakahira to pursue a critical media capable of somehow breaking apart the closed circuits that undergirded this homogenized surface. For Nakahira, photography offered the possibility of a critical media practice that did not seek to rediscover preestablished meanings within the impermeable stasis of circulatory networks, but instead traversed an unexplored intermediary zone of intertwining gazes, dismantling and rejecting the asymmetries and expanding forms of violence through which the closed network was secured. Despite the success of deriving a method to redeploy and refashion the futile assaults of *Provoke* into a multiplex textual accumulation of an irruptive discourse in *For a Language to Come*, a fundamental limitation remained by the very nature of the original photographs that imbued the resultant indeterminate world as an instance of landscape itself.

Nakahira's self-critical stance after the publication of *For a Language to Come* in 1970 highlighted the limiting conditions of the emergent urban-media environment indexed by critical reconceptualizations of landscape and brings us closer to an understanding of the conflicts that would inform his subsequent works. Maintaining a perpetual lock on the changing contours of this emergent environment, Nakahira's subsequent work delineated a pursuit of a suitable method for deriving other transformative possibilities embedded within the entangled relations of urban materialities and media systems that occupied his interest thereafter. Even at the time of *For a Language to Come*, Nakahira's landscape essay outlined the vague traces of a transformative method for traversing such an environment in a provisional sketch.

Today, the world exists as an expressionless, uniform landscape before me. Moreover, becoming increasingly beautiful, its coherence will become progressively more perfect. To tell the truth, I am like a scrawny dog sniffing about for a weak crevice that may not even exist; what I seek is the remote possibility of a single crack in this complete landscape. Is there no hidden opening that gives me a sign of cracks within this flat, beautiful landscape? If I could only find such a crevice, the city as landscape would be destroyed by my angry gaze, just like the "city of the dunes" broken into thousands of pieces in Antonioni's film. This is just a crazy delusion however. There is no such fissure or anything like it. Perhaps such an opening can only be revealed by flames, by stone, or by rifle.

For the time being, there is no other method for me than to cease-lessly gaze at this landscape. Yet, at the limits of my perpetual gazing, could flames, my real fire, be igniting? I won't know without trying. What I can say for sure is that this is only possible through my com-plete transformation into this very same fire of mine. After all, seeing is unrelated to doing. This is true even if doing something becomes clear only by first seeing something.

Urban rebellion. It is an unlimited personal act of aggression against the landscape. It is the realization of the dream that has been endlessly repeated by each person to somehow change the political system, a system that cannot be expected to change on its own.[38]

The emphasis here was upon seeking out a transformative locus of mediation within the relations of visuality, finding an embedded means of confronting the homogenizing forces at the limits of an unflinching stare, and at the same time, confronting the staring observers them-selves. A profound powerlessness permeates such a pursuit. But at the same time, in delineating the forces at play that render such powerless-ness as a landscape that subsumes the field of visual relations, Nakahira's pursuits effect a redistribution of what can be sensed and acted upon.[39] Seeking out critical forms of relation from the photographic residues and fragmentary remnants of Nakahira's traversals of and resistance to the emerging landscape, the contours of the entangled urban-media environment become clearer.

INTERROGATIVE STRATEGIES

Of course Nakahira was not alone in isolating the landscape as a crit-ical focal point for seeking out alternative strategies of critique and inquiry.[40] Nakahira's efforts contributed to Matsuda Masao's speculative interrogations of the landscape in writings that would later be described as *fūkei-ron*, or theories of landscape. In the midst of these exchanges following the publication of *For a Language to Come*, Nakahira's photographic practice soon changed, shifting away from the previous modes of confronting the urban landscape. Through his pursuit of a suitable method for grappling with the challenges this landscape posed, Nakahira would perform a rapid evolution of styles and approaches that produced a crucial turning point in his work around 1973. At the same time, Nakahira took an increasing interest in film and produced a prolific body of writings on image media during this period.[41] Throughout the shifting trajectory of Nakahira's formative efforts after 1970, we discover a consistent inquiry into the entanglement of urban forms and media environments, culminating in the 1973 publication, *Why an Illustrated Botanical Dictionary? Nakahira Takuma's Collected Writings on Visual Media.*[42]

As Gō Hirasawa notes in the afterword of the recently republished and expanded edition of Matsuda's essay collection *The Extinction of Landscape*, Nakahira and Matsuda's attempts to mobilize the term "landscape" to interrogate a shifting constellation of power remain instructive in many crucial ways. Although their interrogations were less exhaustive conceptual models than a nexus of interrelated questions, their shared pursuit of a critical vocabulary for contending with the changing environments of power, as well as questions related to an emergent, and as yet fully realized world system, offers important hints for understanding ongoing transformations and crises that inform our contemporary moment. "In the present, reexaminations of the politics and culture of the 1960s and 1970s, symbolized by the upheavals that shook the world in 1968, have continued worldwide in search of historical points of reference for grasping, or better yet, points of departure from, the violence unleashed by the nation-state and capitalism as they envelop the world in the wake of the devastations of the Cold War."[43]

Nakahira's efforts to reassess the critical role of photography within the context of a broader reconceptualization of landscape, or *fūkei-ron*, played a profound role in traversing seemingly disparate dimensions of his practice between *For a Language to Come* and *Why an Illustrated Botanical Dictionary?* To put it simply, the paradoxical term "illustrated botanical dictionary" emerged from the embryonic formulation found in the ambivalence of the "irruptive discourse" performed in *For a Language to Come*. Just as the latter served as accumulated photographic residues that made sense of the violent coherence of the sealed-up surfaces of an expansive landscape, the speculative form of an "illustrated dictionary" indexed a changing strategy of relation/mediation fundamentally at odds with the closed networks of communication and accentuated violence disclosed in this crucial moment of Japan's Cold War urbanization.

Just a few months before *Why an Illustrated Botanical Dictionary?* was published, Nakahira offered a particularly lucid commentary about the emergence of the discourse on landscape and its implications. Assembled within another kind of dictionary, the essay "a dictionary of keywords of contemporary film practice" ("*Gendai eiga jōkyō jiten*") appeared in the December 1972 issue of *Film Quarterly* (*Kikan firumu*). Among the entries by Nakahira, Matsuda, and many other figures of the period, Nakahira reflected on the stakes involved in both confronting and questioning the changing conditions of power evidenced by the reconceptualization of the landscape.

> What they discovered was the binaries of the urban-rural, and the modern-native are merely formalistic concepts of classification imported from the West by capitalism rapidly developed spreading over Japan in the present, whose essence consists of a structure that produces the relations whereby the urban rules the rural, the modern rules the premodern, and vice-versa, even though such classifications were only formalistically possible. What penetrates through all of these relations is the logic of Japanese monopoly capitalism itself. This spreads out from the urban centers to the frontiers. By its very nature, its vantage point is that of the landscape. Within this context, the discovery of landscape comes to rest upon the stage of epistemology. Inevitably before the landscape, this forces us to recall each of our own actions as the exploited of this national monopoly capital. How to crack open this landscape in a deeply practice-based way is the task at hand.[44]

This entry further illuminates the orientation of the "illustrated botanical dictionary" as Nakahira's response to the "epistemological" implications of landscape had provoked. Although Nakahira had quickly moved away from direct usage of the term "landscape" in his writings after 1971, the barrage of critical writing and changing photographic methods that culminated in the publication of *Why an Illustrated Botanical Dictionary?* embodied his own "deeply practice-based way" of attempting to put an enduring fissure in landscape elaborated through Japan's Cold War urbanization. By ascertaining a potentially disruptive locus of contradictory force embedded within the secured and securing relations between seer and seen, Nakahira discovered a dynamic kernel of critical energy capable of contesting the enclosure and entanglement of Japan's urban sensory experiences and infrastructural media after 1970.

As interrogative methods, moreover, these critical theorizations of landscape emerged from a pivotal moment of transition within a global history of power, situating the Japanese archipelago's transformations within a worldwide horizon of change. Even though as questions, they merely evidenced a profoundly limited and bounded understanding of the sociohistorical transformations at hand, they continue to afford novel perspectives on our own profoundly limited and bounded understanding of transformations that define our own moment. Just like the whirling scraps of paper and waste that captivated Abe Kōbō's detective, the residues produced in Nakahira's shifting interrogations afforded a critical knowledge of the otherwise invisible currents of power. "They cheated one's expectation, caught one by surprise, suggesting the swimming of certain kinds of fish. By them one was made aware that air was matter."[45] The seamless enveloping of worlds, selves, and others within the luminous enclosures of the landscape that were made sensible in the process necessitated a different strategy, a different arrangement derived by learning how to "swim" and traverse this landscape without succumbing to its stultifying immobilizations and disempowering violence.[46] In Nakahira's turn from problems of language to those of landscape, the act of reading continued to play a crucial role, forging a critical interrogative locus for thought that was embedded among the accumulation of photographic residues, and the mediating relations among selves, worlds, and others. As such, Nakahira's *residual* vocabulary offers a way of seeing the holes and fissures within the seamless environments materialized and virtualized by capitalist state power. With such a vocabulary, we might begin to ask how to forge new arrangements of relations from such cracks, fragments, and residues therein, and how to derive new vocabularies from such a fraught totality, despite, or because of, the fact that it is always in crisis, always incomplete. As we shall see in the following chapters, this potent locus of interrogative force would generate a range of ecological forms of inquiry.

CHAPTER FOUR

An Illustrated Dictionary
of Urban Overflows

In the previous chapters we saw how infrastructure, visuality, and land-scape afforded expanded elaborations of critical vocabularies of urban transformation. Here, through a passage from writer Abe Kōbō's photographic novel, *The Box Man* of 1973, in the chapter, "From Within the Mirror," I'd like to raise the problem of how to read the mediating structures that span across these layers of the constellations of urban ecologies proliferating in the early 1970s.

> When anyone comes into contact with the scenery around them, one tends to see selectively only those elements necessary. For example, though one remembers a bus stop, one cannot recall the willow trees nearby that have repeatedly been there. One's attention is caught willy-nilly by the hundred-yen piece dropped on the road, but the bent and rusty nail and the weeds by the wayside may just as well not be there. On the average road one usually manages not to go astray. However, as soon as one looks out of the box's observation window, things appear to be quite different. The various details of the scenery become homogeneous, have equal significance, Cigarette butts . . . the sticky secretion in a dog's eyes . . . the windows of a two story house with the curtains waving . . . the creases in a flattened drum . . . rings biting into flabby fingers . . . railroad tracks leading into the distance . . .

sacks of cement hardened because of moisture . . . dirt under the fingernails . . . loose manhole covers . . . but I am very fond of such scenery. The distance in it is fluid and the contours vague, and thus perhaps it resembles my own position. The gentleness of a garbage dump. One never wearies of looking at such a view as long as one is peering out from a box.[1]

In the novel, readers experience the perspective of the occupant(s) of a cardboard box. These occupant(s) disappear from their normal every-day lives into the invisible inner lining of an urban expanse. As a telling example of Abe's ongoing efforts to render the sensory abstractions of literary language into a nonvisual written work that paradoxically con-sists in visually mediated relationships, the novel explores the limits of visuality as a means of knowing the world, the other, and one's position therein. The passage describes a perspectival shift that accompanies the framing of vision, which in this case results in the rendering equivalent of all objects within a visual field delineated by the edges of the window of the cardboard box occupied by the narrator. It captures the break-down of the habituated hierarchies and orderings at play in the "normal" operations of a subject-centered gaze. Bounded yet undifferentiated, the singular details within the homogenized field of view from the box fail to congeal into the given meanings and values of a human-centered perspective. Instead, displaced from the selective visuality habituated in the everyday view, the box dweller is afforded a somewhat "unsettled" position coexistent among an accumulation of fragmentary remnants.

As Atsuko Sakaki has pointed out, Abe's deep entanglement with photography infused his writing with an acute sensitivity to the equaliz-ing effects of framing. Sakaki notes how Abe's attention to framing awak-ens the reader/viewer's role in "making sense" of the framed material, in an act of "enabling a non-selective vision and revealing the uneven attention afforded the naked eye."[2] In this sense, the framed views of this peculiar perspective are akin to those of photography, that mechanism of "optical unconscious" celebrated by Walter Benjamin for its ability to disclose the world beyond the capacities of the human vision to its spectator.[3] Seen through the thresholds of the box as a kind of cam-era, the world indeed looks different, depleted of its everyday patterned hierarchies of visually mediated relations. This, Kaja Silverman reminds us, is photography's "ontological calling card," one that "helps us to see that each of us is a node in a vast constellation of analogies."[4] Silverman explores early photography's revelatory capacity for grasping how such analogies not only structure the world and our place within it, but also the changing distributions of mediating relations among human and nonhuman subjects therein. There is much at stake in Silverman's assertion that early photography was "disclosive" of analogical relations among human and nonhuman worlds, and not merely a representational form of mediation between presence and absence. The analogical relations operative at the outset of photography's histories, Silverman suggests, offer an antidote to a potent form of melancholy derived from an explicit emphasis on an indexical understanding of photography, constrained to its evidentiary or representational function as a medium of an absent referent located in the past.[5]

Likewise, in the passage from *The Box Man*, we obtain a brief glimpse of how the photographic sensibility that informs the novel discloses a nested set of analogical, rather than indexical, relations at the heart of the text. From the framed view within the box, looking out onto a landscape derived by a nonselective visuality, the reader is exposed to a defamiliarizing perspective on the urbanized social relations normalized beyond the thresholds of perception. Moreover, as one of the "things" that come into view as a result of the novel's photographic visuality, the box is inscribed within a landscape stripped of human-centered meaning in the act of being seen. As the reader learns later, the novel itself has been derived of fragmented passages of text that the box's inhabitant(s) have recorded on the inner cardboard walls. In the act of assembling these scraps of text together in their experience of reading it, the novel interpolates the readers themselves into a position of negotiating the play of reversals among human and nonhuman landscapes, seer and seen, sensory intensities and sensing subjects. Thus, the novel's photographic visuality was constituted by the nesting of framed and mediated relations, rather than merely by the coexistence of photographs and photographers among its pages.

A marginal degree of dislocation—not merely an act of defamiliarization but that of disappearance—is made available in the act of reading through the "nonselective" visuality derived by the box itself. In this sense, the novel dramatizes a decentering of visually mediated relations that govern an individual's subject-centered matrix of meaning and being in the world. Moreover, the novel's accentuated way of framing, and thus exposing, the reader's relation to the acts of seeing depicted in the novel make sensible a decentered set of mediating relations among human and nonhuman subjects rendered equivalent elements of an urban landscape. In the context of an inquiry into the expansive forms of capitalist state power associated with the term "landscape" (as discussed in the last chapter), *The Box Man* elaborates an embodied view of the frames and limits of such a landscape's visually mediated social relations.[6]

In this chapter, I seek to understand how specific mobilizations of photographic visuality come to make sense of a set of mediating relations and the thresholds of an all-encompassing landscape of power in the early 1970s. I will chart how the act of seeing became a problem in Nakahira Takuma's interrogations of the inundating urban materialities and informational economies as he maneuvered through the critical impasse posed by the conditions of landscape. Moving beyond the problems of language and landscape that we explored in the previous chapter, I expand my inquiry into the prospects and limits of seeing that informed Nakahira's work that followed the publication of *For a Language to Come*. This reading of a period of Nakahira's work that remains largely overlooked in existing scholarship is an attempt to make legible the compelling problems it posed. In addition, through the dynamic lens of Nakahira's writings and photography, we learn how seeing itself became a potent source for critical reflection on the changing distributions of sensory economies among a wide range of literary and visual media during these years.

On the one hand, we will learn how Nakahira reoriented his work from the pursuit of a critical photographic vocabulary wrought from an all-encompassing landscape toward a self-critical photographic recycling and remediation of fragmented materialities of a changing urban world. At the same time, I will attempt to situate these remarkable shifts and turns through Nakahira's pursuit of what can be described as a decentered visuality, a way of seeing derived within the very relations of mediation and circulation that informed the historical transformations of Japan's urban ecologies. Though critical studies of visuality have developed a rigorous understanding of the sociohistorical constructedness of visual meanings and codes, Nakahira's work further revealed a critical grasp of how circulatory and communicative infrastructures came to systematize and organize specific ways of seeing. By exploring the decentered forms of visuality afforded by Nakahira's work, articulated across the often discontinuous and disparate practices of photography and writing, we discover a shared set of limitations and possibilities that informed diverse practices of literary and visual media during the 1970s and beyond.

INTERROGATIVES

This chapter examines the development of an "illustrated dictionary," or *zukan*, form of photographic thought and practice, tracing the changing contours of Nakahira's inquiry into decentered ways of seeing. While Nakahira himself described a "slump" in his interest in photography following the publication *For a Language to Come*, Nakahira would further question the urban everyday through new forms of color photography and media criticism first published in diverse periodicals between 1971 and 1974. The publication of Nakahira's first essay collection, *Why an Illustrated Botanical Dictionary? Nakahira Takuma's Collected Writings on Visual Media*, in 1973 materialized a deepening of his interrogative inquiry.[7] The ideas and concerns engaged by the essays explored how visuality itself played a crucial role in the urban and media pathways of circulation sustaining the reactionary contours of power in the wake of the 1968 upheavals worldwide. As a central component of his interrogation of power, Nakahira would forcefully criticize his own black and white photography of the late 1960s, and in the volume's title essay, openly call for a new photographic methodology. However, how might we begin to understand the shared questions and problems that sustained both Nakahira's vigorous self-criticism as well as his remarkably diverse photographic output of the 1970s? I will explore how intensified interrogations of power and visuality informed the development of Nakahira's "illustrated dictionary" form as evidenced by the essays, installations, and publications of the early 1970s.

As I touched upon in the previous chapter, the existing reception of Nakahira's work overwhelmingly has focused on the "iconic" black and white work without attending to his subsequent diversification of writings and photography. Not only does such a limited reception in effect disavow the vast majority of Nakahira's photographic output, more problematically, it fails to engage with the very questions and concerns that initially motivated Nakahira to problematize his own work. In this context, it is necessary to grasp not only why Nakahira undertook a continued process of self-criticism of his own work (the early stages of which I began to outline in the previous chapter), but also, to chart the evolving problem of seeing itself that informed both the process of self-critique and the diversification of his photographic praxis, which not only traversed the sprawling Tokyo metropolitan area, but would also extend to the islands of Okinawa, Amami, and Tokara. Thus, if the essay collection, *Why an Illustrated Botanical Dictionary?*, embodied a profound shift in the contours of Nakahira's photographic thought and practice, how might we read the manifold trajectories of Nakahira's work from the writings collected together in this volume? In order to shed some light on these questions, I will outline Nakahira's persistent inquiry into the shifting contours of power and modalities of mediation of photographic visuality. At the heart of Nakahira's "illustrated dictionary," we will discover a sustained pursuit of decentered ways of seeing as a locus for continuously regenerating critical knowledge *of*, and forms of relating and becoming *in*, a world in constant flux. Moreover, I hope to illustrate how the shifting geopolitical and aesthetic dimensions exposed in the fissures, fragments, and fractured totalities of Nakahira's work defy easy containment within narratives of the so-called end of the politically engaged literary and visual media in Japan.

In order to grasp the paradigmatic contours of seeing as a problem spanning Nakahira's diversified critical and photographic praxis, I will delineate the formal and conceptual specificities of *Why an Illustrated Botanical Dictionary?*, and outline how it operated as a text informed by the entangled problems of power and visuality that Nakahira extracted from the changing infrastructural pathways of urban and media systems. Seeking to understand how the text was shaped by his ongoing efforts to develop a novel practice-based photographic response to capitalist state power, this chapter will explore the prospects and problems of seeing articulated by Nakahira across discrete media and moments that informed the "illustrated dictionary" form first introduced in his essay collection. With the exception of the title essay, the essays in *Why an*

Illustrated Botanical Dictionary? were drawn from the five-year period between 1967 and 1972. The text encompassed and expanded beyond the range of themes and topics that culminated in *For a Language to Come*. With the exception of the title essay, the essays are assembled into three sections, "Part One: The Incessant Reaping of Visuality," "Part Two: Date, Place, Events," and "Part Three: Today, What is Seeing?" As Nakahira wrote in the afterword, the title essay and longer essays in the first part focused on his photographic methodology and the social conditions that informed it, whereas the second part assembled together fragmentary shorter texts on daily realities that vividly reflected his response to news media, photography, film, television, and art. Nakahira identified these fragmented, one-off, pieces to be the "prototypes" (*genkei*) of the ideas that are fleshed out in the longer essays.[8] The third part encompassed Nakahira's perspectives as a photographer on the diverse domains of theater, jazz, tourism, and journalism, areas that, although Nakahira was not an expert of, he considered to be interesting sites for expanding his critical inquiry into "seeing" in the early 1970s.

By its very nature, much like the photobook format, the usual essay collection form assembles together a variety of texts drawn from disparate contexts and levels of editorial intervention. More often than not, such collections tend to be organized chronologically, allowing readers to appreciate both the development of particular motifs, themes, and arguments over time, as well as the author's command of a wide range of different topics. Nakahira's collection is organized differently. First, the title essay stands apart due to the structural differences mentioned above, as the only text from after 1972, and preceding the three main divisions in the text. Secondly, the essays of the first and third sections were not organized by chronology or any other explicit logic. At most, they can be read as having an inferred linkage with their respective section headings. Also, the second section is organized chronologically, for reasons we will explore below, as an exercise in assembling fragmentary writings mediated by date, place, and events, rather than a continuous development of themes and ideas. Moreover, the ideological construction of authorial authority, including the notion of the photographer as "author," is consistently problematized by Nakahira's writings in the collection, performing an outright dismantling of historical notions of authorship, which renders an author-centered organizing logic of the text to be profoundly fraught at the very least. Thus, on the formal level, much like the pursuit of a critical language found in *For a Language to Come*, the text of this collection is rendered from the decentering and displacement of two dominant organizing logics of the essay collection form itself: chronological development and authorial center. So how might we go about making sense of the collection as a text without detracting from the particular formal and conceptual interventions that Nakahira wrought from this decentering and displacement? What's more, how might these writings offer clues for reading the overlay of continuities and discontinuities among Nakahira's photography, essays, and installations as a manifold text of an "illustrated dictionary," one mediated by the singular-lived language of Nakahira himself, but not the propertied manifestations of a singular author?

Nakahira, in fact, addresses these and other doubts in the exceptional essay at the outset of the collection. More than a mere introduction to the themes and problems raised by the collection, the opening essay constituted a metacritical framework that illuminated the heterogeneous makeup of the text. Itself divided into three parts, the opening essay moreover modeled the specific textual incompleteness that permeates the collection as a whole. Though fragmentary, and at times ambiguous, the changed contours of Nakahira's photographic praxis and the stakes for interrogating seeing itself as a model of critical inquiry into the entangled conditions of the urban and media milieux are rendered in stark clarity by the essay. In its most basic outlines, the essay set out to confirm for Nakahira himself his own reasons for being unable to take photographs as he had before, instead spending more time questioning the social foundations of photography as a form of media in the two years since the publication of *For a Language to Come*. In part, this "confirmation" took the form of a response to the specific claim that Nakahira's photography had lost its "poetic" qualities and that the critical essays that Nakahira was publishing were mere compensation for this loss.[9] However, the self-critical tone taken in Nakahira's essay went beyond merely defending his writing practices from the author-centric ideologies of photography as art.

Drawing on a rich plethora of literary and critical discourses, we discover Nakahira employing the radical leftist practice of self-critique to outline the shifting geopolitical and aesthetic stakes of photography as a form of media, rather than as artwork.[10] In what reads like what we might describe as a performative self-critique, Nakahira's essay dismantled the closed circuits of photographer as author/artist, photography as art/work from "within," as a photographer embedded among the different economies where his photographs circulated. From this specifically situated position, Nakahira instead sought to conceptualize photography as a form of media, and in so doing, to embed an interrogative locus of inquiry within the visual relations governing mediations of self, world, and other. In this sense, Nakahira undertook a critical form of inquiry into seeing itself that sought to traverse the thresholds governing medial forms, by displacing photography from categories of art to those of media, and locating an embedded means of disintegrating the privileged subject of the "author" shared among them. For Nakahira, as we shall discover, photographic mediation constituted a radically open modality of seeing, a decentered relational medium of knowing and becoming in the world. Like the box in Abe Kōbō's *The Box Man*, photography afforded Nakahira a marginal form of displacement *within* the mediating act of seeing, one that constituted the changing contours of his work as it traversed the transforming pathways and boundaries of Japan's urban social spaces.

THE MAGNETIC FIELDS OF VISUALITY

The central, yet perplexing, term that emerges in the opening essay to indicate this displacement was the "illustrated dictionary" (*"zukan,"* or in this case, "shokubutsu zukan," an "illustrated botanical dictionary"). Although the term was mobilized by Nakahira to index a novel photographic method, I think it can moreover be read as a crucial aspect of the larger critical inquiry into seeing itself, which informed both the unusual organizing logic of the essay collection as well as his pursuit of an ever-changing photographic praxis. As I will briefly outline here, Nakahira derived the prospects of an "illustrated dictionary" through an ever-shifting engagement with the processes of photographic mediation of material reality and human visuality. The thresholds delineated by the strange term were a crucial component of Nakahira's critical inquiry into seeing as both problem and possibility. My reading will explore how Nakahira's use of the term "illustrated dictionary" sought to enumerate the contours of the power and possibility coursing through Japan's urban and media systems. Among his continued explorations of the uncanny mediations of self, world, and other afforded by photographic media, we can grasp how Nakahira turned his attention to how visuality had become a systematized and managed kind of environment itself as well as a resource for critical forms of relation antithetical to such controlled environments. Nakahira's use of the term "illustrated dictionary" is often taken at face value as corresponding to his aim to "clarify" the photographed subject in a prospective new method described at the end of the essay.[11] But if we explore how this term emerges as part of a displacement that spans a broader critical inquiry into the act of seeing, we discover a crucial shift in the role of photography in shaping the geopolitical and aesthetic stakes of knowing and becoming in the world. In one of the most striking passages of the essay, Nakahira delineates the entangled visuality that would constitute this shifted locus of inquiry:

> We fix our gaze at things, and charge after them to possess them. Yet against this, material reality makes no response. Our gaze is merely repelled by the solid surface of material reality. The material reality before our gaze always recedes. From exactly this point, the point where our gaze is repelled, this could be said to be where the gaze of things starts to be thrown back toward us.
>
> The world consists of this magnetic field where our gaze and the gaze of things become intertwined.[12]

By locating an immanent zone of magnetic forces among human and nonhuman gazes, Nakahira situated the camera as a powerful tool capable of harnessing this magnetic field to clarify the visible and invisible relations of mediation that structured the world.[13] Noting the ideology of human as operator of the world sustained by the optical technology of the camera, "the superlative product of modernity," Nakahira unleashes these (in)visible mediations to erode the static schema structuring the world from this single-point perspective.

> When we restrict ourselves to a single photograph, it merely exhibits a space one-sidedly peered at from the single point of the self.

But, if we do not limit ourselves to the space of a single photograph, and instead consider an infinite number of photographs that have been mediated by different times and places, the perspective of each individual photograph gradually loses its meaning. That is, accordingly, it becomes possible to clarify the structure of the world as the place encompassed within the binary opposition of world and self, precisely that which infinitely exceeds them and mediates them through time. There, the static schema of self and world vanishes, forming continuously moving and multiplying points of view.[14]

Thus, for Nakahira, it was through photography itself that the evolving forms of mediation governing the relations among humans and material reality could be mobilized to clarify the structure of the world. Moreover, Nakahira grasped the multiplicity and fluidity of perspectives afforded by photography as a critical tool for enumerating the changed contours of urban social spaces and media ecologies themselves.

The contemporary city is like a behemoth that breaks us into pieces. Each of our identities have been shaken at their foundations by the city. Our everyday selves are continuously invaded by a flood of commodities, a flood of information and a flood of material things. [. . .] We must dare to turn the tables. We must recognize the defeat of "humanity," in a world where things exist as things, humans exist as humans, absolutely unprivileged. We must first perhaps find out our proper place.
The city is flooding. With the flood of things, a revolt is beginning.[15]

The erosion of a centered subject by the deluge of urbanization and mediatization was not lamented by Nakahira. But rather, this inundating flux of materialities and informational flows seemed to compel him to seek an equally dynamic locus of critical inquiry, as situated within the expanding circulatory infrastructures and economies that sustained them. We discover throughout this period Nakahira's pursuit of an intermediary form of knowledge embedded within the flux of material and virtual forms of mediation and relation among self, world, and other. For Nakahira, it was the methodological possibility of an "illustrated dictionary" that emerged as the modality such a photographic inquiry would take, one that could capture the dynamic energy of disintegration and reintegration informing the urban transformation and mediatization of social space.

> The illustrated dictionary is never a whole that has been constructed by privileging something and making that its center. That is to say, its parts are not parts permeated by the whole but rather the parts always remain parts, there is nothing on the other side of them. The method of the illustrated dictionary is absolute juxtaposition. It is this method of juxtaposition, or enumeration, that must be my method.[16]

The socialized totality of "meaning" that operates in the circulation of images was thus interrupted by such a definition for the illustrated dictionary, torn asunder in the "absolute juxtaposition" of remnants, fragments—and perhaps residues—of an always incomplete "text" that was photography for Nakahira. Although I have rather roughly enumerated the features of this metacritical inquiry into seeing that marked the term "illustrated dictionary" cited here, I begin to flesh out the import of such a strange term by engaging with the changing ways this idea can be located in Nakahira's work, both prior to, within, and after the publication of his essay collection. This peculiar "illustrated dictionary" form first emerged in Nakahira's practice-based response to the conditions of landscape. As I attempt to demonstrate below, the layering of questions regarding visuality together with those of urban and media power posed by the metacritical essay at the outset of this collection, was deeply related to a shifting set of problems disclosed in Nakahira's photographic practices. What's more, by clarifying the stakes of decentering the single-point perspective, the textual heterogeneity of the essay collection opened the contours of Nakahira's photographic praxis to interrogate the prospects of seeing the incompleteness of such environments. Hence, if the essay and collection took an interrogative form, as indexed by the title's question, what kind of knowledge or critical understanding might be derived from reading Nakahira's "illustrated botanical dictionary"?

As discussed in the previous chapter, the problems that informed this "illustrated dictionary" arose from an expansion of the leftist geopolitical imaginary indexed by the radical discourses of "landscape" of the early 1970s. Seeking out the changing contours of power beyond the spectacular confrontations with capitalist state violence became a crucial source of methodological and theoretical innovation for a wide range of activists, artists, filmmakers, journalists, and writers as a result. While our ability to "read" and make sense of the extensive "text" elaborated by Nakahira's resultant "illustrated botanical dictionary" depends upon recognizing the geopolitical urgency of this moment, we might position the essay collection among others from this moment to clarify the stakes at hand.[17] Other contemporary collections such as Matsuda Masao's *Media of Impossibility*, Tsumura Takashi's *The Politics of Media*, Adachi Masao's *Strategies for Cinema*, and even the lesser known collection of Miyauchi Kō's architectural criticism, *Attack the Landscape: The University 1970–1975*, illuminated a set of discursive vectors that arose in response to this shared crisis of the new left geopolitical imaginary.[18] On the one hand, we can identify a shared set of questions regarding media power, both in the sense of how capitalist state power circulated and proliferated across increasingly controlled media environments, as well as how to adapt critical strategies through novel media practices. On the other hand, we find a shared interest in thinking about the changing contours of power that informed urban forms, particularly in how to sustain critical forms of urban practice even as administrable networks of communication, transportation, and control expanded across the archipelago.[19] While many historical narratives monumentalize the 1972 Asama Mountain Lodge incident as the "end" of the Japanese new left, as Nakahira and others noted at the time, the monumentality of such a narrative betrayed the (ongoing) operations of power at the time.[20] Thus, Nakahira's "illustrated dictionary" embodies the elaboration of a manifold inquiry into seeing itself that informed his ever-changing critical writings and photographic praxis. And, moreover, we discover a shared context of critical inquiry into the everyday informed by the "afterlives" of radical leftist thought as it illuminated the shifting geopolitical and aesthetic stakes of contesting novel circulations of power that congealed within the 1970s and beyond.[21]

One of Nakahira's primary responses to the limiting horizons of the landscape that he had previously confronted in *For a Language to Come* was first performed at the 1971 Paris Biennale. There, Nakahira's process-based installation titled *Circulation: Date, Place, Events*, mounted an assault on the institutional practice of art by mobilizing the myriad forms of mediation that Nakahira distilled from his traversals of post-1968 Paris.[22]

Occupying a crucial turning point between *For a Language to Come* and *Why an Illustrated Botanical Dictionary?*, the installation *Circulation* revealed the changing orientations of Nakahira's interrogation of power. For this installation, Nakahira photographed, printed, and displayed a vast number of images documenting his daily experiences in Paris, adding more each day, and overflowing the allotted exhibition space. The photographs represented Nakahira's attempt to record the entirety of his everyday experience within the installation space, and to forcibly disrupt the safe distance between the viewer and the

FIGURE 4.1 Nakahira Takuma, *Circulation: Date, Place, Events*, Seventh Paris Biennale, 1971.

photographed realties. Following his return to Tokyo (after a brief, but important, visit to Morocco recounted in the essay "Returning from Africa"),[23] Nakahira described in detail the process-based performative nature of the installation, as well as the unexpected theoretical and practical insights that resulted, in several essays that were included in *Why an Illustrated Botanical Dictionary?*[24] Though unable to expand his installation beyond the confines of the exhibition space, into the streets themselves, as Nakahira originally intended to, *Circulation* materialized a crucial set of problems that would inflect the format and thematic contest of the essay collection itself.[25]

At the most basic level, the installation disclosed a critical form of photographic mediation through the "remediation" of the inundating flows that constituted the urban and media infrastructures he himself encountered in Paris. As a process-based text, Nakahira's *Circulation* assembled scattered photographic fragments of Nakahira's traversals of the everyday flux of mediated realities, inducing a feedback loop of accumulating residues within the exhibition space. Appropriating and remediating the otherwise habituated circulatory pathways that sustained Paris, the installation decentered and displaced the generalized structures of meaning that integrated and ordered singular dates, places, and events within a transparent and seeming coherent totality. Nakahira momentarily "hijacked" the privileged space-time of the exhibition, and engulfed the exhibition space with an overflow of photographic detritus, which as he described, was wrought from his specifically mediated experiences each day. "I sought to momentarily record the biases of my everyday existence through the camera, the encroachments, changes, and violations I myself continuously inflict in the world, in order to abandon them. Thus, the process of taking pictures and exhibiting them day after day was a single act of expression, and the hordes of photographs that were accumulated as a result, were mere *remnants*."[26] These photographic remnants (*zanshi*) resembled a substrate in biochemical process, playing a key role in a chain of exchanges, but lacking worth in themselves. Day by day, Nakahira expanded and reassembled the installation with the noisy, heterogeneous remnants he "recorded" from within the patterned flows of people, information, and things. In the process of dismantling and abandoning the biases of the single-point perspective of the "self," Nakahira produced a stream of photographic feedback from the streets, traffic, print media, television screens, art installations, signs, teletype news feeds, subways, crowds, and so on.[27] As an event, the fragments imported daily into the exhibition space recast the status of both the recorded realities as art (as proprietary images to be consumed as such) and the photographer as artist, unable to be seamlessly reintegrated within the given totality.[28]

Read as a performative critique of institutionalized art practice as well as how it staged a specifically expanded form of mediation delineated therein (where, "the static scheme of self and world vanishes, forming continuously moving and multiplying points of view"), we discover a set of questions connected to those that informed the essay collection's performative elaboration of the notion of the "illustrated dictionary" form, as described in the opening essay. Read together, the installation and essay collection can be recognized as discrete parts of a nonetheless shared and radically open kind of inquiry into the changed relations mediated in the act of seeing. Fragmentary and full of holes, the manifold inquiry was derived from the remnants and residues of flux that informed urban transformation in Japan and worldwide. At once contestations of the discursive structuration of artist, artwork, and art, and performative events, the installation and essay collection modeled a critical practice for interrogating the circulatory pathways and bounded distributions of the urban and media infrastructures that governed subject-centered modes of seeing. While the photographic installation did not simply "illustrate" the ideas of the essays in any basic sense of the word, nor did the essays simply explain or define the conditions revealed by the installation, together they constituted the parameters of the "illustrated dictionary" form that came to inform Nakahira's work thereafter. However, if the functions of "illustrating" or "defining" were not operative in ways that such terms suggest, how can we as contemporary viewers or readers grasp the activity at play in such a critical inquiry into the act of seeing and the prospects of displacement that constituted this multiplex text?

OVERFLOWS

Another instance of the "illustrated dictionary" will be necessary to elaborate the specificity of this paradoxical form: Nakahira's large-scale

FIGURE 4.2 Nakahira Takuma, *Overflow*, 1974. From the collection of the National Museum of Modern Art, Tokyo.

installation *Overflow* from the 1974 exhibition *Fifteen Photographers Today* at the National Museum of Modern Art, Tokyo.

Measuring approximately five by twenty feet, consisting of forty-eight color photographs distributed in expansive horizontal array, *Overflow* was the first exhibition of Nakahira's color photographs. It is remarkable not only for its impressive formal scale, but also for the near-complete absence from the existing accounts of Nakahira's work. Unlike *Circulation*, which impelled Nakahira to write and reformulate the insights gained from the installation in *Why an Illustrated Botanical Dictionary?*, *Overflow* embodied a seeming nonevent within the expansive elaboration of Nakahira's ever-evolving photographic interrogations, generating no new critical writings on the subject of the installation itself. However, with the inclusion of *Overflow* in the 2003 Yokohama retrospective and 2015 exhibition *For a New World to Come*, it has become increasingly clear that the work had a sizable role to play in the elaboration of the "illustrated dictionary" form.[29] In many ways, despite (or because of) Nakahira's silence regarding *Overflow*, our reading of the "illustrated dictionary" depends upon engaging with the installation as both a crystallization and critical disavowal of the problems that informed the shared conceptual and practical dimensions of *Circulation* and *Why an Illustrated Botanical Dictionary?*

In its impressive scale and title, *Overflow* (*Hanran*), which is also a homonym for "revolt" or "rebellion," distilled Nakahira's grasp of a photographic platform of critique as a central stake in his self-reflexive interrogation of the urban materialities and sensory intensities accumulated through the camera. Like the photobook and essay collection, the installation confronted its beholder without the preestablished conventions and codes that accompanied the specific form taken by the work. It presented no obvious "logic" by which spectators could order and organize their experience of viewing the installation. The photographs were distributed in adjacent columns of different arrangements of vertical and horizontal prints in groups of two, three, or four, and in two cases, as single photographs. Though lacking a coherent structure, the installation was asymmetrically divided into two sets of eight columns on each side of a single photograph positioned in the center, consisting of twenty-one photographs on the left and twenty-six on the right. The contiguous sprawl of glossy photographic prints made viewing the images in isolation profoundly difficult. Moreover, the diverse arrangements and orientations distributed vertically and the dispersal of the columns across a wide horizontal span of twenty feet made viewing the images in whole nearly impossible. How then might the viewer make sense of the photographs installed in *Overflow*?

It seems fitting to commence our reading of *Overflow* as an instance of the "illustrated dictionary" at random. Starting from the left, I am drawn to the single photograph of remnants caught in a drain, the threshold between the elimination and accumulation of urban residues. Projecting the viewer's gaze down upon an empty asphalt expanse, the photograph captured the wrought iron grill of a drain that has entrapped fragments of concrete rubble, and perhaps a discarded bottle cap, too large to pass into the invisible depths of an underground drainage network. The simple photograph curiously inscribed both the things left behind and the flows that carried them there, no longer present but suggested by their distribution along the drain and the pale vestiges congealed in the channel that terminates there. On its own, such a photograph offered the viewer little more than a literal portrait of some anonymous urban residues, like the rubble caught in a drain of any urbanized place, perhaps anywhere and anytime in the past half century. But this photograph was not meant to be viewed in isolation. When viewed in its immediate context, the drain photograph was adjacently surrounded by five others, and depending on one's distance, could be viewed together with up to about twenty photographs on the left side of the installation. Clustered among other analogous kinds of surfaces and residues, the anonymous fragments of distributed photographs invited their viewer to organize and relate them together. How did these things relate to the other things presented? Along with fissures, openings, surfaces, and other unidentifiable scraps of detail, there were identifiable parts within the installed images, such as the shiny parts of a motorcycle, the wheel of a large truck, a fire near a rocky seashore, and a partial glimpse of a crudely painted advertisement featuring the nude body of a woman flanked by fragments of katakana script reading "yo-ka" (perhaps part of a sign that read "New Yorker").[30] What was the logic that connected these parts together? Why were they assembled in such an arrangement? Yet the sprawling and uncoded distribution of photographs installed put the viewer all the more at a loss, thwarting any attempt to further grasp these parts within the context of the entire work at hand.

Like a collection of views wrought by the "nonselective" vision obtained in Abe Kōbō's *The Box Man*, the act of seeing was itself framed in a novel way by the unwieldy form and dizzying accumulation of residues, surfaces, and detritus. "The distance in it is fluid and the contours vague, and thus perhaps it resembles my own position. The scenery has the gentleness of a garbage dump." Confronted with such a multitude of fragments, the single point of view crumbled away, and with it, the ordering hierarchies of "meaning" broke down. Compelled to move around and seek out novel resonances among the uncanny materiality of light and shadow, unaided by the projected "meanings" of an "artist," the

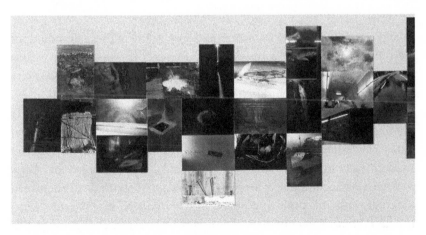

FIGURE 4.3 Nakahira Takuma, *Overflow*, detail.

viewer's gaze was invited into the installation itself. Yet unlike the box dweller of Abe's novel, who "never wearies of looking at such a view as long as one is peering out from a box," the thresholds that both framed and separated the positions of seeing and being seen were seemingly absent for the viewer of *Overflow*.

How then, could the viewer make sense of the residues and fragments that inundate the interpretative faculties, assembled together in a cluttered array of recognizable and unintelligible fragments? More than the straightforward clarification of transparent objects depicted by a conventional illustrated dictionary, the residues of *Overflow* disoriented more than they defined. If it resembled an illustrated dictionary at all, it would more accurately be an illustrated dictionary of residues wrought from fleeting and contingent encounters with disordered and intentionally obscured fragments of urban flotsam and jetsam. As entries in this paradoxical kind of illustrated dictionary, what exactly was clarified through the uncannily illuminated surfaces of things in revolt, and the photochemical vestiges of Nakahira's traversals of the urban expanse? To get a better sense of ways we might begin to make sense of *Overflow* both in its immediate context of the exhibition and within Nakahira's pursuit of "illustrated dictionary" form, we must trace the layered problems that informed the installation itself, and we must return to the printed pages where Nakahira's uncanny residues first circulated.

ILLUSTRATING DICTIONARIES

Like the collection *For a Language to Come*, many of these photographs were first published as a series of installments in the popular weekly news magazine *Asahi Journal*, between 1971 and 1973.[31] In fact, Nakahira had commenced this work with the "Illustrated Botanical Dictionary" ("*Shokubutsu zukan*") in the August 1971 installment of the journal's photographic series entitled, "Another Country." Though subsequent entries each had different titles and a range of approaches and subject matter, each installment of Nakahira's color photography for *Asahi Journal* was accompanied by a short passage of writing.[32] When read together with the problems posed by *Circulation* and *Why an Illustrated Botanical Dictionary?*, this series of writings and photographs enumerated another dimension of the "illustrated dictionary" as a set of problems arising from the relations between the viewer and the material world mediated by the urban as a kind of all-encompassing and fear-inducing environment. Furthermore, the fact that these earlier elements were reassembled in *Overflow* was a crucial index of how Nakahira's efforts to derive new possibilities for photography not only sought a multiplex form of seeing that was capable of sustaining an open form of relating in the world, but also worked through and against the increasingly closed networks informing the transfiguring social spaces of capitalist state power in Japan.[33]

The first installment of the series, where the term "illustrated botanical dictionary" first emerged, disclosed a defining concern for a visually mediated confrontation with the self-propagation of a particular "botanical" form of material reality:

> At some point I came to be gripped with a sensation close to that of terror for the rampant growth of plants. There is no clear reason why. Yet, while these are clearly living things, and no matter how hard I try to feel intimate for them, they always escape ownership by me, and remain a strange living thing continuously rejecting so-called personification. Indeed they do have sap like our blood, veins like our veins and in that sense they can relieve my mind with something human-like. But that is only the appearance of a single leaf of a tree, the encounter with rejection of the brilliant "water-proof surface," instantly transfigured into delusion. In this way what should be affinity becomes animosity. The affinity instead increases my terror.[34]

These dimensions of demarcation and the uncanny encounter with "botanical" forms were articulated throughout this series by means of a color photographic engagement with urban material reality that shifted away from the predominant mode found in *For a Language to Come*. Dispossessed of a safe distance and lacking a suitable language that can speak against the landscape, the "botanical" indexed a provisional method that pursued the potentiality of intermediary forms of relation that arose within the encounters among human and nonhuman worlds. The urban, the "botanical," and the fragmentary delusions that they incited, served as a multidimensional zone of repulsion and attraction through which Nakahira refined a photographic means of displacing a subject-centered visuality. In one example of the mode of writing that accompanied each of these installments, we find Nakahira describing the urban terrain of this encounter in a distinctly surrealist vocabulary:

> The city: all the things that constitute the city, ivy creeping over a wall, manhole covers, or a solid steel-frame structure seen from a moving car, once momentarily illuminated by a single flash of light within the darkness, they seem to be beginning to rise up in revolt on their own perhaps. But this is nothing more than a fleeting hallucination. When morning comes, blanketed with daylight, these again return to "things" as the necessary conditions constituting the city.[35]

Both text and photographs were filled with contrasts of light and dark, as fleeting encounters with disorder and the perpetual restoration of order, together with the inundation of material objects. The uncannily illuminated surface of things in revolt, reflected back into the camera where they are frozen as the photochemical traces of Nakahira's encounter with a regulated world of light and shadow, these oblique exteriors materialized a refractory threshold between the seeing subjects and the world they saw. In another installment Nakahira continued to index the expanding landscape as a new scale of mediation, circulation; an always incomplete totality:

> Going off to nature or the countryside away from the city is merely to escape from the decomposing center of the city. The wheel of a long distance transport truck speeding through the city, or a shark captured in an aquarium, they are not mere hard material objects, or "natural" living things. The city is unmistakably engraved even on the white underbelly of the turning shark. The city, it has almost all of the resonance of when we mutter the word "history."[36]

Like the looming tire, the pale belly of a shark floating in transparent darkness, visible yet forever severed from the seer, each of these surfaces reflected a mere fragment of an urban reality that has overturned all boundaries between city and countryside, human and nature, history and fiction.[37] The urban had become an all-encompassing reality from which escape was no longer possible, one that furthermore constituted as much a destructive force as it did a "constructive" force. Once accumulated as discrete moments of encounters among gazes, sheared from the infinitely expanding totality through the mechanism of the camera, a repulsive tension can be registered by the viewer, the same way one can feel the force of a magnetic field by moving small magnets around each other by hand. One begins to sense in these early color photographs how Nakahira worked to reorient, or remediate, the charged flow of the photographic gaze as the "operator of the world." These uncanny surfaces seem to repel their smooth alignment within the ordering language of the city as the "landscape" that subsumed all differences. The single-point perspective of the photograph was "hijacked" and transported away from the realization of the coherency of the landscape. There, the play of gazes elaborated by the mediated relations among materiality, the mechanism of the camera, and the spectator, disintegrated the thresholds among them, and openings ominously emerged from the breakdown of a knowable totality. In a later of installment of this series, Nakahira wrote:

> The city is like something living, the city continues to propagate in the daylight. This is perhaps on the surface proof of the wholesome activity that continues and the health of the city in which we reside.
>
> But, within the crevices of this kind of city, there are hole-like openings here and there. These are like openings that pass into the reverse lining of the city. Stopping on the landing of a somewhat dark "negative" stairs, the wind begins to blow. If you descend from here where exactly would you end up? The terror of being ensnared in a trap and the anticipation of an anti-world; perhaps it is the "healthy city" that surrounds us that is a mere momentary hallucination.[38]

These installments were published as much as three years prior to the *Overflow* installation, and suggested the wholly undeveloped character of Nakahira's initial efforts to break from his prior photographic praxis. However, they also revealed how Nakahira's questioning of seeing itself was initiated from his continued pursuit of fissures or cracks embedded within the emergent landscape of power. Within the immediate context of *Asahi Journal*'s news, commentary, and criticism, these abbreviated and ambivalent fragments of text and photography likely could elicit nothing more than a fleeting moment of confusion. However, Nakahira's continued contributions to the *Asahi Journal* in the early 1970s played a crucial role in fleshing out a changing set of questions that informed both his photography and writings thereafter.[39] Both the text and photographs evidenced a consistent questioning of the changing contours of urban materiality, which was telling of the ways Nakahira pursued visually mediated relationships as a foundation for groping toward a broader totality, however incomplete.

The compounded parameters of this inquiry into visuality, urban materiality, and mediation, moreover indexed a pursuit of knowledge as a key component of the "illustrated dictionary" form that Nakahira was developing through these fragmentary installments. These attempts at forging knowledge of and in the world through a mode of photographic visuality that consisted of fragmented surfaces and uncanny pieces of urban materiality, disclosed an intermediary platform for rendering novel relations within a broader totality. Nakahira's installments took their interrogative form because critical knowledge of such a totality itself was never preestablished as a coherent system of meanings or concepts, such as "capital" or "state power." Instead, by posing the question of how to grasp a totality from within the visual mediations among each remnant of an all-encompassing urban materiality, the installments participated in displacing the immediately given meanings of such concepts, as openings for novel forms of knowledge of and in the world. In one of the essays included in part three of *Why an Illustrated Botanical Dictionary?* Nakahira problematized the commodification of knowledge and the loss of any attempt to relate increasingly specialized knowledge to any form of totality. Rather than asserting some nostalgic claim to having once had access to such a totality prior to the commodification of knowledge, Nakahira instead sought novel forms of mediation among the increasingly fragmented particularities of which an incomplete totality consisted.[40] Thus, however ambiguous and illegible the fruits of Nakahira's rudimentary entries in an "illustrated dictionary" were, we can grasp how the relation to a non-immediately established totality remained a central concern for Nakahira. In part, the use of uncanny residues and remnants of urban materiality in the "very attempt to know," situated Nakahira's installments within a context of emerging critical urban discourses.

Questionings of urban spaces and media systems emerged precisely because critical knowledge of the mediating structures (whether linguistic, aesthetic, geopolitical or otherwise) that constituted totalities of relations (the broader social relations of production) had become a central stake among diverse struggles of the late 1960s and early 1970s. The untarnished vision of boundless growth and prosperity of capitalist modernity that had structured Japan's Cold War remaking rang hollow in the wake of the successive "shocks" to the geopolitical order in crisis worldwide.[41] Moreover, reactionary police violence erupted across the archipelago in an effort to extinguish ongoing struggles against large-scale state and corporate "modernization" projects, such as the construction of Narita Airport, the 1972 Sapporo Winter Olympics, and projects preparing for Okinawa's reversion to mainland Japan in the early 1970s. Thus, we can situate Nakahira's attempts within a broader constellation of intellectual exchanges that sought to derive a critical mode of knowledge distilled from the urban ecologies of this moment. For even as these became totalized environments in the consolidations of capitalist state power, critical knowledge of—and intensive modes of encounter with—the diffuse totality of relations in crisis was rendered increasingly difficult.[42]

KNOWING THE URBAN NEBULA

One such set of exchanges was demonstrated by another regular series published in *Asahi Journal* from 1973–1974. The series, entitled "The City" ("Toshi"), was organized by Taki Kōji, Nakahira's coeditor and collaborator on *Provoke*. As an early instance of the sustained interdisciplinary analysis of urban form that would characterize Taki's later work, the series approached the city from multiple symbolic, discursive, ideological, material, and linguistic layers of inquiry. Photography scholar Yuko Fujii has described the formal and conceptual outlines of Taki's project as part of an inquiry into the social functions of photography within society. "Taki attempted to devise methodologies for analyzing the ideology that is the city. In Taki's view, the 'city' does not merely mean the collective entity of architecture and infrastructure but also signifies

the site of social, cultural, and political interactions and associations."[43]
Along with Nakahira's photographs, included often anonymously or
without attribution, the series involved architect Isozaki Arata (b. 1931)
and graphic designer Kimura Tsunehisa (1928–2008), who designed the
cover of *For a Language to Come*.[44]

A few examples of the subjects and sites treated indicated the broad
scope of Taki's series and the expansive nature of the urban under inquiry
therein. Encompassing somewhat predictable topics such as "my home,"
"my car," and "mass illusion," the series often turned to more unpredict-
able sites of inquiry such as "coin lockers," "message boards," and "vend-
ing machines." To briefly enumerate some of the more interesting topics
here, I will simply list a number of titles and provide a short summary
of their analysis: "electro-graphic architecture," on neon signage; "lab-
yrinths," on the multilayered structure of cities; "spaces that have been
left behind," on the heterotopic residues and ruins of earlier formations
of urban space; "the sexual city," on the urbanization of sex, which rather
than producing the "liberation of sex," integrated sexuality within managed and administrated systems; "poverty," on the new forms of poverty
coming into being with enduring forms of "classical" poverty concealed
within the image of Japan's new prosperity; "underground passages," on
the contradictions between surface and underground cities; "mobile
tent theatre," on the 68/71 Black Tent mobile theatre group and the indeterminate forms of mass resistance to state power that began after 1970;
"the homecoming rush," on the contradictions of "returning home" after
the "home" has been rendered a mere image of the city-dwelling masses;
"vestiges: the flyer," on the residual traces of political and nonpolitical
flyers that wallpaper the streets and how they work on the subconscious,
appealing to our pleasure principle as described by Marcuse; "the perception of the environment," on the lived environment and the process
of encoding, decoding, and recoding; "uniforms," on the uniform as
diverse cultural forms including fashion and the contradictions of the
pursuit of identity through collectivity; "Tokyo," on the orthographical
use of English in signage; "artificial nature," on the contradictions found
in forms of humanmade gardens and decorative plants; "mysterious dis-
appearances," on the rapid increase of sudden vanishings of individuals,
like those depicted in Abe's *Moetsukita chizu* discussed in Chapter 2;
"surveillance organizations," on vigilante neighborhood self-defense

organizations from their origins in the 1923 post-Kantō earthquake massacre of Koreans and anarchists sponsored by the police; "the possession of space," on zoning and fictions of property development; "the seat of power," on the desks and chairs of mayors; "citizen power," on the handmade signs of citizens movements blocking development projects; and "identity crisis," the final entry in the series that closes with the claim, "the urban is not a 'work of art' but rather 'a text' consisting of the processes of being continuously formed, learned, reconstructed by its citizens."[45] In many cases, as Fujii points out, a number of these installments would serve as starting points for Taki's later studies of visuality, architecture, urbanism, and power. Motifs from "The City" series can be found taking a more developed form in Taki's expansive studies such as *The Lived House* (*Ikirareta Ie*, 1976, and the revised version of 1984, a largely different text with the same title), *Metaphor of the Eye: Phenomenology of the Gaze* (*Me no in'yu: Shisen no genshōgaku*, 1982), *The Poetics of Things: The Rhetoric of Furniture, Architecture, and the City* (*Mono no shigaku: kagu, kenchiku, toshi noretorikku*, 1984), and even two decades later, *The Politics of the City* (*Toshi no seijigaku*, 1994).[46]

Yet, in contrast to Taki's comprehensive project, the early instantiations of Nakahira's "illustrated dictionary" seemed to resist any accumulation of knowledge more than evidencing an imperative of attempting to know and think about urban materiality through photographic visuality. Nakahira's own theorizations on the nature of urban form would be made clearer in an essay precipitated by his contributions to the covers of the magazine *Modern Architecture* (*Kindai Kenchiku*) during the year 1974, spanning the period of *Overflow*'s installation in the *Fifteen Photographers Today* exhibition. Nakahira's cover photographs presented striking critiques of both modernity and architecture. Much like the *Asahi Journal* color series, each cover featured oblique urban surfaces, suspended between states of being under construction or being dismantled, dim crevices, shadowy underground passageways, forms of residues, uncanny objects, and the disintegrating materiality of an incomplete urban world. Four of the cover photographs would be included in the *Overflow* installation itself. When asked by the journal's editors to give a commentary on his cover work, Nakahira provided a lucid and similarly provocative essay that described his pursuit of the urban, its influence on his photography, and a critique of the architectural discipline stirringly entitled, "Can an Anarchist become an Architect?" ("Anākisuto wa kenchikuka ni narieruka").[47] While openly admitting his lack of interest in and prejudice against the professional field of architecture (arising from his distaste for the inhuman stasis of the modernist architectural vision), Nakahira invited critical reflection on the fruits of modern architecture, raising the paradoxical image of the anarchist architect together with introducing his own unique perspective as a photographer of the city. As such, the essay fleshes out critical developments in Nakahira's "illustrated dictionary" form, revealing a focus on the relational nature of urban social space, where bodies and material reality collided.

> For me the city is always a dark nebula, nothing more than the utterly mixed relations among people, things, and space. No matter how much the city is dissected, it can never be reduced to a single architecture or building. It's just like if you were to divide the ocean into equal parts, then divide it again and again repeatedly, this water that would remain in the end would not be the ocean. This splash of water would just be a splash of water, without any relationship to the ocean at all.
>
> The city is something that encompasses me, something synonymous with a history which continuously violates me. The city is something that always exceeds my grasp, something opaque, yet something certainly existing; a totality of invisible relations.[48]

This vast dark cloud of intermixing, interconnectedness, and conflict was for Nakahira precisely what the visibility of the architectural field remained blind to. Only in its blindness could the historical formation of this hostile zone of tense relations be neutralized within the closed circuit of buildings, "authors," and "works," severed from the social space of mediation and exchange it sought to "express." The fluidity of this dark nebula, an ocean of invisible relations that exceeded, yet encompassed, the subjects and material reality of an urban history was posed as a radical contrast to the highly specialized discursive practices of producing architectural objects or monuments that divide and fragment these relationships. Escaping the immediacy of a preexisting discourse, however, the invisible urban form and the invisible totality of relationships articulated here by Nakahira, could not be located outside the infrastructural intervals of capitalist state power. The urban could never be a neutral plane of transparent becoming, abstracted from the living fabric of fluid social relations. Instead, Nakahira saw the urban as the contested intermediary where subjects and objects were integrated within, or repelled from, an ever-expanding landscape, entangled within a vast networked lattice of codified relations that induced a regulatory way of seeing on the subjective level. Attuned to the workings of power operative within the environmental field of view rendered by this regulatory gaze, Nakahira turned to the fragments and flux of the everyday reproduction of the contemporary city.

> However incapable of grasping the reality of such an urban nebula, the city in which we are living swells up like the throat of a gigantic toad. It has been completely transformed into a massive web, a multitude of interlacing webs lacking that core of a human center [the once shared sensibility of all city dwellers]. That is my concrete sense of the contemporary city. Within the very innermost depths of our dreams, at the very foundation of our existence as urban people, the city functions as the unseen binds that ceaselessly regulate, oppress, and violate us.[49]

Moving beyond his earlier theorizations of landscape, Nakahira furthermore pointed to a blind field enveloping our very perception of the urban's expanding entanglements with power. The urban was the mediating place of exposure to a growing mass of entangled webs that permeated even the depths of our unconscious, naturalizing a sensory order that ceaselessly reproduced a totalized environment.[50] However, typical of the paradoxical optimism that we find in Nakahira's criticism in *Why an Illustrated Botanical Dictionary?*, among the profound forms of exposure that "ceaselessly regulate, oppress, and violate us," Nakahira located the transformative possibilities harbored within the "dark nebula" of an expansive urban reality. Stated as the heading of the concluding passage of the essay, Nakahira's notion of the urban nebula remained a tense magnetic field of relations: "The city is first of all a 'relational form,' an 'intermediary' between people, things and space."[51] As an intermediary of *other* relationships, qualitatively different forms of relation, the figure of a dark urban nebula indexed an embedded source of inquiry that permeated throughout—yet is not contained by—the given contours of urban forms and media systems.

At the end of the essay, seeking out a starting point for an inquiry inflected by this intermediary form, Nakahira reassessed the assaults on the landscape by the student movements. Reorienting a self-reflexive critique of architecture toward the destructive forces of capitalist state power, Nakahira delineated the form such an inquiry must take.

> Perhaps the revolts of the students at the end of the 60s and their "destruction for destruction's sake" can also be considered the stately work of architects. These were tied to the "city" at least, in the sense that these were actions that brought us closer to reality of the "city."
>
> But unfortunately, in the present state, the destructive force of architecture, of the city, is performed on behalf of power itself. Today the "Remodeling the Archipelago" is progressing with the coopera- tion of construction, architectural and wrecking industries. How can the dismantling and destruction of the city from our side take shape against power's destruction of the city?[52]

Though posed as the perspectives of an outsider to architecture, the self-reflexive critique modeled here paralleled the one Nakahira himself mobilized in pursuit of a photographic visuality capable of unfolding, unraveling, and opening the intermediary zone of urban materiality in the "illustrated dictionary."[53] Moreover, the stakes of performing such a critical architecture are clarified in opposing it with the totalizing visions espoused in Tanaka Kakuei's 1972 bestseller, *On Remodeling the Japanese Archipelago* (*Nippon rettō kaizō-ron*). As an ideologically charged "blueprint" for envisioning the heterogeneous parts of the archipelago within a networked and homogenized landscape itself, Tanaka's text laid bare the discursive outlines of an environment seam- lessly enclosed within the workings of capitalist state power.[54] Efforts to produce critical knowledge in and of the urban were thus enmeshed within an asymmetrical struggle over how to see and sense other ways of relating among self, world, and other. In this sense, the essay clarified how the "illustrated dictionary" form emerged within a self-reflexive and embedded critique of seeing the urban itself, as part of such a critical inquiry, one that sought knowledge in and of the urban as an incomplete totality, rather than a totalized environment.

SEEING INCOMPLETENESS

Bringing the development of such an inquiry to bear upon our reading of *Overflow*, how then did the rearticulation of the basic elements of the illustrated dictionary inform the installation? How might the rudimentary form of illustrated dictionary given to the *Asahi Journal* work have been further refined in the remediation and translation of such photographic detritus from the domain of print journals into the museum installation? As we saw with *Circulation* and *Why an Illustrated Botanical Dictionary?*, Nakahira would increasingly pursue the prospects of the "illustrated dictionary" through the circulations of photography across thresholds among domains of architecture, art, journalism, and media more generally. So what traversals did Nakahira's illustrated dictionary form afford *Overflow* as a large-scale installation? As I hope to make legible here, the installation in fact enumerated the thresholds that defined a way of seeing Nakahira had developed across manifold layers of critiques. That is, Nakahira's installation modeled how seeing itself not only mediated and related together each of the embedded loci of critique that he had unearthed through his writings (including his critiques of architecture, art, journalism and television, travel and Discover Japan, and documentary cinema, among others) but also a critical form of knowing and becoming in the flux of the self, world, and other. First we must seek clarification of what we are seeing when we look at *Overflow*. Then we can approach how seeing *Overflow* performed a critical form of illustrated dictionary.

As described above, on first look *Overflow* confronted viewers in ways that forced them to engage with the installation differently from that of a passive consumer of an artist's selective views of the world. Within the specific context of the *Fifteen Photographers Today* exhibition, the format and content of *Overflow* would immediately look different. From published photographs of the exhibition, it was clear that many of the installations emphasized large-scale prints, each occupying at least as much wall space as *Overflow*, if not more, as in the case of the massive floor-to-ceiling prints of Shinoyama Kishin's "A Sunny Day," and

Araki Nobuyoshi's "Photographs."[55] Others, such as Naitō Masahito's "Heta Village" installation incorporated multiple layers and numerous prints, with one continuous panel consisting of 132 portraits of Sanrizuka farmer-activists, offset from fifteen contiguous landscape photographs mounted on the wall behind.[56] Moreover, other installations explicitly indexed the urban as a constituent element of their work, most notably Takanashi Yutaka's *To the Cities* (*Toshi e*), which incorporated photographs originally published in *Provoke* and *Asahi Camera*.[57]

Unlike the stunning and varied "windows onto the world" that were centralized around the intermediary gaze of the photographer, Nakahira's decentered installation made the viewer's gaze operative as the organizer of the work. From *Overflow*'s interplay of seemingly random distribution of fragments, surfaces, and residues, a discernible process could be detected: the undifferentiated enumeration of parts of an incomplete whole. This was, if you recall, the definition of the "illustrated dictionary" that Nakahira provided in the essay "Why an Illustrated Botanical Dictionary?":

> Its parts are not parts permeated by the whole but rather the parts always remain parts, there is nothing on the other side of them. The method of the illustrated dictionary is absolute juxtaposition. It is this method of juxtaposition, or enumeration, that must be my method.

In its most basic form, *Overflow* was merely the enumeration of parts that "always remain parts": sky, sea, street, wall, body, vehicle, passage, shadowy surface, animal, reflective surface, portal, crevice, fire, spill, and so on.

The enumeration of *Overflow* afforded an exploration of the photographic capacity to disclose a vast, incomplete totality that exceeded—yet mediated—each of these residues and fragments. On the one hand, we can clearly see how *Overflow* materialized the very form of "illustrated dictionary" provisionally named in both the original series of photographs and text from which many of the installation photographs were drawn, as well as further articulated in the essay collection. But only in *Overflow* do we learn how seeing operated in the "illustrated dictionary" as an accumulation of fragmented urban scenes wrought from

FIGURE 4.4 Nakahira Takuma, *Overflow*, detail.

the reflective surfaces of an expansive urban reality that had overturned all boundaries between city and countryside, human and nature, history and fiction. These photographs were the scattered residues of an urban world that pervaded and yet escaped each photograph; a looming tire photographed through a windshield, a pale belly of a shark floating in transparent darkness behind glass, an uncanny growth of vines spreading out over an unnoticed corner of the city. Enumerated together, they indexed a totality of which these residues were parts, but one that was discontinuous and incomplete to say the least; they did not add up to an immediately signifying whole.

Constituted by remnants extracted—or excreted—from the circulatory flux of an urban ecology, the incompleteness of *Overflow* not only refused any total view, it moreover exploited the possessive logic of a penetrating gaze to deplete the safe remove of a totalized visual field. Displaced from a closed visual system of seeing "parts permeated by the whole," the incompleteness enumerated by *Overflow* decentered the static gaze as an assimilatory locus of "meaning." Drawn into the magnetic field emanating from the fragments, flows, and residues of material things accumulated in *Overflow*, the viewer's gaze becomes a mobile and transient contact among a polyphony of possible relations. As such, exposed to—and together with—the manifold of *Overflow*, the viewer's gaze becomes caught up in an interminable enumeration of the contours of an urban totality full of holes and flows. We thus discover how the "illustrated dictionary" form operated at the very thresholds through which we see the world and see in the world. In rejecting the totalized urban environments and media systems of its age, *Overflow* made sensible a proliferation of relations among human and nonhuman worlds wrought in the flux of the incomplete totality they held in common.[58]

NAKED EYE REFLEX

Although Nakahira remained silent about the installation itself, offering no reflections upon *Overflow* in his own critical writings, we can discover modalities of the way of seeing obtained in the "illustrated dictionary" form taking on different articulations across his work.[59] I will conclude this chapter by examining a parallel development to this way of seeing found in *Overflow*. One decisive characteristic of Nakahira's subsequent work, which continued to question how seeing mediated our capacities for knowing and becoming in the world, was the challenge of critically reading other photographers' ways of seeing. If photography afforded an embedded inquiry that disclosed how the act of seeing itself could be grasped in other ways, then other thresholds of knowing and becoming captured by other photographers could also be "read" and exposed differently.

We can locate another source of inspiration for Nakahira's "illustrated dictionary" in the photography of Eugène Atget.[60] In an important 1973 essay that outlines his discovery of a latent tension harbored in Atget's works, Nakahira is confronted with another *critical* threshold embedded within photographically mediated visuality. Describing the paradoxical allure and repulsion of Atget's photographs, Nakahira draws attention to the suspension between these antithetical forces from which Atget's work derived its lasting and intense interactions with viewers of his photographs.

> In the end, the images of Atget reject my own memories and feelings; the streets indifferently stare back at me as streets and the material objects stare back as objects. In these images my attempts to ascribe significance or sentimentalize cannot penetrate into them. They entwine themselves within my memories, and yet ultimately they reject these completely with a kind of twisting.

Atget's photographs hang suspended in midair between this kind of attraction-catharsis and repulsion-alienation. This is where the unique characteristic of Atget's photography lies.[61]

This tense suspension between attraction and repulsion that Nakahira ascertained in Atget was a product of Nakahira's own pursuit of an embedded locus of inquiry that could serve as an intermediary among the urban materialities and media ecologies that governed sensory experience. As we noted above, in enumerating an "illustrated dictionary," Nakahira repeatedly accentuated the thresholds of attraction, reflection, and repulsion within photography as a means of revealing the systematization of the gaze within the daily deluge of image media that constituted the urban everyday. Although born out of different historical contexts, Nakahira's pursuit exposed him to other moments when the stakes were heightened for seeing and sensing changing forms of relation within urban materiality.[62] Nakahira's essay emphasized the fact that by the very property of remaining in suspension between the poles of attraction and repulsion, Atget's photography served as an intermediary locus of conflicting gazes that did not comfortably "return" or "resolve" these intertwining gazes in favor of one side or the other, but instead profoundly threatened the coherence of the subject and objecthood on both sides of the relation of seer and seen. As Nakahira described in this essay, Atget's photographs exhausted the viewers' gazes as they are confronted with the naked, indifferent materiality of city streets and the hostile gaze of a once-familiar world stripped of its familiar, human significance. Nakahira would point out that this was less a product of the historical or cultural distances between post-Commune, fin de siècle Paris and 1970s Japan, and more a function of Atget's photographic practice itself:

In this sense too, his photographs were not photographs that had been permeated by his own consciousness. Instead, it was the elements that Atget was not conscious of, the elements of the unconscious, which decided the nature of his photographs. The fact that we are moved when we see his photographs is precisely because the world ruled by this "unconscious" conveyed through Atget's camera stirs our consciousness even today.[63]

As a photographic intermediary between unconscious and conscious states (also celebrated by Benjamin in his treatment of Atget), Atget's work heralded a model of photographic praxis that surrendered the photographer's desiring and knowing gaze, and instead, invited the opposing gazes of an indifferent world of material reality into the photograph, thus serving as a medium where the dynamically tense zone where antithetical yet overlapping worlds collided. For Nakahira, grasping Atget's photography as a materialization of conflicting gazes was not only a product of his inquiry into photographically mediated modes of seeing, but it furthermore offered a crucial means of sustaining his self-reflexive critique of photographic visuality.

By seeing how Atget's work operated in the tense suspension of both the photographer and viewers' possessive gazes, it could be read as a model for questioning the photographer's role in reproducing the operations of power that congealed through the urban pathways and media ecosystems of Nakahira's moment.

> The first chapter of Eugène Atget's collection of photographs, *Paris du Temps Perdu* is entitled, "Looking at the City." But now, this must be properly restated as the "Looking from the City." This is because these are not the images of the city, images of the world grasped by means of a gaze towards the city from a firmly established ego, but rather a collection of photographs that have succeeded in a curiously plain inscription of the world and the city that leaps at us from that side, with what might be called a vacuum, concave eye.
>
> In this sense, for those of us photographers (self-described or so-called by others), Eugène Atget persistently continues to ask us to return to the starting point and reconsider what is the photographer, what is photography?[64]

The concave eye that circulated the city streets like a ghost to draw out the hostile gaze of urban materiality in Atget's work resounded with Nakahira's continued pursuit of a decentered modality of photographic visuality. The vacuum gaze that Nakahira observed in Atget's photographs afforded a way of seeing the thresholds of power embedded in the act of seeing within the sealed up landscapes of Japan's Cold War remaking. The stakes of seeing as such were not merely those of an aesthetic problem of how to "represent" a reality "out there" nor how to "express" an "internal" image. But rather, as the "illustrated dictionary" form attempted to enumerate, seeing itself was an increasingly critical political platform for securing—as well as for decentering—the administrated and managed exploitation of human and nonhuman coexistence. Thereafter, Nakahira would confront the streets of the urbanized archipelago, and beyond, with a concave eye, pursuing photography deeper into the tense zone of intertwining gazes as an enduring catalyst for critical knowing within an incomplete totality that encompassed human and nonhuman potentialities for collective modes of becoming.

CHAPTER FIVE

Photography as Threshold and Pathway After Reversion

The way of seeing wrought by Nakahira's "illustrated dictionary" played a crucial role in articulating novel ways to render visible the changing geopolitical and aesthetic contours of Japan's urban ecologies. As this chapter will reveal, Nakahira expanded the geographic and historical scope of his interrogations of photographically mediated visuality in the late 1970s. We will discover the diverse ways Okinawa's reversion to Japan in 1972 had a profound impact on Nakahira's photographic theory and practice. Asking how the conditions of postreversion Okinawa, Amami, and Tokara Islands occasioned a refiguring of the literal and figural thresholds of Nakahira's work, I explore how the photographic thresholds of the "illustrated botanical dictionary" form, which played a key role in the last chapter, were reworked through a series of engagements with the redistribution of the material contours and cultural boundaries of the postreversion Japanese archipelago. The geopolitical and aesthetic conditions of Okinawa's reversion, as this chapter seeks to illustrate, reveal a crucial dimension of the broader changes in the urban ecological contours of Japanese literary and visual media.

We encounter a crucial shift in the trajectory of Nakahira's inquiry by exploring the relationship between his writings and photography concerning postreversion Okinawa on the one hand, and his expanded interrogations of Japan's urban ecologies and media systems on the other.[1] Moreover, as this chapter argues, Nakahira's work reveals a crucial set of geopolitical and aesthetic limits at play within the postcolonial relations governing postreversion Okinawa and Japan. Examined through the thresholds of differing orders of visibility exposed by Nakahira's writings and photography, the diverse forces and forms of violence subsumed within the landscapes and archipelagos of postreversion Japan become clear to us. What's more, the broadening of the geographic and historical horizons of Nakahira's appraisals of the thresholds of visibility after reversion sheds critical light on the shifting relations of production and consumption that characterized the literary and visual media of the late 1970s in Japan.[2]

During 1974, the same year of *Overflow*'s installation (examined in the prior chapter), Nakahira published a series of short installments of reportage-like investigations of postreversion Okinawa in *Asahi Journal*. Covering a range of issues that laid bare the geopolitical and economic forces operative in reversion, such as the extraction of Okinawa labor and environmental devastation of the postreversion development projects, Nakahira's reportage evidenced a stark degree of clarity in contrast to the array of murky surface and residues of *Overflow*. But how can we grasp the connective tissues that spanned these singular parts of a shared enumeration of thresholds that came to define Nakahira's work in these years? Was the geopolitical transparency of his experiences documenting postreversion Okinawa irreconcilable with the turbid aesthetics of *Overflow*? He had confronted both the dark urban nebula of the urbanized mainland and the violent dispossession of postreversion Okinawa with the same way of seeing, but the prospects of seeing the relationships that tied these together were profoundly difficult. It is this kind of threshold that I would like to trace through this examination. By exploring the fits and starts of Nakahira's writing and photography as his gaze traversed the seemingly irrevocable divisions and distributions among these disparate worlds, we discover how such thresholds exposed the changing stakes of the problems of seeing, knowing, or relating after reversion. Such problems, I argue, are telling of decisive changes in the expansive urban matrix of mediating patterns of relation and infrastructural pathways that emerged after Okinawa's reversion.

(RE)VERSIONS OF OKINAWA

The event horizon of Okinawa's reversion of administrative rights from the U.S. military government to Japan in 1972 has played a major role in literary and visual media produced both in Japan and Okinawa in the decades before and after reversion.[3] Often described as the end of Japan's postwar occupation with the "restoration" of sovereignty over Okinawa, reversion was a key moment in the Cold War remaking of the archipelago. The logic of reversion materialized a naturalization of the novel territorial boundaries of postwar Japan, rendering a complete, sovereign unit, fully integrated as a partner state within the U.S. geo-political order. But for Nakahira, the problem of reversion revealed a profound crisis in the critical vocabularies available to think about the shifting fault lines in the geopolitical remaking of the archipelago. As Nakahira wrote after two years of visits to Okinawa, what he encountered shook the roots of his very existential basis.

> The lives of the Okinawan people are confronting a critical situation—a crisis—in the most precise sense of the word. Every-thing is visible. This crisis is visible at any restaurant on Naha's International Street. It can be seen driving down the road out to Motobu. It can be seen from the bogs of Kin bay where they are constructing the CTS facility. In addition, it can be seen at the U.S. military bases that occupy the centers of the Okinawan main island, or at Naha airport where the Japanese Self Defense forces repeatedly practice touch and go's landings. The impoverishment and dismantling of Okinawa, as well as the catastrophic impact on the Okinawan peo-ple's lives, are completely visible to the eye, leaving no room for any ambiguity whatsoever. The Okinawans called Okinawa's "Reversion" on May 15, 1972, the "Third Annexation of Okinawa." Yet, if we, the Japanese who must inevitably be *Yamatonchū*, can borrow this word, we could say the "Third Annexation of Okinawa" did not end on that date. In fact, it is now being made a reality.
>
> What do the people of Okinawa think confronted with this much destruction, this visible of a crisis? "Why has the retaliation of Oki-nawan people not erupted?" I know that such questions are like that of mere onlookers. We impose our stereotyped thought upon

them, the Okinawa people. The fact that this is true of both Japanese monopoly capital and the so-called "Left wing of Japan," is indeed a cruel paradox. We throw out our ill-conceived questions like these, and they are swallowed up within the midst of Okinawa, disappearing without a trace.[4]

In Nakahira's account, the profound crisis exposed by Okinawa's reversion was one of visibility itself. Before the naked violence of the U.S.—Japanese occupations of Okinawa, the polarizing thought of the Japanese left was just as complicit in the exploitation of Okinawa as the monopoly capital they so vigorously had opposed. The geopolitics of this visible crisis had seemingly depleted the very critical vocabularies that sought to confront and reject the military-economic logic of reversion. The hypervisible sites and scenes indexed the materialization of Okinawa's reversion to Japan, yet the preexisting geopolitical imaginary of many mainland leftists left them blind to the actualities of reversion, reflected by the silence of the Okinawans themselves.

In Nakahira's eyes, the "stereotyped thought" of mainland capital (sustained by a neocolonial paternalistic development logic) and

FIGURE 5.1 Nakahira Takuma, Okinawa, 1974.

orthodox leftism (sustained by a romantic third-world revolutionary liberation logic) was bankrupt before such visible materializations of the destructive force of reversion.[5] So what meaningful critique—what critical knowledge and forms of relating—could be derived from the gaps revealed in the breakdown of such ideologies before the visibilities of a changing geopolitical order's reconstruction of both the Okinawan and Japanese archipelagos? This was, as we saw in the previous chapter, precisely the critical threshold of knowing and becoming through which Nakahira derived the "illustrated dictionary" form. Thus, we must explore the fine contours of Nakahira's encounter with postreversion Okinawa, tracing the workings of a photographically mediated form of visuality as it traversed the distributions and divisions that defined the thresholds of the Cold War remaking of Japan's archipelagos in the late 1970s.

Nakahira's deep engagement with the questions of Okinawa's reversion had long remained outside the purview of both photographic histories and Okinawan studies. However, with the 2012 publication of the volume, *Nakahira Takuma: Okinawa, Amami, Tokara 1974–1978*, the extent of Nakahira's efforts to interrogate the thresholds of visibility through the conditions of reversion is gradually becoming much clearer.[6] Nakahira was drawn to Okinawa at a key moment during a profound transformation in his photographic praxis from 1974 to 1977.[7] The primary impetus for his first trip to Okinawa in 1973 was the framing of a student activist as a murder suspect during a large 1971 demonstration. A massive protest had attracted student and citizen activists opposed to the bilateral reversion agreement, which allowed both the U.S. and Japanese military to occupy Okinawa in perpetuity. During the protest, a riot police officer was tragically struck down and died, despite the efforts of nearby protestors to assist in his rescue. The front page of the November 11, 1971, edition of the *Yomiuri Shinbun* contained two photographs that were captioned, "Violently beaten by radicals, OFFICER DIES ENGULFED IN FLAMES."[8] These photojournalistic images served as the sole evidence for the incarceration and protracted trial of Matsunaga Yū, who was charged with the murder of the police officer depicted in the photographs. Matsunaga was later acquitted by the appeals court who judged from photographic and film footage that he was attempting to help the officer by putting out the fire, as the defense argued. Prior to his support of Matsunaga, Nakahira had written essays critiquing the ideology of "objectivity" sustained by the belief in photography's capacity to record or document reality directly.[9] However, in addition to the Matsunaga incident, Nakahira was deeply troubled by how the police's selective assertions of the evidentiary status of photographs could be supported by a misreading of his own assertions that photography was documentary not expression.[10] In the 1972 essay, "The Documentary Illusion: From the Document to the Monument," Nakahira had problematized the evidentiary status of photography as an objective record and questioned the socialization of the myth that reality was directly accessible through photographic records.

> Because of the immediacy derived from the fact that photography reflects reality, we have succeeded in remarkably reducing the distance between us and reality. If we consider the tremendous potentiality photography has had compared to other media, it would be nearly impossible to eliminate this immediacy. In particular, once photographic technology, which developed as the essential technological reproducibility of modernity, was joined with print to multiply technological reproducibility all the more, the latent potential that the camera had was transformed into an explicit power. This succeeded in forcibly bringing close and showing a reality once distant from individuals for indeterminate numbers of readers for the first time within the circulation of printed materials. Thereafter, in a more acute, and much more extensive way, the inescapably spellbinding power it held was transferred to film, and then television. By means of our acceptance of the fact that these images are surely the images of reality, reality confronts us with immediacy, and simultaneously all of reality is forced upon us as individuals.[11]

For Nakahira, visuality was always already sociohistorical, and urban ecologies and media systems were increasingly informed by systematized ways of seeing wrought by the overflowing circulations of images afforded by the developed capacities of reproducibility. Paradoxically, as these capacities developed, and the more reality had been made immediate and intimate through specificities of hegemonic media apparatuses, the less reality was "seen." As Nakahira noted, the revolutionary potential that Walter Benjamin asserted for the same historical development of technologies of photographic reproducibility, had been depleted, restoring the cult value of images as the monumentalized icons of systematized visuality.[12] The managed and manipulated realities wrought through the overflowing image media that constituted the urban everyday took the place of other ways of seeing and relating within such totalized environments. Moreover, before the hypervisible overflows of images, seeing was increasingly rendered as a form of subjectively induced unseeing, a defuse and pervasive form of nonrelation. Although he had set out for Okinawa with these critical concerns in mind, Nakahira's experiences in postreversion Okinawa accentuated the stakes of confronting this problem of visuality, deepening his engagement with the photographically mediated forms of visuality he had pursued in the "illustrated dictionary" form. At the same time, as part of his self-reflexive critique of his role as a photographer, it became difficult for Nakahira to continue to produce photographs. He came to describe his profoundly conflicted attitude with the curious expression, the "naked-eye reflex." This was derived from the Japanese term for a single-lens reflex camera, "*hitogan refure*," or SLR, in which a mechanical mirror reflects the light into the viewfinder to see through the lens of the camera, as opposed to the twin-lens reflex, rangefinder-style, or other camera. The "naked-eye reflex," or "*nikugan refure*," by contrast, indicated not an unmediated naked-eye view of the world, but instead sought to sustain the way of seeing derived through the intensive forms of photographic mediation pursued in Nakahira's ever-changing praxis. The term indexed a paradoxical visuality that was embedded within the tense relations of photographic mediation without necessarily producing photographs for the overflowing circulations of images that Nakahira increasingly saw as complicit with power itself. Nakahira would test the prospects for seeing through such a "naked-eye reflex" to think across the distributed and divided thresholds that constituted the geopolitical remaking of the mainland and Okinawa.

During his subsequent trips to Okinawa in 1974, Nakahira produced a four-part series of photojournalistic reportage articles that confronted diverse aspects of the Okinawan experience of reversion as military-economic annexation. Along with the mainland left's abandonment of Okinawa as a political cause, Nakahira moreover documented how the postreversion landscape itself had become the subject of large-scale infrastructural and construction projects aiming to remake the material and imaginary topography of Okinawa, such as the CTS (Central Terminal Station, a massive fuel-supply depot for the U.S. military) and Okinawa Expo '75.[13] In the final installment, "Okinawa: The Bases That Will be Forgotten," Nakahira noted that with the dissolution of continued protests by the various factions of leftist activist groups after the official date of Okinawa's reversion, the "Okinawa Problem" had become old news.[14] While documenting these remade contours of the postreversion landscape, Nakahira's reportage work revealed the tensions lingering within the ruins of Okinawa's fraught reconstruction.

> In New Koza I came across an abandoned ruins where graffiti covered the entire surface of the walls. "Yankee go home!" "Okinawa Banzai!" "Annihilate one-hundred million *Yamatonchū* [mainlanders]!" I'm unable to say whether or not these words are appropriate politically. However, they are the unmistakable eruption of the passions of Okinawan people who have repeatedly experienced annexation and discrimination. This graffiti will only disappear by means of a force capable of spanning both the mainland and Okinawa to carry out the removal of American and Japanese military bases.[15]

From silent ruins within the landscape of reversion, Nakahira's reportage work disclosed the thresholds of a visually mediated form of relation that grappled with the limits of the language available to critique the geopolitical forces at play in Okinawa's remaking. Like the silence that swallowed up the stereotyped thought of mainland leftists, the scrawled graffiti of indeterminate absent Okinawan subjects delineated the conditions of possibility and impossibility that governed the inscription of reversion's geopolitical force upon the built environments of Okinawa.

Moreover, rather than reproducing the irreconcilably polarized divisions between the mainland and Okinawa, Nakahira's "naked-eye reflex" exposed—and was exposed by—the residues of these absent subjects as a tense suspension, an indelible threshold among distributed and divided subjects (the graffiti artists, the photographer, and the reader of the article), that mediated and brought them into relation, however

FIGURE 5.2 Nakahira Takuma, Okinawa, 1974.

fraught. This suspension did not subsume the articulated sentiments within a romantic narrative of anti-imperialist struggle, nor did it privilege a singular locus of geopolitical critique with one term over another among the mediated subjects. Like the "illustrated dictionary" of *Overflow*'s urban residues, by turning the photographer's gaze inside out to expose the world not "as it is," but as a tense magnetic field of attraction and repulsion, Nakahira's reportage materialized a kind of geopolitical threshold embedded within the relations of seeing itself.

Despite the insurmountable differences in the perspectives, sentiments, and languages among those entangled by Nakahira's reportage work, this geopolitical threshold delineated a shifting topography of struggle, one born of a shared desire for decolonization and demilitarization, albeit one whose risks and costs were distributed in an extremely uneven manner. Even so, this mode reveals the prospects of obtaining a critical vocabulary for seeing how such geopolitical and aesthetic thresholds brought world, self, and other into relation. However, Nakahira's reportage managed to bring into view how this threshold was at play in remaking the relations among Okinawans and mainlanders who confronted—differently and unevenly—the postreversion landscape encompassing them as a totalized environment, despite (or more accurately, because of) the fact that the geopolitical transformations of reversion were profoundly incomplete.

The stereotyped realities that such a shared struggle confronted in the postreversion landscape were laid bare on the final pages of Nakahira's reportage piece. There, he simply reproduced an ANA travel tourist map of Okinawa side by side with a map of the military installations on the main island of Okinawa. The tourist map was titled with two segments of text "Land of Serenity," with the superscript "easy and lighthearted journey by jet" and, "Kyushu," with the smaller subscript "Okinawa guide map."[16] The map itself appears to be a topographic roadmap, primarily of the main island of Okinawa, with no clear indication of the areas occupied by the U.S. and Japanese militaries. The map of military installations, produced under the supervision of the external affairs division of the Okinawa Prefectural Administration, was densely packed with blacked out areas of military occupied areas and a cluttered mass of lines and text indicating the specific facilities located therein. In the parallax between the two maps, Nakahira disclosed the stereotyped visuality that governed the realities of reversion. As Nakahira's juxtaposition of maps suggested, this bifurcated projection of neocolonial rule over Okinawa as a base outpost and/or resort paradise effectively dissolved the hypervisible destruction materialized in Okinawa's reversion within a seemingly transparent totality of the Japanese nation-state. In so doing, the stereotyped logic of these maps naturalized the violence of reversion by eradicating the very prospects of seeing, relating, and knowing in traversal of the thresholds shared by mainlanders and Okinawans.

Stylistically, the reportage form taken in these installments would seem to have been a considerable deviation from the enumerations of urban residues found in the *Overflow* installation of the same year. However, the problems and possibilities of photographically mediated visuality articulated in Nakahira's writings such as the "Documentary Illusion" essay, and *Why an Illustrated Botanical Dictionary?* more generally, clearly informed both approaches. On the conceptual level, the wide range of problems materialized in the sites and projects exposed in each installment read like *Overflow's* enumeration of singularities of an incomplete totality. Nakahira's reportage accumulated a range of

unsettled doubts, contradictions, and fissures within the lived experience of reversion, eroding the schematic projections of military planners, developers, and romantic revolutionaries-turned-tourists who
sealed up the realities of Okinawa's reversion within their stereotyped
forms of thought and visuality. On the level of photographic praxis itself,
Nakahira's photographs did not all operate as "straight" illustrations of
the realities that he encountered.[17] The installment on the economic,
social, cultural, and material damages wrought by preparations for the
Okinawa Sea Expo '75 included an eerily Atget-like photograph of the
mannequin displaying an Expo '75–themed shirt, capturing the English
signage of a murky landscape reflected in the surface of the store window.[18] In the installment on the extraction of Okinawan labor power in
the group transport of youth laborers to the mainland for short-term,
low-wage work, Nakahira's photographs of a deserted rural road and solitary middle-aged farm workers were laid out together with a photograph
of a poster of mainland pop singer Aoe Mina (1941–2000) adjacent to a
farmer's association sticker protesting the sugar cane industry's sliding
system.[19] Among the installments we find a consistent effort to reveal
the accumulated specificities of reversion's contradictions and tensions,
including those exposing the photographer/writer to the inadequacies
of merely recording the visible vestiges of the geopolitical forces that
encompassed the photographing subject and photographed objects. As
the products of Nakahira's process of confronting the potent integrative
capacities of a photographic technology of reproducibility—the pre-
sumption of the "documentary illusion" that all that is photographed
is reality, and all reality is photographed—the installments moreover
documented his efforts to expose the thresholds embedded within the
relations of mediated visuality. Suspended between the hypervisible
destruction materialized in Okinawa's reversion and repelled from the
stereotyped forms of thought that could "explain" away these realities,
these records exposed the limits of the "naked-eye reflex" where the
geopolitical forces encompassed both seer and seen.

In a little out of the way corner of Naha, toward Yogi from Heiwa
Dori, is the so-called "stomach of Okinawa," the Nōren central market. In the early hours of morning, before the sun comes up, the
movement of people begins. With the entire surface of the ground

lined with *goya*, eggplants, cucumbers, winter melons, etc., the old people sell their wares in silence. What does their silence speak of? Or the old women who sit at their places of worship, what does their silence speak of? Our questions are drawn into their silence, suspended in midair. But once these men and women start to speak, is this not the moment when Okinawa will come to possess its language as Okinawa?

In the predawn skies the cumulonimbus clouds that herald the sweltering heat of the day to come were already gently billowing upward. Walking the streets of Naha all night in a sleepless state, limbs utterly exhausted, these thoughts entered my mind. Okinawa/"mainland," 1974, summer. What had my naked-eye reflex—not single-lens reflex—in fact captured after all?[20]

That Nakahira left Okinawa with profound doubts about the capacities of his "naked-eye reflex" was telling of the magnitude of thresholds he encountered there. Within the silent exchange of figures and material forms flourishing in the dimness of the predawn marketplace, we can locate the workings of Nakahira's "naked-eye reflex." In exposing the threshold where both language and silence were suspended together, he described a vacuumlike force that threatened to consume both the "mainlander's" privileged distance as onlooker and the dispossessed state of Okinawans themselves.[21]

In this sense, as part of his self-reflexive critique of photographically mediated visuality, we can grasp how Nakahira's "naked-eye reflex" expanded the bounds of the "illustrated dictionary" form wrought from the mainland's urban materialities and infrastructural media to confront and make sensible, the geopolitical thresholds at play in Okinawa's reversion. However, the reportage format materialized here was abandoned by Nakahira thereafter, just as he would abandon the museum installation format of *Overflow*. But rather than treat Nakahira's abandonment of these attempts as signs of failure, we must ask how as limitations—as thresholds—they framed and exposed Nakahira's pursuits to an ever-shifting set of thresholds that would, in turn, reveal another set of limitations and prospects for his writing and photographic praxis. In some way, this would require recognition that the tense contradictions and suspended force fields exposed by one instance of the "illustrated dictionary" form were not resolved within the subsequent instance of Nakahira's praxis.[22] The enumeration of such thresholds remained the definitive trajectory of Nakahira's work, plunging his "naked-eye reflex" deeper within the flux of geopolitical and aesthetic boundaries and pathways of an incomplete totality. The dynamic sense of incompleteness exposed by the changing thresholds of Nakahira's "illustrated dictionary" afforded a way of thinking through of the distributive forces, critical limits, and potentials of a given assemblage of materialities and sensory intensities. As we have seen, a crucial stake in Nakahira's work was the discovery of ways of seeing, knowing, and relating in traversal of the geopolitical thresholds that he exposed—and exposed himself to—in the enumerative form of the "illustrated dictionary." As such, when we examine Nakahira's work after his encounter with Okinawa's reversion, we find thresholds that delineated the contours of distinctly *other* distributions among the forces at play in the remaking of Japan.

AMAMI AS (IN)VISIBLE BOUNDARY

We see this interest in distributive thresholds most vividly in "Amami: Waves, Graves, Flowers, and the Sun," a series of sixteen photographs with a short descriptive essay for *Asahi Camera* in 1976.[23] In 1975 Nakahira set out to the Amami Islands between Kyushu and Okinawa where he sought to delineate a dynamic zone where worlds collided. The results of Nakahira's journey were published with an accompanying text replete with rich subtleties of a counter-topographical project that seeks to reimagine the boundaries and dimensions of Japanese social space from within the zone of encounter between Okinawa and "mainland" Japan.

> My interest in the islands that trace a dotted arc from the southern extremes of Kyushu to the main island of Okinawa began the moment I saw their coral-reef-enclosed shapes. I first saw them from a distance high above, on repeated trips back and forth to Okinawa, on a now familiar flight I first made in the spur of the moment.
>
> My experiences in Okinawa taught me that Okinawa was neither culturally nor politically homogeneous with "the Japanese mainland." On this trip, the reason I departed for the Amami Islands was that

I was convinced that I could discover an invisible line that divides Japan [*Yamato*] and Okinawa on these islands. There's no reason it would have to be a line. These islands are more like an invisible zone where cultures mutually intertwine, collide, and encroach upon one another.[24]

That the starting point for Nakahira's encounter with the Amami Islands was embedded within the particular vantage point of his earlier travels between the mainland and Okinawa was related to how tense thresholds exposed in Okinawa continued to play a role in revealing subsequent loci of inquiry for Nakahira. That is to say, the image of the Amami Islands as a zone where cultures collide, confront, and interpenetrate one another, was discovered from a particular vantage point produced from on high within the postreversion tourism circuit, an intermediary site embedded within the split poles of the "mainland" and Okinawa that had informed Nakahira's photographic practice up to this moment. Thus, Nakahira's journey to Amami can be seen as plunging into the fissures exposed within the geopolitical and aesthetic gulf between his Okinawa reportage installments and *Overflow* installation.

The text as a whole, consisting of the short essay and photographs, offers a crucial look at how the "illustrated dictionary" took on a different set of thresholds without seeking to resolve the tensions among these sides of his prior work, even as Nakahira sought to break down, and further expose himself to, the conditions of photographically mediated visuality. Furthermore, in a remarkable shift from his prior efforts, Nakahira explicitly confronted the naturalized ethnic contours of the nation-state and the occlusions of ethnic others within the homogenized and "flattened out" dimensions of the postreversion Japanese landscape.

Japan is not the ethnically homogeneous nation it is usually thought to be. It was a multiethnic nation-state that included the Ainu, Gilyak, and Orok people in the North and Okinawans in the South. However, due to the fact that at some point this was substituted with the myth of an ethnically homogeneous nation, my interest in these southern islands drastically increased by reading Shimao Toshio's concept of *Yaponesia* (who, until recently, lived in Amami), as well as poet Kuroda Kio's comparative research on the folk songs of Northern Japan and the traditional ballads of Okinawa.[25]

The two bodies of literary work cited as influential points of reference further situated Nakahira's journey within what could be described as discourses of alternative ethnic imaginaries that emerged in the wake of the so-called end of politically engaged cultural practice after the peak of radical student movement in the late 1960s.[26] Dynamic remappings of cultural traditions like Shimao Toshio's (1917–1986) "Yaponesia" had since the early 1960s been born from the urgent need to question the given geopolitical horizons of the Cold War Japanese nation-state. Shimao's influential notion of "Yaponesia" conceived an arc of archipelagos, intertwining cultural spheres whose profound differences relativized the dominant vision of ethnic-national homogeneity at the heart of the Cold War remaking of Japan. For Shimao, this imaginary redistribution of centers and peripheries served as a foundation for reimagining the historical and contemporary forces suppressing Japan's peripheral communities. Thus Shimao's "Yaponesia" opened new possibilities for a collective questioning of the limitations of the homogenized ethnic-national boundaries, and inspired a wide range of thinkers and writers.[27] Nakahira's interests in Kuroda Kio's writings, according to Kuraishi Shino, were spurred by the attempt to confront the fiction and concept of a Japanese identity or sensibility from the perspective of the heterogeneity of those who had been marginalized out of existence by Japan's centers of power.[28]

Although he does not index it here, Nakahira's mentor and celebrated photographer Tōmatsu Shōmei had produced a photographic version of the "Yaponesia" vision in his 1975 photobook *The Pencil of the Sun, Okinawa and S.E. Asia*.[29] The majority of the work takes an ethnographic documentary approach, traversing the marginalized peripheral communities throughout the Okinawa Islands. Tōmatsu captured shamanistic rituals, impoverished but smiling children, uncanny animals inhabiting the landscape, and a highly refined attention to light, shadow, surface, and texture in a photographic record of "timeless artifacts." Despite Tōmatsu's clear desire to reencounter Japan's own archetypical landscape, long since lost to the tides of modernity, the work ended in a vibrant color photographic portrait spanning Okinawa, Taiwan, the Philippines, Singapore, and Indonesia. Indiscriminately juxtaposing together the spaces and faces of lifeworlds as disparate as Koza and Bali, for instance, Tōmatsu photographically reproduced Japan's imperialist geographic imaginary of Southeast Asia, and at the same time rendered a continuous photographic space and time that evoked a startling sense of contemporaneity in vivid color. Tōmatsu brought the nativist ethnographic gazes that were crucial influences on his work, such as Yanagida Kunio, Okamoto Tarō, and Shimao, into a tense force field that delineated a continuous and contemporaneous expanse of marginalized spaces within the pages of the photobook.[30]

What set Nakahira's journey apart from Shimao, Kuroda, and Tōmatsu's imaginaries of cultural difference was a shift away from a comparative ethnographic methodology that drew upon literary, folk, and historical forms of cultural production. Instead, what defined Nakahira's Amami text was an effort to map a tense zone where overlapping yet different cultural worlds intermixed, encroached, and resisted one another. Rather than seeking to document ethnographic differences, Nakahira described his motivation as the pursuit of learning how these different worlds might have delineated an "invisible" threshold along which a multiplicity of relations could be found. If we further situate Nakahira's stated motivations as an attempt to reframe the locus of his inquiry from within the tense geopolitical and aesthetic thresholds that spanned his prior work on Okinawa and the "mainland," the "invisibility" of the cultural threshold he sought in Amami marked a new frontier for testing the capacities of his "naked-eye reflex." How does one "see" such an invisible threshold by means of a self-reflexive and photographically mediated mode of visuality? Moreover, how might the "illustrated dictionary" form itself have to be transformed to interrogate the visible residues of an invisible threshold between worlds? What then would be the stakes of such a transformation and what other forms of relating and knowing could be derived through exposing such a threshold? We gain a clear sense of the changed contours of Nakahira's reframed inquiry in another passage of the accompanying text.

This time I made a two week trip from Naze on Amami Island proper to Tokuno Island and Okinoerabu Island. The southern islands in early winter, bathed in the brilliant rays of the sun, confronted me in silence, as though disappointing these yearnings of mine. I saw the waves, flowers and the sun. I saw many graves of the island people that differed by period and style there. Open air burial, burial in the earth and most recently, cremation, these diverse manners of burial commingled there. It was a creole culture that bulged out from between the Ryūkyū and "mainland" cultures.

Yet, most of the graves had dissolved into nature. Graves covered with beautiful flowers, burial mounds bleached with the light of the sun. In these places, even the slightest traces of the darkness of death was nowhere to be found. Perhaps here one's death meant their return to nature. Death coexisted with life.[31]

Fleshing out the thresholds between worlds, a diversity of graves and burial methods captivated Nakahira, and we see the camera repeatedly turned to sites where opposing worlds become entangled and intertwined. More importantly, the burial methods narrated here modeled the text's photographic subject: the thresholds of a shared existence of worlds that delineated a zone of mutual intermixture, encroachment, and resistance. As we examine the Amami photographs, we discover a consistent focus on the intermixing of botanical forms, aquatic forms, mineral forms, all subsumed within a landscape that teemed with thresholds and boundaries—between light and dark, human and nature, life and death—islands seemingly suspended between states, both inhabited and deserted. Nakahira captured these tensely intermingling worlds in photographs whose picture planes have been seemingly toppled forward or backward by the charged zones where waves, plants, roads, shadows and light come into contact.

The text's avowed interest in the diversity of burial methods, each suggesting a different relationship between the worlds of life and death, was not merely that of a documentary impulse to enumerate the ethnographic differences overlapping upon the Amami Islands.[32] Instead, taking Shimao's and Kuroda's poetic reimaginations of cultural geography as his point of departure, Nakahira photographed Amami as a zone of contact where the mutual intermixtures, encroachments, and resistance among cultures had materialized a lifeworld radically other to the images and imaginaries naturalized in reversion itself. Moreover, as a redoubling of the overlay of thresholds at play in the photographic mediation between worlds and subjects, Nakahira's Amami work performed a subtle redistribution of the very hierarchies of photographically mediated visuality. In Nakahira's photographs, botanical forms, aquatic

FIGURE 5.3 Nakahira Takuma, Amami Islands, 1975.

forms, and mineral forms entangled with, and encroached upon, the fixed distance of the photographic gaze. The possessing eye had instead been possessed by its object, becoming irrecoverably entangled within thresholds and boundaries replete with a transformative energy arrested between states. As though capturing the viewer off guard, the photographic angle of view had been toppled forward or backward, as if jarred by the charged zones where waves, plants, graves, roads, shadows, and light have collided. Once disarmed and dispossessed of a privileged distance, the photographic gaze was here opened up to other distributions by a zone of contact wrought from the materiality of Amami itself.

For instance, take the graveyard photograph in the *Asahi Camera* installment. The sharply focused photograph captured the cleanly piled stones of the low walls that divided the grave plots, receding on a steep incline that drew the viewer's gaze toward the horizon where the blue sky and downy clouds lingered over the varied patterns of stones and graves woven with wild grasses and plants. The subtly cropped printed photograph obtained a kind of symmetry between upper and lower halves of a picture plane that was evenly divided, neatly splitting the foreground and background. However, more than an ethnographic document of burial practices that could support the evidentiary value of the invisible zone of cultural differences that Nakahira indexed as the objective of his text, we encounter a vivid enumeration of material boundaries, both within the photographic frame and of the photographic framing itself. That is, the split plane delineated not only the details of the piled stone walls and graves, but also elaborated a matrix of tensions that set the gaze of the viewer at odds with the photographed subject matter. For the juxtapositions wrought by the perpendicular orientation of the foreground abutting with the horizontals of the receding walls of the upper background suspended the vertical movement of the viewer's gaze while inviting it to consume—and be consumed by—the proliferation of details, resplendent and yet devoid of immediately legible meanings.

The vivid clarity of the Amami photographs posed a stark contrast to Nakahira's *Overflow* photographs that accentuated the limits of legibility and confronted the viewer's gaze as a murky obstruction of its advance into the photograph. While unobstructed, the gaze nonetheless became ensnared within the uneasy force fields wrought in the distributions of accumulated rocks, plants, and limpid skies. Moreover, in the discord between the textual framing of the work as a diagramming of the invisible thresholds among cultural spheres, and the actualities of the unadorned materialities of the photograph, the viewer was exposed to a refined visibility, which did not illustrate the text, but evidenced a play of gazes, things, and worlds that constituted the thresholds of the text. Read as a further development of the self-reflexive form of the "illustrated dictionary," the framing of the text itself constituted a crucial dimension of how such a text could be read. Rather than opening a photographic window that looked out upon the entangled worlds of Amami, the proliferation of details and thresholds threatened to pull the viewer out from behind the safe distance established by the ethnographic frame of the text.

Among the other Amami photographs, we discover myriad literal and figural residues of threshold forms: walls that delineate boundaries, doorways and roadways that arrest the movement of the gaze, waves that engulf the field of view, and plants that delimit the entangled boundaries of human and nonhuman landscapes. Moreover, despite the clarity of the contours of the figures and material forms revealed by the camera, the photographs rendered their "subjects" with considerable uncertainty.

Whatever ethnographic details we as viewers may have anticipated finding based on Nakahira's textual points of reference, nothing in the photographs could immediately elicit legible traces of cultural difference. None of the photographs declared to have discovered some essential Amami cultural artifact, or could be made to support any definitive claim to have captured the "invisible" boundary between Okinawa and the "mainland." In this sense, it was clearly not an ethnographic mode of knowledge that was at stake in Nakahira's Amami photographs. However, on the level of the photographic mediation of the viewer's gaze, seeking to know and "see" such legible differences among the enumerated forms of landscapes, plants, waves, and graves, the photographs delineated the very thresholds of visibility and legibility that pertain to the distributions of power marking such differences. By drawing in the viewer's gaze, and suspending it within the playful indeterminacy of the material specificities vividly exposed therein, the photographs repelled and depleted the desire for ethnographic meanings. In part, this can

FIGURE 5.4 Nakahira Takuma, Amami Islands, 1975.

be read as the continuation of Nakahira's effort to break down the "stereotyped" patterns of thought through which Okinawa's reversion was consumed by "mainlanders." By frustrating the photographic capacity to make such ethnographic differences intimately knowable as such, Nakahira's "illustrated dictionary" upset the hierarchies of power that sustained and are sustained by modernity's myth of the photographic reproducibility of ethnographic knowledge.[33]

Nakahira revealed an unsettled distribution of relations along this threshold where myriad differences and differentials were distributed and subsumed within the hierarchies of power that sustained the postreversion landscape spanning both Okinawa and the "mainland." Embroiling the viewer within this invisible geopolitical boundary, embedded within the photographically mediated forms of visuality incited by the text, the distributions, displacements, and divisions of reversion at play could be made sensible. Instead of the ethnographically differentiated markings of cultural difference, Nakahira's Amami photographs were emptied of human forms. While framing the photographic suspension of gazes as an effort to locate the northern boundaries of a Ryūkyū cultural sphere at the outer limits of a "Yamato" cultural sphere extending south from Kyushu, the refractory materialities of the photographs hardly sustained the geographic abstractions of such a cultural cartography. What then, did such a text reveal? Through the overlapping of cultural, botanical, and historical thresholds with the proliferation of uncanny material things enumerated together in the photographs, Nakahira captured a zone where worlds continued to encroach upon and mutually inform each other, even as their myriad differences are refracted and retained. Nakahira's photography thus exposed the distributive thresholds shared among visible and legible orders of geopolitical, ethnographic, cultural-cartographic, and other forms of knowledge wrought from photographically mediated forms of visuality. And as thresholds, they exposed the viewer to a proliferation of differences that could not be easily assimilated within such totalized orders, but nonetheless could be seen together as parts of an incomplete totality, as related through the mediated visuality of the photographs.

In this sense, the forms of seeing and relating among such sensible thresholds operated differently from those indexed by Kuroda and Shimao's prior literary and nonfiction counter-cartographies. Like

Shimao's notion of "Yaponesia," and Kuroda's marginalized peoples, Nakahira's Amami text questioned the relations among Japan's shifting centers and peripheries.[34] However, rather than seeking to elaborate a new distribution through the mediations of cartographic or literary imaginaries—although these are made present in the essay as the frames of reference engaged by Nakahira—the "naked-eye reflex" that operated in the Amami text can be read as an evolved instance of the "illustrated dictionary" form.[35] That is, the thresholds enumerated among Amami's waves, graves, flowers, and sun demonstrated how Nakahira continued to seek out ways of seeing, relating, and knowing after reversion, as embedded within the fraught conditions of photographically mediated visuality.

AT THE LIMITS OF THE GAZE

The publication of Nakahira's Amami text can be read as part of a reinvigoration of his writing and photographic praxis, thus marking a boundary within the trajectory of his work.[36] The text was published in *Asahi Camera*, a journal that served as a central platform of Nakahira's work from 1975–1977.[37] We can locate the starting point for Nakahira's expanded engagement with *Asahi Camera* in his contributions to the monthly installments of a "New Encyclopedia of Photography" ("Shinsetsu shashin hyakka") along with those of Taki Kōji and Suzuki Shirōyasu (b. 1935), a multimedia poet and filmmaker.[38] As suggested by the title, the series had a stated intent to produce a new form of knowledge about photography and images more broadly.[39] With each author taking on a different set of keywords each issue, the entries of varying length covered a wide range of topics and issues. Nakahira's entries included more theoretically oriented topics that offered critical reflection on many of the predominant themes of his prior work, such as "author," "expression," "landscape," "*provoke*," "realism," "situation," "thing," "concept," and "media." He also contributed shorter entries that were often humorously critical on basic aspects of photographic practice, such as "exhibition," "photography school," "photobook," "group photoshoots," and "problem consciousness," as well as individual photographers such as, "Araki Nobuyoshi," "Diane Arbus," "Moriyama Daidō," and "Richard Avedon."

In some ways, Nakahira, Suzuki, and Taki's encyclopedia participated in redrawing the discursive boundaries that constituted the photographic text.[40] Spilling over from the medium's ambivalent institutionalization as both art and documentary record, the series emerged within the redistribution of the geopolitical and aesthetic horizons of photography as a discursive practice. The entries spoke to the need for an expanded terminology, if not a critical grammar, for grasping changes in photography's conditions of possibility. As might be expected from Taki and Nakahira, this often required destabilizing established meanings and uses of existing terms. Moreover, in traversing a number of crucial boundaries, such as public and private domains, sincere and ironic language, journalistic and artistic artifacts, the discursivity of the photographic text took on renewed importance for the series' aim of constituting a "new mode" of thinking about image media. In this sense, we could locate this attempt as a form of "metacritical" knowledge production that sought as its object not a definitive understanding of what constituted the photographic text but took the form of an inquiry about how the photographic text was constituted.[41] This may seem like an overly minute distinction, but by seeking an understanding of the forces at play in redrawing the horizons of photography, the metacritical encyclopedia revealed the shifting stakes of thinking about, and with, image media.

These stakes were made clear in Nakahira's subsequent contributions for the same magazine. In 1976, the year his Amami text was published, Nakahira commenced a collaboration with photographer Shinoyama Kishin, serialized monthly in *Asahi Camera*. Nakahira's critical essays were paired with a wide range of Shinoyama's photography as part of a series titled, "Duel on Photography" ("Kettō shashin-ron," later collected in a volume of the same title in 1977). These writings proved to be some of Nakahira's most important thinking on—and with—photography, revealing the shifting boundaries and thresholds of the photographic text constituted by profound changes wrought through Japan's (and Okinawa's) social spaces. A central question repeatedly posed by these essays was the possibility of seeing derived through the mediations of precisely the forms of thresholds that Nakahira had enumerated in his Amami text.

Consider, for instance, the two-part essay "The Limits that Consume the Gaze" ("Shisen no tsukiru hate"),[42] which is full of rich accounts of how visually mediated encounters with the world can be made to disintegrate the ordering functions of sight. The essay begins as a narrative of how the process of reading can break down through an intensified visual encounter with the text as material things rather than coded signs. This is immediately followed by another account of an intense visual experience that Nakahira experienced while in Okinawa. Described in vivid first-person detail, Nakahira recounts a sleepless night after an exhausting day of agitating in support of Matsunaga, on trial during the summer of 1974. As part of a twenty-member activist collective, some of whom were as young as ten years old, he had spent the day in the burning heat raising funds and protesting, becoming sunburned to the point of blistering in the process. The collective had piled together in a small lodging place to sleep before another day of tireless struggle; while the others slept, Nakahira was wide awake. In that exhausted but sleepless state, his attention was drawn to a gecko on the ceiling, slowly creeping toward a moth. Describing the intensive distortions of scale and the dissolution of his immediate surroundings as he stared intently at the gecko, Nakahira felt a profound sense of dread and discomfort arising from this visual event wholly at odds with the act of seeing that grounded the everyday experience of reality. It was not a hallucination in the sense of perceiving something that was not present, but rather a kind of deep seeing in which the gaze itself consumed the frame of reference that constituted the seeing subject's embodied context, unsettling the given distributions of scale, distance, and duration.

These experiences are established as the basis of Nakahira's claim that the gaze itself can be transformed into a medium for the perpetual deconstruction and reconstruction of the self. "Seeing is the act of causing the breakdown of the meanings and significance of our mental projections of what we think we have seen by rendering oneself as a single look itself. And in so doing, to bring about the breakdown of the self, and go on limitlessly recreating the self."[43] This central theme was further posed against two important counterpoints that informed Nakahira's writings at the time: the systematization of sight fostered by travel (the geopolitical aesthetics of the orientalist gaze, or the "stereotyped" vision he described regarding Okinawa), and the surrealist aesthetics of illusion or fantasy (the introspective turn away from the realities of material things to augment the human-centered subject). Against these codifications of visual mediation that impede the transformative processes of the gaze, Nakahira enumerated the specificity of the dreamlike visuality of Eugène Atget's photography. For instance, Nakahira outlined the temporality of dreams as the basis for understanding the resonance they have with Atget's photography.

> In dreams everything is in the present tense. What's more, time has no complete flow. Time consists of fragmentary instants, each broken up and isolated, that rise up vertically in succession without any connective thread among them. Without any thread to join them together, they exist on their own as "moments isolated like islands." The division between each instant is vividly clear. As such, in dreams, the center of the self, the self that gives order to the world and controls it, has been lost. So the threads of the present in our dreams that span and connect the past and future together are severed apart. A constant present tense from moment to moment. These are forced upon us in our dreams. We can do nothing more than expose ourselves in our dreams.[44]

The fragmented time and what Nakahira described as the spatial enumeration of details in dreams, constituted a visually mediated mode of experience (in Japanese the verb to dream is in fact "to see a dream" [yume o miru]), which also informed the way of seeing found in Atget's photography. Moreover, in his reading of Atget's dreamlike photography, Nakahira derived an account of how this visual mediation operated through the photographic text based upon the division of seeing acts between the moment of taking and moment of reading a photograph. It was within the limitless cycle afforded by such a way of seeing that Nakahira posed the possibilities of a "permanent revolution of the gaze."[45]

While there are a number of striking aspects about this essay, I would like to highlight here the role of the term "threshold" or "limit" ("hate," or "gai" 涯) that served as the framing interval between the two moments of the photographic text. The term marked the point of inflection within each isolated moment of "seeing," embodying the limit where the ordering gaze became exhausted and exposed the viewer to the bare contours of material reality.[46] However, the threshold of one moment was not merely an indexical referent of the threshold of the

other. That is, Nakahira saw photography not as a medium of reproduction or equivalence, but of translation among analogous forms of
bounded relations. Spanning discrete thresholds that constituted an
incomplete totality, each threshold consisted of the fragmented temporality and spatially enumerated difference of dreams as "moments
isolated like islands." Related by their shared incompleteness, as linked
thresholds embedded in the cycles of photographically mediated visuality, the relation between seeing and photography was thereby opened
up to the intervals among discrete moments to render a "permanent
revolution of the gaze."

More than merely extolling Atget's photography, Nakahira's essay
in fact offered vivid models of the operation of the thresholds of visual
mediation at play in delineating the ways of seeing found in his own
photographs. The dangers of isolating the prospects of transforming
relations among bounded subjects within an intensive visuality were of
course clear to Nakahira. In his continued critiques of the systematized
forms of visuality secured within the patterned and distributive infrastructural media of Japan's urbanized social spaces, Nakahira repeatedly sought to historicize and contextualize the naturalized modes of
sensory manipulation that rendered such transformative prospects
increasingly fraught, if not impossible.[47] However, when we examine the
photographic texts that Nakahira produced in elaborating the prospects
of a "permanent revolution of the gaze," we are confronted with a set of
thresholds seemingly very different from those first encountered in Okinawa. How do the ways of seeing elaborated by "The Limits that Consume the Gaze," offer a mode of reading Nakahira's photography? What
novel thresholds were brought into view in the workings of these later
texts? How might we situate the ways of seeing, relating, and knowing
that we encounter therein within the changing discursive boundaries
of literary and visual media in the second half of the 1970s? To begin to
answer these questions, it turns out, we must follow Nakahira to some
of the most isolated islands of the Japanese archipelago.

ISOLATED ISLANDS LIKE MOMENTS

At the remotest thresholds of Japan's integrated sensory systems, the
Tokara Islands became a significant launching point for a series of

travel-related photographic texts that would occupy Nakahira from 1976 to 1977. Two different publications resulted from Nakahira's travels to the Tokara Islands in December of 1976.[48] These Tokara texts can be seen as playing a crucial role in testing the prospects of a self-reflexive photographic praxis that first fleshed out his work on the Amami Islands as well as the ways of seeing under development in the critical essays of "Duel on Photography." Shortly before traveling to Tokara, Nakahira had commenced a collaborative travelogue series with writer Nakagami Kenji (1946–1992), which found them traveling together to Hong Kong, Singapore, Morocco, and Spain.[49] Nakahira originally set out for the Tokara Islands as a continuation of his pursuit to discover an invisible boundary zone between postreversion Okinawa and "mainland" Japan commenced with his Amami work. These works can be read as both reaching the end of his journey to locate a threshold between overlapping worlds at Japan's most local limits, and the start of a phase of intensive travel worldwide. Moreover, as a model of the traversal of thresholds and intervals that informed Nakahira's writings at the time, the Tokara text sheds light on the broader trajectories of literary and visual media, many of which increasingly sought ways to reach beyond the naturalized boundaries of Japan.[50] In the critical destabilizations of the "permanent revolution of the gaze," we discover how even the most violent distributive forces at play in the remaking of the archipelago could expose—and be exposed to—ways of seeing and reading in traversal of the thresholds that seemingly consumed all prospects of transformation.

Like the Amami text, Nakahira first approached Tokara following in the footsteps of a prior literary text. "*Tokara rettō*, the Tokara archipelago, the first time I heard of the existence of these islands with the strangely resonate name was fourteen or fifteen years ago from Tanigawa Gan's essay, 'Death Watch Beneath the Palms.' Of course I was fascinated with the intricate writing style produced by Tanigawa's assertive narration and extravagant images."[51] The two pages of sparse text that accompanied the color and monochrome photographs of Nakahira's series, "National Border The Tokara Archipelago: The Islands of Uninhabitation," open and close with direct linkages with Tanigawa's 1959 essay on these remote islands located between Amami and Kyushu.[52] While Nakahira's journey to Tokara shared with his Amami work a literary impetus, the context and nature of Tanigawa's original essay further contributed to this series as the literal and theoretical itinerary that served as the guide for Nakahira's journey. As we will see, the overlay of the two texts itself constituted a set of historical and geopolitical thresholds that informed the aesthetic approach of Nakahira's text. To bring this aspect of the text into relief, we will need to grasp the contours of Tanigawa's text, and consider how it exposes and is exposed by the thresholds of Nakahira's text. Paradoxically, this will require briefly going back to the starting point of Japan's Cold War remaking, even as Nakahira's work began to look beyond the limited horizons of the "environmentalized" ecologies of urbanized social space and infrastructural media that had resulted.

Tanigawa Gan (1923–1995) was an influential poet and activist who was most active in the late 1950s and early 1960s. He was best known for his work in the collaborative poetry journal *Circle Village* (*Sākuru mura*), which embedded itself within the coal miner labor struggles in Northern Kyushu as a kind of social network for assembling together the voices of rural farmers and industrial laborers who represented the substrata of Japanese society in an accentuated moment of flux.[53] Tanigawa coedited the journal with poets and nonfiction writers Morisaki Kazue (b. 1927) and Ueno Hidenobu (1923–1987). The journal also featured contributions from both amateur and emerging writers such as Ishimure Michiko (1927–2018), who contributed poetry and reportage on the outbreak of Minamata disease.[54] Situated in the midst of the struggles of the anti-ANPO movement and the restructuring of Japan's energy policy evidenced in the shutdown of Kyushu coal mines, the work of Tanigawa and *Circle Village* sought to reveal a range of remnant contradictions and fissures that endured along the margins of Japan's Cold War remaking.[55] Read as elaborations of the shifting geopolitical thresholds that would inform the restructuring and remaking of the Japanese archipelago, their collective efforts proved to be an influential model for writers and activists for many generations to come, not the least of whom was Nakagami himself.[56]

Tanigawa's lesser known journey to the Tokara Islands at the end of the 1950s, nearly two decades earlier than Nakahira's, sought to locate a remnant model of human community at its most extreme limits. In the midst of the tense struggles of the coal miners and anti-ANPO movement, Tanigawa's interrogative approach to the residual potentials of organizing marginalized people had led him to ascertain for himself the minimum thresholds of human habitation, as the first lines of his original essay announced.

Do you know about it? The nation of just fourteen households, population sixty-four, that sits in the middle of the Black Tide? Rocks, dugout canoes, and the gods. The minimum human world where people cannot exist with any more, they will diminish, or they become isolated. I have just drifted ashore as if I had banished myself from that place. To where? To that familiar landscape I had grown accustomed to until a month ago, to Japan's civilization in the early summer of 1959. I have not come back to it. I have escaped from it. There the communal society that for us has become nothing more than a phantasm and tattered fragments, still exists writhing with the colors and sounds of lived fundamental principles, in that sense it is not just our "mother country."[57]

The essay was a reportage-style account of the remote community on Gajajima, which faced depopulating pressures as well as the effects of a state policy to depopulate remote islands for more efficient administrative aims. Tanigawa's essay delineated his embodied vision of Gajajima as a model of communal habitation at the very limits of human existence. In part, this reflected a desire to locate alternatives to the limitations he had encountered in organizing the marginalized strata of North Kyushu. At the same time, the essay posed a series of potent questions to the aspirations of the mainland left's Okinawan reversion movement gaining momentum at the time. Because the Tokara Islands were historically the first set of islands "reverted" to Japanese rule by the U.S. military government in 1952 (followed by the "reversion" of the Amami Islands in 1953, the Ogasawara Islands in 1968, and Okinawa in 1972), Tanigawa's text can be read as seeking to locate a potent starting point for a genealogical inquiry to the implications of reversion. Thus, while set in a now-remote past from Nakahira's moment of seeking out the cultural and geopolitical thresholds of the postreversion archipelago, Tanigawa's own brand of alternative cultural cartography was a crucial factor in how he approached the Gajajima community. Moreover, the

Tokara Islands served both texts as a related threshold approached from these two different perspectives, embodying a pivotal linkage between two discrete moments within Japan's Cold War remaking.

In Tanigawa's moment, the marginalized communities of Tokara embodied a challenge to nationalistic visions of reversion as well as the centralizing logic of the mainland left. Tanigawa's work traced the profound questions raised by the island inhabitants' continued habitation at the limits of the national community, demonstrating the need to critically reflect on the collusion of capitalist state power and the dominant leftist political parties. Reimagining the prospects of an indigenous communist alternative from a remote form of communal dwelling faced by a perpetual crisis of survival, Tanigawa's Tokara sought to dismantle the predominant geopolitical center-periphery hierarchies shared by these ostensibly opposing forces from its very foundations. Depicting an actually existing community on Gajajima as taking the archetypical form of a virtually propertyless village commune, Tanigawa's text elaborated the geopolitical thresholds informing his moment from a locus immanent to the vast contradictions of capitalist modernity and the systematized vantage points securing the Communist Party's "monopoly rule" over manifold forms of opposition rising up against the ANPO treaty at the time.[58]

Upon Gajajima's reversion to Japan, the government planned to turn it into unmanned grazing land for livestock, thus offering the community a means of enjoying the offerings of modern life as resettled individuals and increasing the productivity and revenue stream obtainable from the island. The logic of reversion clearly spelled the death of the collective forms of inhabiting Tanigawa found on Gajajima, the "death watch" ticking away under the palms of this subtropical utopia. Moreover, Tanigawa was impressed with the resistant stance of the islanders whose continued presence on Gajajima, when faced with the dispersal of the community, embodied a living and contemporary prototype for a "Japanese people's commune."[59] As an archetypical commune, Tanigawa's Gajajima served as a counterpoint to expose the mainland left's attitude toward Japan's peripheries. Therefore, while the vast majority of reversion movement supporters were not complicit with a government policy of depopulation, Tanigawa questioned the contradictions subsumed within their calls for reversion. Instead of "return" to a nation that eradicated such communities, Tanigawa sought to render Gajajima as an alternative model based upon residual forms of nonnational identification harbored within the immanent contradictions of capitalist modernity.[60]

In the case of the Tokara archipelago, the persistence of many people's belief that they were descendants of the defeated Heike clan served as a starting point for Tanigawa to reflect on the need for a counterimagining of belonging suitable to Japan's urbanizing social spaces. As we saw earlier in Chapter 1, the Cold War remaking of the archipelago had unleashed a limitless tide of displaced people, who flocked to the cities like refugees from the margins. For Tanigawa, who advocated recreating marginal communities as fictional constructs that could resist the outflow to Japan's swelling urban centers, it was a question of how such fictional identifications could be sustained against the geopolitically induced tides of change. The pride of the self-described descendants of Heike was a fictional mode of identification, and as Tanigawa noted, was one found across Japan wherever generations of deprivation gave rise to an oppositional structure of struggle. In this case the sustained claims of Heike descent were directly opposed to the Shimazu rulers of the Satsuma domain, which had administered the Tokara Islands since the Edo period. The endurance of such a fictional relation on the Tokara Islands was not evidence of a premodern "residue," but rather was a remnant product of the island community's experience of capitalist modernity itself. As such, the remaining community's existence evidenced a model of resistance to the forces of reversion that threatened to evacuate its collective forms of symbolic and social belonging.

Tanigawa's text documented Gajajima to reveal the *critical* thresholds of a double structure of identification, dependency, and belonging that constituted the shared conditions of the ever-rising tide of displaced urban "refugees." As such, Tanigawa saw in Gajajima's fictional form of residual identity a redistribution of the forces at play in the double structure governing the geopolitical thresholds of Japan's Cold War urbanization.

This superior consciousness is sustained by the fictional authority of the Heike legend, and behind this there exists a kind of republican system that cannot be harmed, overthrown, or monopolized.

While being driven away from their social economic foundations, the double structure captures the consciousness of Japanese people with infinite and unlimited power, and thrives within a vast ocean as a system that has taken root in reality. It is resistance that has taken the shape of dependency, and thus dependency that has taken the form of resistance. In order to break this circuit, we must respond to the question of how Gajajima will proceed from here. Because that is where the generative locus of contradiction is, whoever finds the key there will control everything.[61]

Tanigawa's Tokara exposed the critical dilemma faced by the inhabitants of the remote island of Gajajima as a means of raising the wider question of the need to break the circuit of Japan's double structure by looking at the alternatives faced by Gajajima, the bellwether of communal identification at the limits of an urbanized social space confronted by all within the sea of the displaced.[62] The identifications of an unassailable republican system produced by—but immune to—the destruction and displacements of capitalist modernity offered a telling example of the paradoxical set of counterforces Tanigawa derived from this locus of contradiction. As romanticized as Tanigawa may have rendered his depiction of the remote community, the refractory thresholds of his text revealed a set of resistant counterforces capable of relating the violence of depopulation faced by the remote and marginalized community on Gajajima, together with those confronted by movements elsewhere that questioned the given identifications and collective forms of dwelling induced by Cold War urbanization. The text mapped together the transformative fissures within the double structure that offered Tanigawa a reimagined horizon of revolutionary possibility, even as the prospects for such resistance seemed so dire in the moment of the late 1950s.

The double structure should be discarded, yet the nation-state and monopoly capital will never be ready to destroy this on their own. The legends of Heike should be discarded, yet no unifying symbol of the small societies exists that can take its place. This is the ultimate affliction of the islands I visited.

Will our civilization progress, stagnate, or empty out and degenerate? This notion again and again caressed my face like the hot winds that resound through the leaves of the palm trees, protruding like giraffe necks. In the end, I decided that this dying epidermis-like landscape is the forerunner of Japanese civilization. Many people will merely think of my words as a paradox. They will agree only in the sense that these islands are the ancient archetypes of our society. Yet, what are considered archetypes of the past can also become standards for the future. Here we find a sensibility of non-owner-ship that has been continuously preserved in the midst of absolute impoverishment throughout modernity. Does this not have the firm degree of resistance to bolster us forward?[63]

But this future did not come to pass for Tanigawa. Framing his own journey with Tanigawa's nearly two decades later, Nakahira's text brings into relief a sense of distance from the possibilities for sustaining such resistant communal forms. After Okinawa's reversion, the prospects of Tanigawa's geopolitical imaginary of resistant marginalized communes were eradicated within the flattened out homogenous landscape of the mainland's tightly sealed up "environments" depleted of political potential. As documented in Nakahira's reportage on Okinawa, rever-sion had indeed spelled the ruin of the remnant patterns of the human and nonhuman ecologies celebrated by Tanigawa. In delineating the gap between their texts as a sensible threshold, Nakahira confronted the changed reality with a very different outlook. As Kuraishi notes, if Tanigawa's text sought to invoke the remote island commune of Gajajima as an archetype for the revolution to come, "Nakahira's text revealed the desolation of the abandoned landscapes after waking from the dream of revolution."[64]

It is in this sense that we find Nakahira situating his journey to Tokara vis-à-vis Tanigawa's, as if returning to a former geopolitical threshold to assess the magnitude of the change rendered in the Cold War remaking of Japan. Between these two Tokara journeys, two thresholds as isolated from their moments as the islands themselves, Nakahira's text elabo-rated a paradoxical movement of simultaneous return, and at the same time, departure from the embedded fissures and contradictions traced by Tanigawa's Gajajima reportage. While seeking to delineate the line of demarcation between Okinawan and mainland cultural spheres, Naka-hira had elaborated the thresholds of intermixture and exchange in his

Amami text. Here, in seeking to further expose the remoteness of Tanigawa's moment from his own, Nakahira paradoxically inscribed a tense zone of connectivity between the thresholds isolated within each text.

> Ten years after reading Tanigawa's essay, fascinated with Ryūkyū culture, the Tokara Islands took on renewed significance for me while traversing the islands of Okinawa and Amami. I began pondering the points of contact between "mainland" and "Ryūkyū" culture, and what could be called an invisible boundary line between them. The Tokara Island chain, formally designated as Toshima-mura of Kagoshima-gun, is one of the Satsunan Islands that dot the sea squeezed between Amami to the south, and Yakushima and Tanegashima to the north. Nakanoshima is the largest among them with a population of 336. There are also islands that have been deserted like Gajajima. For just over twelve and a half days I traveled to both Nakanoshima and Kuchinoshima. Among the inhabitants of Nakanoshima there is an ongoing rivalry between the self-described decedents of the defeated Heike clan and the people from Amami; even the public baths and youth corps are segregated. On Kuchinoshima, just eighteen kilometers to the north of Nakanoshima, there are no signs of Amami and Ryūkyū culture.[65]

Between Nakanoshima, located at the outer limits of the zone of conflicting and intertwining cultures first mapped in the Amami Islands, and the fully "mainland" landscape of Kuchinoshima, Nakahira had traversed a boundary between worlds. Like Tanigawa's text, Nakahira's traversal had purposefully eschewed the production of a neutral collection of ethnographic details and minutiae of remote island lifeways as some primordial *furusato* archetype that has escaped the forces of modernity. For Tanigawa, the thresholds wrought by his text delineated an archetype for the future, a model of communal life born of the fissures and contradictions of Japanese modernity for the revolution to come. Nakahira's traversal of the invisible threshold located within an eighteen kilometer span between Nakanoshima and Kuchinoshima brought into relief the contemporary living contours of reversion, depleted of any future but that of abandon. As a text wrought from such traversals, the violence of reversion was made sensible in at least two ways. First, Nakahira's text revealed the magnitude of the literal dimensions of change from the utopian prospects of Tanigawa's margins, a critical view of the center from a reimagined fictional community surviving just beyond the reach of the state. Although Nakahira's original plan was to go to Gajajima, ultimately the weather prevented him from seeing the deserted conditions himself. As Kuraishi insightfully points out, Nakahira's Tokara photographs read like someone following in the reportage-like pace set by Tanigawa's text.[66] Thus, Nakahira's texts performatively demonstrated that literally following in Tanigawa's footsteps, one could not directly access such a utopian place, for that village and its patterns of inhabiting the margins no longer existed. Moreover, as a self-reflexive confrontation with the violent forces of reversion, Nakahira's traversals exposed how the sublation of prior distribution of centers and peripheries had consumed both margins and centers within a seamless landscape of power, erasing the differential prospects of transformation those relations once harbored. Thus the figural prospects of Tanigawa's village no longer afforded any traction against the workings of power.

In this sense, both Tanigawa and Nakahira confronted the geopolitical thresholds of their respective moments from the vantage point of the tense contradictions they derived in traveling to Tokara. Rather than orienting their respective readings of these thresholds toward an ahistorical past, nostalgically celebrating the marginalized island communities as possessing what the modern has been deprived of, both texts traversed the distributive forces of the historical and geopolitical asymmetries at play in each (undeveloped-developed, center-periphery, and islander-mainlander, for instance). While both Tanigawa and Nakahira's Tokara journeys can be read as texts that rendered these thresholds legible as the operative contradictions of a moment shared across such distributed inequalities, Nakahira moreover modeled a reading of these thresholds that afforded ways of seeing, knowing, and relating that exposed and were exposed to "the permanent revolution of the gaze." That is, the thresholds disclosed by Nakahira's Tokara (including the interval it delineated between itself and Tanigawa's moment), were wrought in the process of "the breakdown of the self, and to go on limitlessly recreating the self." The hypervisible violence of reversion and the destruction of remote villages (as well as the depletion of Tanigawa's archetypical communes for the revolution to come), were made sensible as an integral part of the photographically mediated forms of visuality that sustained this process. Seeing served as the crux of a set of geopolitical and aesthetic transformations that delineated the thresholds of the postreversion landscape itself.

What did a photographic text rendered within this crucible of relations look like? Interestingly enough, Nakahira produced both color and monochrome photographs while in Tokara, marking a dualistic approach he had not taken previously. The *Asahi Camera* installment included both color and monochrome, while the *Ryūdō* installment consisted only of monochrome photographs.[67] In all of these, we encounter a pervasive sense of desolation and ruin rather than the delineation of discrete cultural worlds. Photographed like ruins left in the wake of a storm, Nakahira's Tokara work draws our attention to an experience of raw exposure again and again. When we take a closer look at the photographs, we discover in Nakahira's journey to Tokara the fraught tensions of residues wrought in the breakdown of the thresholds between the exteriority of the "outside," and the interiority of the "inside," embedded within the photographic act of seeing the world. For instance, one Tokara photograph captured a dismal island roadway where a sliver of the indigo sea lingered in the distance. Instead of an ethnographic portrait of life on a remote island, we encounter the unremarkable, bare surfaces of an earthen road that stretches toward the sea.

The narrow roadway had been violently carved through dense entanglements of plants, and the viewer's gaze, closed in upon by the bare earth of the surrounding slopes, is drawn toward the threshold between the road's end and the distant seascape. A pervasive sense of exposure clings to this crudely hewn path to the sea, all the more accentuated by the uncanny photographic framing of the sea and land, which has excised the shoreline boundary between them. In this crude perspectival distortion, the shore, which should delineate the division of land and sea, has been dissolved, disturbing the perspectival sense of distance and scale. The vista arrests the viewer's gaze within this passageway between the land and the sea, at once occluding and displacing the "outward" trajectory of its line of sight. Instead, the strong diagonal lines of the bare slope and muddy road draw the gaze to the middle of the photograph where the plane of the sea and the slope of the roadway

FIGURE 5.5 Nakahira Takuma, Tokara Islands, 1976.

uncomfortably abut each other. With time, the distortions wrought by this tense threshold vex its beholder. The difference collapses between seeing as a traveler looking "out" over an unfamiliar road to the sea over which they came, or seeing as an islander looking across the intimately familiar road to the wall of the sea that encloses them from the "outside"; here the pathway becomes a threshold and the threshold becomes a pathway within the photographically mediated acts of seeing.

The photographs similarly confronted each encountered subject as a kind of threshold. We find abandoned homes, reduced to rubble and exposed stones where foundations once stood, the graves between states of abandon and disrepair, the tattered leaves of storm-thrashed *bashō* fiber banana plants, the uncanny encounters with people, children cleaning harvested daikon radishes in a communal well captured with eyes closed midblink, or the fishermen spreading their gleaming catch on the bare concrete pier as the sun sets, one caught in a tense suspension of movement and stasis precariously balanced on the far edge of the pier, the exposed earth after a landslide on a slope once thickly covered with trees and plants now piled at the base of the slope in a tangle of branches and roots, the wall of uprooted trees with clusters of their intricate roots drying out in the sun, a discarded television face down amidst stalks of brightly blooming red flowers protruding from a thick entanglement of aloe. In many cases, it was difficult to ascertain the status of the encountered subjects, as each was rendered as in a tense suspension between such states as abandon and habitation, wreckage and restoration, living and dying, nature and culture.

Moreover, the monochrome photographs further accentuated the barrenness of such scenes, evidencing a subtly refined approach to the granulation of the picture plane once mobilized in the *are, bure, boke* methods of *For a Language to Come*. Although he eschewed intervening into the act of seeing in the way he once had (grainy, shaken, and out-of-focus), Nakahira's black and white Tokara photographs did not simply return to the reportage style of his *Asahi Journal* work either. Instead, these exceptional photographs captured a vivid set of thresholds by materializing a more excoriating form of exposure through the washed out and gritty materialities of the subject matter itself. High-contrast, sharply focused, and largely upward or downward oriented, the photographs deprived the gaze of a deep field of view. They confronted the

FIGURE 5.6 Nakahira Takuma, Tokara Islands, 1976.

viewer with a flattened and curiously dimensionless proliferation of miniscule points of light and shadow.

While by no means could such an approach be described as an attempt to photographically render a direct, unmediated indexical trace of the world "as it is," little remains for the gaze to consume but the harsh material contours of the vast accumulation of fragmented things, made equivalent through the monochromatic abstraction of the photographic rendering of the world. Depleted of the gradation of gray tones, the detailed contours of each thing were abstracted within the binary polarization of black and white tones. If the human photographer had intervened into the photochemical rendering process at all (recalling that the ostensible reason Nakahira had previously abandoned black and white photography was because it afforded too much human manipulation), it would be the amplification of the granulation of light into a high-contrast field of sharply detailed things. The resultant image exposed the viewer to a high degree of contact with the photographed materialities by paradoxically subtracting the color, depth, variation, and tonality from the scene itself. Rendered as polarized densities of black or white optical datum through the amplifications of photographic mediation, the bare contours of Tokara's landscapes of raw exposure assaulted the safe interval between them and the viewer.

READING THRESHOLDS

When viewed together in light of the overlay of geopolitical and aesthetic questions raised by Nakahira's interrogations of Okinawa's reversion, the proliferation of material things and thresholds accumulated in traversal of the two modalities of Nakahira's color and monochrome photographs delineated a deeply unsettled text. How might we begin to read these landscapes of exposure and harshly rendered materialities? As developed in his essays for the "Duel on Photography" series, such as "The Limits that Consume the Gaze" discussed above, Nakahira's work can be read as modeling a transformative mode of reading described by the term "permanent revolution of the gaze." In the suspension of both the dissimilating ethnographic gaze looking "outward" sustaining the other, and the "inward" looking of an assimilating gaze sustaining the self, these thresholds were exposed together in the photographically mediated acts of seeing. Moreover, Nakahira's Tokara text can be read as part of a broader redistribution of the discursive contours of photography, modeling its own redistribution by modulating each of the crucial intervals between photographer-photographed and photograph-viewer in this acute way of making sensible the thresholds among each of them. This manifold of thresholds and mediating layers, as I discuss in the final chapter, are the hallmarks of an emergent urban ecology that would inform the conditions of possibility for literary and visual media from the late 1970s to the present. Nakahira's writings and photography offer a vivid resource for recognizing how the tense postcolonial dimensions of this expansive ecology of material, discursive, and affective relations are continuously displaced and disavowed in the given imaginaries of urban centers and tropical peripheries that govern the archipelago today.

CHAPTER SIX

Residual Futures

As we have seen, the transformed urban ecologies of the infrastructural media of Japanese society, made sensible through the changing modes of critique found in the works explored in these chapters, disclose the crucial stakes of elaborating geopolitical and aesthetic vocabularies wrought from the churning flux of material and sensory transformation. Urban ecologies disclosed through evolving literary and visual media praxis during a formative period of the Cold War are suggestive of how we might map or diagram other relations among the fleeting prospects of sensing and knowing within acute sociohistorical transformations. The works explored here grapple with the codification of senses and signs that accompanied Japan's Cold War remaking, and reveal the changed contexts and prospects for an urban ecological understanding of the (im)possibilities the Cold War materialized worldwide. Here I will close this study by briefly delineating the afterlives of these urban ecologies and how they may be mobilized hereafter in expanded lines of inquiry.

Nakahira Takuma remained committed to the possibility of photographically mediated ways of seeing as dynamic means of perpetuating those transformative vectors of a "permanent revolution of the gaze" described in Chapter 5 of this volume. Tragically, Nakahira was stricken with partial loss of linguistic and memory functions after having nearly died from alcohol poisoning in September of 1977. In one of his last critical essays, published while he was still in the hospital, "Preemptive Strike: Seeing and Reading," Nakahira would powerfully restate this fraught possibility as a problem of critique itself.

> When "seeing" becomes the same as "not seeing," as "seeing" is already tied to an established code, we fight against this world by concerning ourselves with the admirable, nonhuman mechanism of the camera. The instant a photograph is taken, a strange looking world unknown to us is inscribed into the film. It takes us by surprise, arising from the boundary zone between conscious and unconscious states. Breaking through the code there, and discovering a small chance to blow away the code, that is the sole possibility for the photographer. It would perhaps be an exaggeration to describe this as the shattering of the world by our gaze. The single tree we see every day, a single pebble, the breaking waves, and most of all, the familiar view of the streets, the crowds of people, the encounter with people, by inflicting a preemptive assault upon these trifling things, and exposing ourselves to their counter attack, our selves are persistently dismantled and we repeatedly reclaim a new self without end; how can we continue to maintain this battlefront of the gaze? That is by critique. Critique against the world and at the same time critique against the self.[1]

Until his death in 2015, Nakahira would continue to evolve his photographic praxis, inhabiting that fraught possibility of waging a dual critique of self and world by means of the camera long after the intensities of the transformative 1960s and 1970s would fade. Nakahira sought a way of leveraging the affordances of photographic visuality to open "both sides" of the sensory and material "battlefront" where the mediating thresholds of selves and worlds could be opened up and enfolded with one another in myriad and shifting ways. And thus, Nakahira was attuned to the possibilities of encounter and exchange in a moment when "seeing" and "not seeing" had become effectively equivalent through the codification of visuality in the systematization and mediatization of the senses. The Cold War remaking of the archipelago not only saw the proliferation of infrastructural networks of transportation and communication, but also by the late 1970s had advanced into the realm of the senses. Accordingly, as the geopolitical and aesthetic contours of the Cold War itself dramatically shifted, critical strategies for mobilizing the gaze(s) afforded by photographic mediation were modulated to confront the workings of capitalist state power materialized through the urban ecologies of the day.

As we find in Nakahira's late 1970s work, strategic modes of seeing and reading, elaborated through a proliferation of discursive framings to break out of the operative codes of the text at hand, were telling of the magnitude of change wrought in the process of urbanization. What had started with the flux of demolition and rebuilding of Japan's urban centers had permeated into the inner linings of the embodied senses. In other words, what was formerly an absent, exterior, or otherwise invisible geopolitical totality that required the mediation of novel aesthetic strategies to become sensible, even if incompletely, had later become operative within the immanent, interior, and immediately given domain of sensory experience. For Nakahira and others, the thresholds of subjectivity had become deeply infrastructured within these changing urban social spaces and media networks. As we have seen in the changing contours of the urban ecologies mapped across these chapters, the generative locus of novel geopolitical and aesthetic vocabularies was displaced from the kinetically charged confrontations with the emerging landscape to that of deeply self-reflexive modes of "reading" the thresholds among selves, others, and material things. Nakahira developed a highly contextualized strategy located within the mediating thresholds of photographic visuality itself. Similarly, when we examine other texts of the late 1970s we find signs of self-reflexive discursivity that inform a highly discontinuous sense of textuality.

For instance, in his exhaustive study of the relationships between science and fiction in Abe Kōbō's work, Christopher Bolton explores the singular intensity of mediation that informs Abe's last novel of the 1970s, *Secret Rendezvous* (*Mikkai*, 1977), which features an extensive audiotape surveillance system within the labyrinthine hospital setting of the narrative. Bolton describes the novel as, "a mingled collection of heterogeneous fragments—shards of space, time, sound, and writing. The novel is like a 'mosaic' to which the narrator compares the tapes, but a mosaic viewed too close: the overall design has become unclear, and the work is often reduced to a collection of bright fragments. It is the task of the narrator and the reader to make sense of this jumble, to step back from it to discern some pattern in the riot."[2] The narrator, much like the detective in *The Ruined Map*, undergoes a process of disintegration in pursuit of a missing person, but here the intensive visuality of the former work is displaced, and much of the narrative is delivered by an acute attention to the sounds captured onto the multichannel tape recordings of the surveillance apparatus. Moreover, despite the visual nature of the metaphor of the "mosaic" Bolton describes, the narrator himself uses the term to describe the terrifyingly intense mode of listening he must undertake to sift through the tapes to discover clues about his missing wife: "The crumbling of his relationship to the outer world, based formerly on his sense of sight, brought on a dizziness like that caused by fear of heights. A time mosaic: moments that existed simultaneously, yet were impossible to experience simultaneously. It was like utter darkness."[3] This mosaiclike temporal intensity, one that recalls Nakahira's reading of the mosaiclike temporality of the "moments isolated like islands," of Eugène Atget's photography (which "consists of fragmentary instants, each broken up and isolated, that rise up vertically in succession without any connective thread among them"), is telling of the profoundly transformed contours of the urban conditions of Japan's media cultures of the late 1970s moment.

In Bolton's reading, the audio surveillance system is a metaphor for the mediatized social relations that accompanied the advanced development of media technologies in the late 1970s in Japan, as a communication system that "brings the world close and simultaneously holds it at bay: the sphere of our experience grows wider, but the experiences themselves become progressively more virtual or mediated."[4] However, the intensity of the mediated modes of listening described in Abe's novel are also suggestive of the potentials for articulating novel forms of subjectivity within the transformed relations among selves, others, and material things wrought by the highly infrastructured urban sensory systems of the late 1970s. As the informational and affective economies of the urbanized consumer/spectator rendered object, image, and language as equivalents, then more intensive and expansive modes of reading (or better, critical modes of sensory attunement more generally, including smell, touch, and taste, as well as listening and seeing) were needed to break through the systematized sensations and signs that encoded these urban ecologies thereafter. We can situate this shift toward a self-reflexive attention to the intensities and thresholds of mediated subjectivities in the late 1970s as part of what Paul Roquet has described as ambient subjectivation. As a response to predominant narratives of the "loss" of reality/politics (although it is often unclear how these are defined in such narratives), and the entry unto the postmodern era that purportedly accompanies the rise of consumer society in these decades, Roquet draws our attention to workings of the self within a pervasive infrastructural and technological environment.[5] "An ambient understanding of self necessarily situates the person in an intimate relation with larger ecologies, affirming our interdependency not only with other people but with the affordances of the objects and environments we live with and through."[6] In contrast to the integrative techniques of "reading the air" suggested by the emergence of ambient subjectivation, the intensive self-reflexivity of Abe and Nakahira's works accentuated a different mode of reading and relating materialized in the proliferation of mosaiclike patterns within a fractured and incomplete urban totality—one akin to what Marié Abe has termed the dynamic relationality of "resonance." "Resonance enables the politics of imagination as not essentially resistant or instrumental, but rather something emergent, diffractive, and indeterminate in need of constant renewal and improvisation."[7] While Abe derives this expansive form of relation from an inquiry into changing articulations among sound, space, and sociality, this form of "resonance" clearly names the open horizons of the kinds of urban ecologies traced through these chapters. The fragmented and residual vistas obtained from the thresholds and intensities of texts like these thus continue to invite intensive, or perhaps "resonant," modes of reading for continued elaborations of an ecological critique of capitalist state power.

RESIDUAL RESONANCES

I would like to close this volume with some brief reflections on a set of problems that are illuminated by this study, even as they span beyond its historical and conceptual framing. These chapters have undertaken a strategy of taking the aesthetic incompleteness of the texts seriously as an index of the geopolitical flux that defined the decades of the 1960s and 1970s, thereby seeking to illuminate the residual futures of the urban ecologies that proliferated therein. Yet, in the interval between the historical and contemporary moments, much has changed, and much has not. On the one hand, the once-vague contours of an emergent worldwide order have taken vividly clear form in the catastrophes of what we might describe variously as regimes of neoliberal globalization, an ascendant control society, and the mass extinctions and environmental disasters of the Anthropocene. On the other hand, despite nearly two decades since the ostensible collapse of the Cold War, and decisive shifts in the nature of military-economic strategic orders worldwide, the Cold War in East Asia is very much alive. Two entangled event horizons inform a present inflected by these developments and reframe not only how we might read the residual futures contained in this volume, but also the potential trajectories of future inquiry we might take in response: the meltdown of the Fukushima Dai'ichi nuclear reactor, and the 2020 Tokyo Olympics. To the degree that the urban ecologies of the contemporary inform how we make sense of these event horizons, we remain in need of critical ways of seeing, knowing, and relating among the contours and thresholds of a post—Cold War world very much haunted by the Cold War remaking examined in this volume. To briefly illustrate the crux of the problems that confront these efforts, I will outline the work of three contemporary Japanese photographers who differently enhance our understanding of such urban ecologies.

Photographer Kanemura Osamu's 2001 photobook *Spider's Strategy* records the seemingly endless proliferation of material objects that clutter the streets and alleyways of postbubble Tokyo, nearly three decades after Nakahira's *Overflow*. Whether the heterotopic vestiges of aging worlds that haunt alluring centers of contemporary youth culture, or anonymous arcades of suburban station towns, Kanemura's photographs strip these spaces bare of their familiar shell of codified meanings. Mobilizing a low-key monochromatic tonality that further depletes the habituated views of a lived Tokyo, Kanemura's street scenes erupt with the excessive details of the alarming clutter that otherwise escape our attention, naturalized beyond the threshold of visibility through the patterned rhythms and flows of Tokyo's everyday. Flooding the picture plane with unassimilable junk and torrents of bodies, words, and things that have been woven together into the flat nonsensical mesh of

FIGURE 6.1 Kanemura Osamu, 2017.

perspectives obtained from within domesticated conduits of work and leisure, Kanemura's photographs render the everyday spaces of Tokyo into an alien wasteland strewn with trash; most of all a cacophony of tangled bicycles, wires, and signs.

Kanemura emerged as a photographer in the late 1990s after graduating from the Tokyo College of Photography in 1993. His work has largely consisted of monochrome street scenes with provocative titles given for the resultant exhibitions and photobooks, such as, "Crash-landing in Tokyo's Dream," "Someday O.K. Prince will Come," "Black Parachute Ears 1991–1999," "Colored Air Blood Black 1999," "Stravinsky Overdrive," "Suzy Cream Oil Cheese," "13th Floor Elevator over the Hill," "Chinese Rocks," "My Name is Shockhammer," "Dante Lobster," "Ansel Adams stardust (You are not alone)," "System Crash for Hi-Fi," and most recently, "Ectoplasm Profiling." He was awarded the top photography prize, the Domon Ken prize, twice, a record for a younger photographer in Japan. In recent years, Kanemura has run a workshop for emerging photographers and continues to issue fascinating essays and commentaries on the conditions of photographic thought and practice today. Kanemura has added color digital video and still-image work to his oeuvre, rather prolifically producing a number of short videos such as, "Elvis the Positive Thinking Pelvis," "Kentucky Fried Benjamin," "Dead Stick Landing," and "Life is a Gift," as well as maintaining a Twitter presence with the intermittent stream of mercurial urban surfaces entitled, "Z-Trash Diary." In addition, Kanemura was instrumental in the republication of Nakahira's *Circulation* installation, providing new photographic prints made from the original negatives for publication in book form, *Circulation: Date, Place, Events* (2012).

However, the photobook *Spider's Strategy* demonstrates the continued relevance of seeking a critical understanding of the entanglements of urban materialities and infrastructural media through photographic thought and practice. As Isozaki Arata, the renowned architect, critic, and former collaborator with Nakahira, described Kanemura's compelling photographic strategy in an essay included in the photobook, these photographic portraits of urban space have captured nothing less than the true urban form of Tokyo, stricken by an invisible meltdown within the core of the metropolis:

> I can't help but see within the alleyways, side-streets, and arcades captured by Kanemura the mountains of garbage of a junk yard and the scattered rubble of earthquakes. These are the excretions of the city, and scraps of structures, all of which are ruins. Nevertheless, as places replete with an everyday sense of déjà vu, they have, after all, been largely left behind and forgotten. What is characteristic of these scenes is that anything suggestive of urban space has been completely enveloped by cluttered-junk-like-things, as within a spider's nest. One might discover outskirts like these in Paris or New York. However, only these fragmentary scenes can symbolize the city of Tokyo where a meltdown is already occurring within its depths, wrapped within the shell of a metropolis.[8]

Even before the 2011 triple disaster became a reality, the urban meltdown suggested here evokes the flux of material and sensory forms that we saw in such works as Tsuchimoto Noriaki's *On the Road: A Document*,

Abe's *The Ruined Map*, and Nakahira's *Overflow*. As part of the larger genealogy of urban ecologies mapped in these chapters, Kanemura's photography affords a way of seeing urban flux that produces a critical knowledge of those visible and invisible displacements, distributions, and dispossessions of an incomplete totality that momentarily congeals and coagulates within these trashscapes. Though Kanemura's photography is similarly unwavering in its refusal of an unobstructed field of view and consistent occlusion of vanishing points, the density of noise and matter captured within the photographs is of a significantly greater magnitude, perhaps an index of the sheer volume of the materialities consumed in the "normal," smooth functioning of urban societies. Moreover, within each of Kanemura's photographs, circulating bodies, things, and information are accumulated as an undifferentiated mess, whereas the earlier texts fostered decentered and often fragmentary and residual perspectives. Yet, more than the many differences in formal style and content, we discover here a genealogy of critical "readings" that offer

FIGURE 6.2 Kanemura Osamu, 2017.

critical perspectives on the forms of mediation shaping the imaginary and material contours of urban life in the decoding, disintegrating, or dismantling of habituated views.

A related strategy of making sense of the urban as an all-encompassing continuum of surplus materialities and nonhuman agencies can be found in the work of Komatsu Hiroko. Her 2017 installation, "The Execution of Personal Autonomy," invites viewers into a gallery space covered in layers of photochemical prints suspended from hanging wires and spread over the walls and floor. Stepping into—and onto—the photographic prints, the viewer is engulfed within a monochromatic space rendered from innumerable photographs of materials and objects from industrial sites found in and around Tokyo. Unsettling the planar surfaces of the gallery walls with messy photographic materials, the installation erodes not only the habituated dimensions of the rectangular exhibition space but also disrupts the set distances and intervals that govern the mediating thresholds of photographic visuality.

By accentuating an encounter with the materiality of photochemical prints, rather than privileging the uninhibited consumption of a

FIGURE 6.3 Komatsu Hiroko, *The Execution of Personal Autonomy*, 2017.

photographed image, a strange set of relations comes into play within the installation space. The ordered distributions of small prints on the floor and wall are compounded by the entropic layering of large roll prints. Both in the installation and within the photographic images installed, we are made witness (twice) to the curious orderings of things. Subordinating the logistical coherence of a human-centered organizing desire, the material objects in the photographs, as well as the prints materialized by photochemical processes, evidence an assemblage of uses and sensory intensities that are telling of our contemporary urban ecologies. This is suggestive of what Jane Bennett has described as a "vital materialism," where things, *"form noisy systems or temporary working assemblages* that are, as much as any individuated thing, loci of effectivity and allure. These (sometimes stubborn and voracious but never closed or sovereign) systems enact real change. They give rise to new configurations, individuations, patterns of affection."[9] Like a three-dimensional expansion of Nakahira's *Overflow*, Komatsu's photographic assemblages render sensible an urban ecology of the "vital materialism" of the contemporary conditions of urban transformation in Japan.

As a new era of Olympic remaking is underway in Japan, one that seeks to erase and contain the actualities of an ongoing nuclear meltdown disaster, the urban ecologies that span these media and moments of inquiry take on renewed significance. In articulating novel ways of seeing, knowing, and relating with/in the mounting problems posed by Olympic "recovery," confronted differently by residents of the Fukushima area and those of the urban centers, we gain a critical understanding of the thresholds and limits of the assemblages of power at play in what might be called the post—Cold War remaking of Japan. It remains urgently important to confront the living conditions of those communities immediately affected, displaced, and forced to live through ongoing forms of exposure unleashed in the disaster. The urban ecologies that permeate Olympic "recovery" and the Fukushima reactor meltdown disaster harbor a vast accumulation of literal and figural residues of Japan's Cold War remaking. As these chapters have sought to make clear, the geopolitical and aesthetic vocabularies derived from such residues, then as now, remain potent resources for illuminating the often-defuse contours of ongoing sites of resistance to—and fault lines within—the operations of capitalist state power. It seems to me that an ecological approach to the urban materialities and media transformations unfolding in the present can gain much from such residual vocabularies, suggesting ways to think differently with them, even as we are just beginning to make sense of them, to sense them.

As a starting point, one that operates quite differently from Kanemura's and Komatsu's, I would like to introduce Akagi Shuji's photography and the ways it reveals the embodied labor of decontamination as an effort to materialize and render sensible some of the magnitude of the Fukushima disaster. Akagi's work emerged from the simple impulse to record what was going on around him from the moment of the devastating earthquake on March 11, 2011. Originally working in the format of a Twitter account where he uploaded photographs with explanatory captions, Akagi documented the unusual everydayness of postdisaster life in Fukushima-city where he lives and works as a high school art teacher.[10] By depicting the largest populated area in the path of the initial plume of the massive release of radioactive materials shortly after the Fukushima Dai'ichi reactor meltdown, Akagi's work records the visible and invisible contradictions of postdisaster everyday life "under control" in Fukushima-city. Among the myriad forms of media coverage that emerged in the wake of triple disaster, Akagi's work was first recognized by author Yu Miri (who moved to Iwaki City in Fukushima in 2013), then followed by art critic Sawaragi Noi, both of whom were vigorous postdisaster Twitter activists. Many photographs from Akagi's Twitter account were later assembled and published with the original captions in the 2015 collection *Fukushima Traces 2011–2013*.[11] In addition to these two formats, Akagi's work has appeared in exhibitions at home and abroad.[12]

As a provisional attempt to trace the unsettling nature of the nuclear material indexed by Akagi's tireless photographic portraits of the uncanny tarp-enshrined mounds wrought by the decontamination efforts, we might consider Peter C. van Wyck's engagements with the strangeness posed by nuclear waste. In his fascinating book *Signs of Danger: Waste, Trauma, and Nuclear Threat*, Van Wyck delineates the problems posed by nuclear waste that trouble the human scale of values and render strange the forms of connectedness found in many ecological understandings of the world:

> Such an ecology is in a sense an ecology of the strange. At least it is from the point of view of an episteme of full understanding, an episteme of interconnectedness and the possible. Yet from another perspective, an ecology of the virtual would be nothing of the sort. After all, the strange is something actual that seems unreal or out of place. The strange is like the Freudian uncanny *(unheimlich)*, the uncanny, something familiar but foreign ("the *unheimlich* is what was once *heimisch*, home-like, familiar"). The strange requires the home, an *oikos*, as a reference and index to its very strangeness. That is, its relationship, its interconnection with the *oikos*, remains both necessary and obscure.[13]

The virtual dimension of nuclear waste remains beyond the human, a threat horizon whose actuality extends beyond the limits of a human-centered ecology, and thus renders strange all the totalities of understanding that govern our capacities to contend with nuclear materiality. However, this strangeness does not eliminate the task of grappling with nuclear materiality, but rather inflects our inquiry with what van Wyck describes as a charge to question the limitlessness of human capacities to know, or otherwise contain, the externalities of radioactive materials.

> Ecological threats and nuclear wastes in particular are perhaps not a call to understanding at all—at least not a boundless understanding of connections or presence. Perhaps the kind of understanding that is called for is that we can come to know such threats only indirectly, only perhaps through our responses to them (here we would ask questions about social meanings and values) and, above all, only through a radical reappraisal of the discourses of ecology and risk that have come to operate as the clearinghouse for questions of social well-being.[14]

This framing of the strangeness of nuclear materiality, seen together with the actualities traced by Akagi's work, is suggestive of how we might marshal an ecological approach to the displacements and disavowals of the ongoing Fukushima disaster at the heart of the mobilizations undertaken in the name of Olympic "recovery." To confront the present, it will be necessary to draw upon an expansive range of geopolitical and aesthetic vocabularies of urban and media critique, including those delineated across these chapters. As a kind of work that brings into view the long afterlives of the radioactive materials released by the meltdown (materials that are further accumulated in the very act of "decontamination" and compounded by the complexities of the restoration of "normal" everyday life that are exposed in the process), the uncanny realities found in Akagi's photography delineate a set of crucial thresholds within contemporary urban ecologies. These limits emerge within the mediations spanning Tokyo's Olympic remaking and the Fukushima disaster, inscribing a resilient fissure, or critical impasse, within the smooth mechanisms operative in the Olympic "recovery." Akagi's photography is embedded within, and makes sensible, the gaps and holes within a seamless landscape of "recovery," troubling the givenness of our capacity to see, know, and relate in response to the realities of this disaster.

FIGURE 6.4 Akagi Shuji, May 10, 2013.

Traversing the gap between life inside and outside the contaminated areas, Akagi's photographs capture the normalized strangeness of scenes filled with tarp-covered mounds, the so-called "temporary containment facilities" that haunt the landscape with their uncanny presence, in varying colors and states of containment. Some are marked with numeric indices of radioactivity, others with more ontologically ambiguous signage such as "under temporary containment" (*kari oki chū*), and others have no signs at all. While we might mobilize such scenes to consider the role of discursive signs that encode such uncanny materiality, and moreover the role of narratives in public efforts to normalize the strange labor of decontamination, here I just want to highlight what might be called the more provocative language of the materiality itself, and think about the ways such temporary containments consistently betray the mythos of "recovery."

What's more, Akagi's work reveals the tense locus between seeing the problem and no longer wanting to see the problem that such material residues pose. In other words, his photographs continually frame the act of seeing as a problem at the heart of the contemporary disaster. At times this takes the form of Akagi expressing profound doubts about the very meaning of his efforts. Other times, this takes the form of photographs of scenes from outside Fukushima-city becoming imparted with the uncanniness of contamination. Through Akagi's self-reflexive mobilizations on the Twitter platform, the strangeness of the radioactive materials that haunt the expansive event horizon of this disaster overflow the hierarchies and intervals of what Mitsuhiro Yoshimoto has called the "state-media-industrial-complex" that work simultaneously to nationalize the disaster and to naturalize engineered forms of security and safety to contain the externalities of the event.[15] As Akagi claims, the strange "traces" of his photography operate differently than hegemonic media portrayals of Fukushima's recovery from the disaster. "I have recorded as much of the surrounding area as I could by myself. No matter how the media cover the boiling, shining city in the glow of recovery, I want to document the traces of my surroundings."[16] Akagi's photographs not only make the normal look strange, but invite us to question those strange futures when such materials are transferred to "intermediate storage facilities," and beyond that to indeterminate "final deposit" sites, when the promise of "recovery" comes and goes, and the realities of the ongoing disaster remain.

The residual vocabularies articulated differently in Akagi, Kanemura, and Komatsu's work, resonate in strangely compelling ways with the ecological mappings delineated among these chapters. As openings unto other critical perspectives derived from the flux of urban ecologies, they "contaminate" the contemporary with their uncanny heterogeneity. Rather than reading such heterogeneous vocabularies as productive of comprehensive answers to shared problems, I have read these as interrogative forms that illuminate the limits and potentials shared among diverse media and moments of critical inquiry. We have traversed a constellation of different modalities of praxis and vocabularies of urban change, ranging from the kinetics of the taxi-driver-camera eye, the topological literary figuration of the disappearance of social relations, the material image-language of photographic landscapes, to the illustrated dictionary of overflows, and the embedded thresholds of postcolonial visual systems. By engaging with the specificities of each text as a crystallization of the immanent material and sensory forces wrought through uneven and contradictory processes of the archipelago's Cold War remaking, we discover ways to work through the smooth teleology sustained by narratives of the postwar period's "miraculous growth" and post-Fukushima "recovery." Thus, I close this provisional inquiry by proposing that such irrecoverable and unassimilable residues remain embedded within the thresholds of the urban ecologies that govern the conditions of possibility today. And with these, we may obtain from such residues a more acutely "resonant" sense of an expansive set of mediating relations and exchanges among selves, others, and materialities made available through an ecological mode of inquiry, as part of the "multidimensional cartographies for the production of subjectivity" once called for by Félix Guattari.[17]

Notes

INTRODUCTION

1. André Sorensen, a historian of Japanese urban planning, has quantified the massive population flows that characterized these decades in *The Making of Urban Japan: Cities and Planning from the Edo to the Twenty First Century* (London: Routledge, 2002). Marilyn Ivy has vividly explored the "vanishing" of rural homelands in *Discourses of the Vanishing: Modernity, Phantasm, Japan* (Chicago: University of Chicago Press, 1995).

2. As Eric Cazdyn reminds us, there remains considerable risk of retaining the very limiting frames we seek to displace in unsettling the given national and disciplinary formations in pursuit of what he describes as unrigorous models of "interdisciplinary" scholarly work favored in the restructuring of universities and disciplinary divisions. "To challenge these limits we cannot simply turn to a mode that ignores the mediation of the nation or that of the university. Rather we must try to organize a different type of inquiry, a rigorous nondisciplined activity that stands on different theoretical ground—one that is not driven by a certain national or academically disciplined epistemology." "Japanese Film without Japan: Toward a Nondisciplined Film Studies," in *The Oxford Handbook of Japanese Cinema*, ed. Daisuke Miyao (New York: Oxford University Press, 2014), 14–15.

3. In English scholarship several monumental studies have laid the foundations for critical understanding of the dynamic histories and resonances of these decades of cultural practice: Abé Mark Nornes, *Forest of Pressure: Ogawa Shinsuke and Postwar Japanese Documentary* (Minneapolis: University of Minnesota Press, 2007); Steven Ridgley, *Japanese Counterculture: The Antiestablishment Art of Terayama Shūji* (Minneapolis: University of Minnesota Press, 2011); Miryam Sas, *Experimental Arts in Postwar Japan: Moments of Encounter, Engagement, and Imagined Return* (Cambridge, Mass.: Harvard University Asia Center, 2011); and Reiko Tomii, *Radicalism in the Wilderness: International Contemporaneity and 1960s Art in Japan* (Cambridge, Mass.: MIT Press, 2016).

4. As Naoki Sakai and Hyon Joo Yoo, the editors of the groundbreaking volume *The Trans-Pacific Imagination: Rethinking Boundary, Culture and Society*, note, "geo-political practice developed by a region inevitably involves a culturally coded categorization of temporal-spatial relations. These temporal-spatial relations are in constant transformation and movement as they generate multiple stakes that encompass the political as well as the cultural. So the boundary cannot be settled as a universal and unified notion. The designation of temporal-spatial boundaries and the concomitant cultural imaginary change as a new configuration of power relation necessitates a new ideological construct." "Introduction: The Trans-Pacific Imagination" in *The Trans-Pacific Imagination: Rethinking Boundary, Culture and Society*, ed. Naoki Sakai and Hyon Joo Yoo (Hackensack, N.J.: World Scientific Pub, 2012), 29.

5. I am not seeking to establish a relation of determinism between Cold War remaking and the vocabularies I examine here. Instead, taking a cue from a crucial distinction that Thomas LaMarre makes in his foundational study of Japanese anime, *The Anime Machine: A Media Theory of Animation*, I am interested in how these media can be read as thinking the urban. LaMarre points out that this difference emerges by distinguishing between determinism and determination. "I refer to technical determination, which is not determinism but a sort of underdetermination. The implication is that determination is at once material and immaterial. Or, put another way, there is indeterminacy to determination, which generates an interval or spacing in which thinking might arise. I might have also said 'anime thinks through technology.' But I favor the expression 'thinking technology' to avoid implying that technologies are neutral mediators whose work is done when the concept appears, or whose operations vanish from the scene of thought and are therefore negligible." Thomas LaMarre, "Introduction," in *The Anime Machine: A Media Theory of Animation* (Minneapolis: University of Minnesota Press, 2009), xxxi.

6. Michel de Certeau, *The Practice of Everyday Life* (Berkeley: University of California Press, 1984), 96.

7. Sakai and Yoo further suggest that a crucial mediating structure that supports the persistence of Cold War geopolitical schema among disciplinary formations is the U.S.–Japan alliance itself; as a result, the elaboration of transverse forms of inquiry that can move across and through this mediating frame—even and especially when we seek to unsettle its established boundaries and pathways—will afford novel redistributions of knowledge about, and across, the Cold War's epistemological distributions. "The geo-cultural project that interrogates East Asia—the geopolitical constellation including the Japan–U.S. alliance and the formerly colonized nations implicated in the neoimperial design, and the West and the Rest opposition—must point to the ways in which various national formations articulate the transnational, that is trans-Pacific, configuration of nation and subjectivity. At the same time, the project must remain mindful of the complex trans-Pacific crisscrossing of ideas and ideologies where America and Japan figure as an epistemological, political, economical, and cultural problem generating different local responses." "Introduction: The Trans-Pacific Imagination," in *The Trans-Pacific Imagination: Rethinking Boundary, Culture and Society*, 36.

8. See Marukawa Atsushi's *Reisen bunkaron: wasurerareta aimai na sensō no genzaisei* (Tokyo: Sōfūsha, 2005), for an important example of how such questions are approached in Japanese Cold War cultural studies.

9. Rita Felski, *Limits of Critique* (Chicago: University of Chicago Press, 2015), 12.

10. Much of what we encounter in these chapters is thus a product of what "reading" is for Felski, "a cocreation between actors that leaves neither party unchanged." Felski, 84.

11. My use of the term "afterlives" here refers to dominant forms of knowledge production that live on after the end of the Cold War from which they emerged. Kristin Ross traces May 1968's "afterlives" across a wide range of discursive and disciplinary formations by illuminating the lasting implications of the literal and figural manifestations of a distributive logic of emplacement, a continual redrawing of social places and functions that sought to contain and displace the eruptive unsettling of such distributions that were instantiated through the events of 1968. Kristin Ross, *May '68 and its Afterlives* (Chicago: University of Chicago Press, 2002).

12. Following Fredric Jameson's efforts to delineate the changed global conditions for knowing one's locatedness within the capitalist world-system, Alberto Toscano and Jeff Kinkle suggest this aesthetic problem continues to necessitate revisiting the possibilities and limits of the practice of "cognitive mapping" as a *representational* practice of recovering a legible image of the totality of global capital precisely because it is unrepresentable. *Cartographies of the Absolute* (Winchester, UK: Zero Books, 2015), 6–12.

13. Jacques Rancière, "The Paradoxes of Political Art," *Dissensus: On Politics and Aesthetics*, ed. and trans. Steven Corcoran (New York: Continuum, 2010), 147. Kristin Ross has delineated the ways that Rancière's redrawing of the boundaries of the political indexed a key dimension of the May 1968 French political upheavals, contesting the distributive social forces delimiting such boundaries. "The movement took the form of political experiments in declassification, in disrupting the natural 'givenness' of places; it consisted of displacements that took students outside of the university, meetings that brought farmers and workers together, or students to the countryside—trajectories outside of the Latin Quarter, to workers' housing and popular neighborhoods, a new kind of mass organizing (against the Algerian War in the early 1960s, and later against the Vietnam War) that involved physical dislocation. And in that physical dislocation lay a dislocation in the very idea of politics—moving it out of its place, its proper place, which was for the left at that time the Communist Party." *May '68 and its Afterlives*, 25.

14. For a critical assessment of how the idea of the rural homeland evolved throughout Japan's modernity and its aftermath, see Narita Ryūichi's "Toshi Kūkan to 'kokyō,'" in *Kokyō no sōshitsu to saisei* (Tokyo: Sokyusha, 2000). In English, see Stephen Dodd's exploration of the literary threads of the *furusato's* discursive constructions, *Writing Home: Representations of the Native Place in Modern Japanese Literature* (Cambridge, Mass.: Harvard University Asia Center, 2004).

15. Paul Virilio has traced many of the key implications of shifting our critical perspective from the distributions of urban/rural difference to the distributive formations of networked infrastructures themselves. On the collapse of such differences that infrastructure has rendered, he says, for instance, "If the metropolis is still a place, a geographic site, it no longer has anything to do with the classical oppositions of city/country nor center/periphery. The city is no longer organized into a localized and axial estate. While the suburbs contributed to this dissolution, in fact the intramural–extramural opposition collapsed with the transport revolutions and the development of communication and telecommunications technologies. These promoted the merger of disconnected metropolitan fringes into a single urban mass." *Lost Dimension*, trans. Daniel Moshenberg (New York: Semiotext(e), 1991), 12.

16. The committee formed for production of the film and then served as the editorial committee for the film criticism journal *Eiga hiyō* 1970–1973. It consisted of Adachi Masao (b. 1939), Aikura Hisato (1931–2015), Hiraoka Masaaki (1941–2009), Matsuda Masao (b. 1933), and Sasaki Mamoru (1936–2006). This was a notably diverse assemblage, with two music critics (Aikura and Hiraoka), a screenwriter (Sasaki), a film director (Adachi), and a film critic (Matsuda).

Not only did the unique configuration play a crucial role in the production of the film, the diverse range of writings that filled the pages of *Eiga hiyō* reflected the exceptional makeup of the committee. Yuriko Furuhata has illuminated the cinematic histories informed by Matsuda's theorization of landscape in the groundbreaking study, *Cinema of Actuality: Japanese Avant-Garde Filmmaking in the Season of Image Politics* (Durham, N.C.: Duke University Press, 2013). For detailed descriptions of diverse aspects of how these collaborations played in the film and the journal, see Michael S. Molasky's *Sengo Nihon no jazu bunka: eiga, bungaku, angora* (Tokyo: Seidosha, 2005) and the long-form interview between Adachi Masao and Gō Hirasawa, *Eiga kakumei* (Tokyo: Kawade Shobō Shinsha, 2003).

17. Matsuda was drawing heavily upon an essay by Mizuki Kaoru, who critiqued the reformist humanism of Hani Gorō, questioning the idealized notion of the renaissance city that Hani celebrated in his best-selling work *Toshio no ronri* ("The Logic of the City") as a model for autonomous self-governance. Moreover, Mizuki engaged with Kurodo Kio's (1926–1984) criticisms of both Terayama Shūji, who celebrated rural youth fleeing their village homes to the city, and Tanigawa Gan, who celebrated flocking to the periphery to create the homeland anew. Kuroda's critique highlighted the ambivalent plight of both depopulated rural communities and the youth who fled them, for both the collectives and runaway youths were all the more deprived of any means of self-sufficiency in the "drama of drifting" ("rurō no geki") that informed Terayama and Tanigawa's modernist literary imaginaries. "Hani Gorō ga Tochiji ni natta toki: ee kakkō no shitai no mirai-ron" ("When Hani Gorō became Governor of Tokyo: On the futurism of a highfalutin corpse"), in *Kakumei to yūtopia: erīto jūhachinin no shisō hihan* (Tokyo: Haga Shoten, 1969), 171–189.

18. Matsuda Masao, "Fūkei toshite no toshi," in *Fūkei no shimetsu* ("The Extinction of Landscape") (Tokyo: Tabata Shoten, 1971), 11–12. "Fūkei toshite no toshi," first published in *Gendai no me* (April 1970), collected in *Fūkei no shimetsu*, 7–21.

19. Yuriko Furuhata, 143.

20. In the early 1960s Jane Jacobs famously problematized the discourse of traffic as a favorite justification of urban planners' brutal dismantling of Manhattan's urban fabric to accommodate automobiles in *The Death and Life of Great American Cities* (New York: Random House, 1961). Meanwhile, Kevin Lynch sought to redefine the sensory vocabulary of the city from diverse vantage points of pedestrians and drivers in *The Image of the City* (Cambridge, Mass.: MIT University Press, 1960). Moreover, as we see in chapter 1 of this volume, the new forms of mobility wrought in this period were celebrated by Japanese transportation historian Kakumoto Ryōhei in *Kōsōkuka no owari: atarashii kōtsū taisei o saguru* (Tokyo: Nihon Keizai Shinbunsha, 1975).

21. "The blindness of the speed of means of communicating destruction is not a liberation from geopolitical servitude, but the extermination of space as the field of freedom of political action. We only need refer to the necessary controls and constraints of the railway, airway or highway infrastructures to see the fatal impulse: the more speed increases, the faster freedom decreases." Paul Virilio, *Speed and Politics: An Essay on Dromology* (Los Angeles: Semiotext(e), 2006), 158.

22. Interestingly, the folk guerilla movement that occupied Shinjuku's underground plaza in 1969 to protest Japan's essential logistical role in the U.S. war in Southeast Asia performed a strategic obstruction of the coordinated infrastructural flows it was specifically designed for as a "flow plaza." As Jordan Sand points out, however, this occupation was, "simply an accident of the available space and the convenience of Shinjuku as a meeting place, the antiwar sing-alongs and discussion groups had occupied the busiest commuter hub in the world— an unsurpassed example of the bureaucratically managed society (*kanri shakai*) that student activists and intellectuals of Japan's New Left, like their counterparts in Paris, saw as the enemy of democracy. Whatever other political factors underlay it, the police action announced vividly that civic gatherings would not be allowed to impede the smooth flow of office workers that sustained Japanese corporate capitalism." Jordan Sand, "*Hiroba*: The Public Square and the Boundaries of the Commons," in *Tokyo Vernacular: Common Spaces, Local Histories, Found Objects* (Berkeley: University of California Press, 2013), 44.

23. The profoundly social forms that Abe's urban visuality disclosed thus reflect a crucial difference with contemporary Cold War discourses of cybernetics, networks, environments, and urban design, articulated by such luminaries as Kevin Lynch and György Kepes. As Orit Halpern notes in her groundbreaking study of visuality in Cold War thinkers such as Lynch and Kepes, "it was the very discourse of society that disappeared beneath the discourse of images and perception, seemingly consumed into the interactive space between the individual and the environment." Orit Halpern, *Beautiful Data: A History of Vision and Reason Since 1945* (Durham, N.C.: Duke University Press, 2014), 122.

24. Toscano and Kinkle have undertaken a provisional mapping of the Euro-American geopolitical aesthetics of intermodal shipping containers in their chapter, "The Art of Logistics," found in *Cartographies of the Absolute* (Winchester, Mass.: Zero Books, 2015).

25. Matthew Fuller, *Media Ecologies: Materialist Energies in Art and Technoculture* (Cambridge, Mass.: MIT Press, 2005), 2.

26. Yukio Lippit, "Japan During the *Provoke* Era," in *Provoke: Between Protest and Performance* (Göttingen: Steidl, 2016), 22.

27. Félix Guattari, "The Three Ecologies," trans. Chris Turner, in *new formations* 8 (Summer 1989), 136.

28. Erich Hörl, "Introduction to General Ecology: The Ecologization of Thinking," in *General Ecology: The New Ecological Paradigm*, ed. Erich Hörl with James Burton (London: Bloomsbury, 2016), 3.

29. Stephen Graham and Simon Marvin, "Introduction," in *Splintering Urbanism: Networked Infrastructures, Technological Mobilities and the Urban Condition* (New York: Routledge, 2001), 11.

30. Swati Chattopadhyay, *Unlearning the City: Infrastructure in a New Optical Field* (Minneapolis and London: University of Minnesota Press, 2012), ix.

31. As Rosalyn Deutsche once illuminated, works of exemplary figures like Fredric Jameson, Edward Soja, and David Harvey, who embody what she describes as an interdisciplinary urban-aesthetic discourse in the United States, often worked to displace the diverse perspectives of postmodern feminist criticism. See in particular the chapter, "Boys Town," in *Evictions: Art and Spatial Politics* (Cambridge and London: MIT Press, 1996).

32. The perpetual displacement and deferral of the realization of urban society was the hallmark of Henri Lefebvre's conceptualization of urban form as a virtual form. As he once declared, "it is the possible defined by a direction, that moves toward the urban as the culmination of its journey. To reach it—in other words, to realize it—we must first overcome or break through the obstacles that currently make it impossible." *Urban Revolution*, trans. Robert Bononno (Minneapolis: University of Minnesota Press, 2003), 17.

33. Raymond Williams, *Marxism and Literature* (Oxford: Oxford University Press, 1977), 126.

1. PRELUDE TO THE TRAFFIC WAR: INFRASTRUCTURAL AESTHETICS OF THE COLD WAR

1. Paul Virilio, *Speed and Politics: An Essay on Dromology* (Los Angeles: Semiotext(e), 2006), 158.

2. Keller Easterling, *Extrastatecraft: The Power of Infrastructure Space* (London: Verso, 2016), 11.

3. Kakumoto Ryōhei's laudatory celebrations of the development of transport technologies pose a stark contrast to more critical studies like those of Wolfgang Schivelbusch, who explicitly sought to map the entanglement of transportation technologies and sensory capacities in the expansion of capitalist modernity. Thus, in contrast to the passive expansion of sensibilities imagined by Kakumoto, we might recall Schivelbusch's insights regarding how the circulatory capacities of human and nonhuman goods remade the given distributions among people, places, and things: "localities were no longer spatially individual or autonomous: they were points in the circulation of traffic that made

them accessible. As we have seen, that traffic was the physical manifestation of the circulation of goods. From that time on, the places visited by the traveler became increasingly similar to the commodities that were part of the same circulation system. For the twentieth-century tourist, the world has become one huge department store of countrysides and cities." *The Railway Journey: The Industrialization of Time and Space in the Nineteenth Century* (Berkeley: University of California Press, 2014), 197.

4. Kakumoto Ryōhei, *Kōsōkuka no owari: atarashii kōtsū taisei wo saguru* (Tokyo: Nihon Keizai Shinbunsha, 1975), 17.

5. Eric Alliez and Maurizio Lazzarato have expanded upon Virilio's notion of endocolonization to explore the prehistory of civil wars that they regard as constituting the present, making available a different perspective on the Cold War's afterlives today: "the Cold War was not only deterritorialization of interstate war aimed at 'Soviet imperialism' and 'communist slavery'; it was, at home and abroad, a new biopolitical regime of *endocolonization* for the entire population subject to the 'American way of life' that must be decidedly inscribed at the heart of the war machine of capital." Eric Alliez and Maurizio Lazzarato, *Wars and Capital*, translated by Ames Hodges (South Pasadena, Calif.: Semiotext(e), 2018), 228.

6. I was first introduced to this film by Mizuno Sachiko, who wrote the English notes for the DVD release by Zakka Films in 2010.

7. Takuya Tsunoda has produced an exhaustive rigorous study of Iwanami Productions in his PhD dissertation, "The Dawn of Cinematic Modernism-Iwanami Productions and Postwar Japanese Cinema," Yale University, 2016.

8. See Justin Jesty's comprehensive introduction to Tsuchimoto's Minamata films, "Making Mercury Visible: The Minamata Documentaries of Tsuchimoto Noriaki," *Mercury Pollution: A Transdisciplinary Treatment*, ed. Sharon L. Zuber and Michael C. Newman (Boca Raton, Fla.: CRC Press, 2012). Christine Marran has furthermore explored Tsuchimoto's ecological cinema in *Ecology Without Culture: Aesthetics for a Toxic World* (Minneapolis: University of Minnesota Press, 2017). For English historiography of the Minamata disaster see Timothy George's *Minamata: Pollution and the Struggle for Democracy in Postwar Japan* (Cambridge, Mass.: Harvard University Press, 2002). For compelling histories of environmental disasters in Japan, see Brett Walker's *The Toxic Archipelago: A History of Industrial Disease in Japan* (Seattle: University of Washington Press, 2011); *Japan at Nature's Edge: The Environmental Context of a Global Power*, ed. Ian Jared Miller, Julia Adeney Thomas, and Brett L. Walker (Honolulu: University of Hawai'i Press, 2013); and Robert Stolz's *Bad Water: Nature, Pollution, and Politics in Japan, 1870–1950* (Durham, N.C.: Duke University Press, 2014).

9. Harada Katsumasa, "Kōtsū jiko," *Sengōshi daijiten* (Tokyo: Sanseidō, 2005), 276.

10. Tsuchimoto Noriaki and Ishizaka Kenji, *Dokyumentarī no umi e: kiroku eiga sakka Tsuchimoto Noriaki to no taiwa* (Tokyo: Gendai Shokan, 2008), 91.

11. Tsuchimoto Noriaki and Ishizaka Kenji, 92.

12. Abé Mark Nornes, *Japanese Documentary Film: The Meiji Era Through Hiroshima* (Minneapolis: University of Minnesota Press, 2003), 223. The significance of PR film as a proving ground in the history of Japanese documentary filmmaking continues to afford critical attention by film historians in Japan and abroad. In addition, see Yamane Sadao's essay, "Changes in 1960s Documentary Cinema: from PR films to Image Guerrillas," in *Japanese Documentaries of the 1960s*, a publication of the 1993 Yamagata International Documentary Film Festival.

13. Tsuchimoto Noriaki and Ishizaka Kenji, 92.

14. Tsutsui Takefumi, "Tsuchimoto Noriaki no henshu gijutsu," *Eiga geijutsu* 425 (Fall 2008): 20. Although Matsumoto Toshio's (b. 1932) fascinating work is beyond the scope of this chapter, the critical shift toward experimental visual forms within the documentary genre that he provoked has been introduced by Abé Mark Nornes in *Forest of Pressure: Ogawa Shinsuke and Postwar Japanese Documentary*, 19–27. Matsumoto's essay collections, such as *Eizō no hakken: avangyarudo to dokyumentarī* (Tokyo: Sanichi shobo 1963, Seiryushuppan 2006), and *Hyōgen no sekai: geijutsu zen'ei tachi to sono shisō* (Tokyo: Sanichi shobo 1967, Seiryushuppan 2006), offer a rich perspective on the influential set of radical challenges to documentary practice that Matsumoto struggled to elaborate from the late 1950s to the mid-1960s. Michael Raine has translated and written a critical introduction to the important essay by Matsumoto, "A Theory of Avant-Garde Documentary," in *Cinema Journal* 51, 4 (Summer 2012): 144–154.

15. From the flier promoting the film, "Dokyumento Rojo no enshutsu ni atatte," *Tōyō shinema*, 1964, accessed from the Tsuchimoto Noriaki online database, http://tutimoto.inaba.ws/top.php.

16. In the words of one critic, "Tsuchimoto is an artist who seeks to examine the 'unseen.' Through film, which consists only of that which can be seen and heard, he perpetually thinks about that which goes unseen." Suzuki Hitoshi, "Mieteinai koto o dōhan suru: shikaku to 'Tsuchimoto Noriaki,'" *Mirai* 424 (July 2004): 10–12.

17. By way of contrast, we can locate a rather different mediating structure of the city in Tsuchimoto's earlier documentary television shorts for the series *Nihon Hakken: Tokyo-to hen* of 1962. Thus, while each instance of Tsuchimoto's filmmaking discretely developed its own methodology based on the documentary subject itself, we might note the consistent effort to mediate a variety of often irreconcilable and contradictory scales of experience across many of his films.

18. Tsutsui Takefumi also highlights this fluidity between inner and external words as a hallmark of Tsuchimoto's methods in this work. "Tsuchimoto Noriaki no henshu gijutsu," 20.

19. Though adhering to a screenplay, the scene of the x-ray was a dramatization based on an actual driver from the participating taxi company with this condition, *Dokyumentarī no umi e*, 97.

20. The Shibuya area underwent some of the biggest transformations in preparation for the 1964 Olympics, in part due to Shibuya being the point where the earliest subway line ended, the terminus of the Tōkyū line, a major suburban line, and its department store, and the Yamanote loop all converged. The overlay of Shibuya's older status as a crucial rail hub of the imperial era of the city and the emerging network of the automobile era of the city is revealed here through the dynamic new vantage points that become available to the camera. For a history of these transformations, see Ueyama Kazuo's "Tokyo Orinpikku to Shibuya, Tokyo," in *Tokyo Orinpikku no shakai keizaishi*, ed. Oikawa Yoshinobu (Tokyo: Nihon Keizai Hyōronsha, 2009), 39–74. In the 2020 Tokyo Olympic rebuilding, the Shibuya area has once again taken center stage in a number of controversial and impactful construction projects. See for instance, Ogawa Tetsuo's essay, "Orinpikku to seikatsu no tatakai," in *Han-Tokyo Orinpikku sengen* (Tokyo: Koshisha, 2016), 110–132.

21. It is also important to note, however, that the privileged revolutionary subject was still predominantly male, and the heteronormativity of leftist labor politics was still unwavering here, as illustrated by the film's instrumentalized and domesticated role for the female character within the primary portrait of the male driver.

22. Sarah Jilani has illuminated the temporalities that characterize the symphonic dynamic of the city symphony film without necessarily rendering a harmonic totality; "This 'dynamic'—the temporal and spatial fragmentation-in-accumulation of the city—is certainly there, but its coherence does not lie in these fragments actually fitting together through different but complementary rhythms. For far from eventually being leveled or abstracted, this is where the temporal layerings of movement are generating a new kind of space; a space we *need*, in order to know the sheer subjectivity of urban temporal experience is *real*. Once it is cinematically articulated along its inherent disjunctions and synchronicities, these accumulated filmic spaces can then perhaps compose (and dissolve) urban modernity in a 'tempo' most akin to its nature." Sarah Jilani, "Urban Modernity and Fluctuating Time: 'Catching the Tempo' of the 1920s City Symphony Films," *Senses of Cinema* 68 (September 2013).

23. Karen Beckman's chapter on the industry-sponsored safety films provides a counterpoint to what she regards as Virilio's "teleological and nihilistic" narrative of the violence of speed shared by cinema and automobiles. *Crash: Cinema and the Politics of Speed and Stasis* (Durham, N.C.: Duke University Press, 2010), 120.

24. While such unremarked contingencies can be seen as a hallmark of Tsuchimoto's methodology, the status of the many fragments of seemingly superfluous scenes in this film cannot be divorced from considerations of the effort to expand the vocabulary of documentary aesthetics. It is, moreover, possible to read the proliferation of such contingencies in this film as an index of the degree to which the film self-reflexively recast the existing relations among filmmaker, documentary subject, and viewer by exposing the PR film's formal codes to the inundating urban forms they encountered in the film's production. As such, the film models what we will discover in these chapters to be the definitive contours of an urban ecological approach by delineating novel ways of seeing, knowing, and relating with/in the flux of the urban terrain.

25. One of the groups of urban dwellers hit hardest by the "traffic war" in terms of injuries and fatalities were children, left to play outside on streets such as these. This led to efforts to create spaces for children to play away from the dangers of cars, to limited success. Kaneko Jun, "Kōtsū sensō no zan'ei: kōtsū koen no tanjō to fukyū," ("Traces of the Traffic War: The Birth and Popularization of Traffic Parks"), *Shizuoka Daigaku shōgai gakushū kyōiku kenkyū: Bulletin of the Center for Education and Research of Lifelong Learning, Shizuoka University* 10 (2008): 21–39.

26. Isozaki Arata, "Dokyumento rojō eigahyō: Tokyo no kōtsū jōkyō o untenshu no me de kiroku," ("*On the Road: A Document*" Film Review: The Traffic Conditions of Tokyo as Recorded by a Driver") *Nihon dokusho shinbun*, April 27, 1964.

27. Isozaki Arata.

28. Isozaki Arata.

29. Yuriko Furuhata, "Architecture as atmospheric media: Tange Lab and Cybernetics," in *Media Theory in Japan*, ed. Mark Steinberg and Alex Zahlten (Durham, N.C.: Duke University Press, 2017), 71.

30. The depiction of irreconcilable coexistences was, in fact, a crucial aspect of his ecological approach more fully developed in Tsuchimoto's Minamata work.

31. Tsuchimoto, "Dokyumento rojo ni tsuite," 1972, accessed from the Tsuchimoto online document database, http://tutimoto.inaba.ws/top.php.

32. As a prominent "turning point" in Japan's postwar history, the Olympic spectacle continues to demarcate the "before" and "after" of Japan's dramatic "rebirth," "restoration," or even "extreme makeover" in contemporary parlance, from barbarous wartime imperialist aggressor to a peaceful, prosperous nation of culture and technology. Even before the selection of Tokyo for a second Olympic Games in 2020, a large body of writings scrutinized the mythical narratives of Olympic recovery. For detailed accounts of the myriad projects deployed to realize this vision, see Katagi Atsushi, *Orinpikku shiti Tokyo 1940–1964* (Tokyo: Kawade Bukkusu, 2010); *Tokyo Orinpikku no shakai keizaishi* (Tokyo: Nihon keizai

hyōronsha, 2009); Noriko Aso, "Sumptuous Repast: The 1964 Tokyo Olympics Arts Festival," 10, 1 (Spring 2002): 7–38; Igarashi Yoshikuni, "From the Anti-Security Treaty Movement to the Tokyo Olympics: Transforming the Body, the Metropolis, and Memory," *Bodies of Memory: Narratives of War in Postwar Japanese Culture, 1945–1970* (Princeton, N.J.: Princeton University Press, 2000); and *Nippon Shindan*, ed. Hidaka Rokurō and Satō Tsuyoshi (Tokyo: San'ichi Shobō, 1964).

33. As a critical node of inquiry into the dynamics of capitalist state power, discourses of Olympics offer a richly self-reflexive ground for contesting the givens of "recovery" narratives. For instance, see the arguments raised in the collection, *Han Tōkyō Orinpikku sengen = The anti-Olympic manifesto: against Tokyo 2020 Olympic and Paralympic*, eds. Ogasawara Hiroki and Yamamoto Atsuhisa (Tokyo: Kōshisha, 2016).

34. The significance of the forced passage of the United States-Japan Security Treaty lies not just with the experience of the "failure" of Japan's nascent institutional democracy. This notion of "failure" merely constitutes an ideologically charged pair to the "recovery" obtained in the Olympic spectacle. The 1960 treaty protests can better be situated as part of a broader set of geopolitical and aesthetic crises that informed the national, regional, and worldwide experiences of the Cold War. Hidaka Rokurō's writings explored the afterlives of the antitreaty protests as a structuring force throughout the postwar, precisely problematizing the separation of domestic and regional scales of the Cold War geopolitical system. See for instance Hidaka's book in Japanese on the protests themselves, *1960-nen 5-gatsu 19-nichi: 19 maj 1960* (Tokyo: Iwanami shinsho, 1960), and in English the collection, *The Price of Affluence: Dilemmas of Contemporary Japan* (New York: Penguin, 1985).

35. For critical commentators at the time, the Olympics were anything but apolitical. The volume *Nippon Shindan* touches upon the international geopolitical context in a number of interesting ways, highlighting, for example, the Tokyo Olympics' role in providing a model of the tangible benefits of alignment with U.S.-centered geopolitical projects of the Cold War. See, for instance, the chapter, "Orinpikku o tsuranuku kokusai seiji no ronri: Orinpikku shinwa no hōkai," *Nippon Shindan*, 29–52.

2. DISAPPEARANCE: TOPOLOGICAL VISUALITY IN ABE KŌBŌ'S URBAN LITERATURE

1. Abe Kōbō, *Moetsukita chizu* (Tokyo: Shinchōsha, 1967), and translated into English by E. Dale Saunders as *The Ruined Map* (New York: Knopf, 1969).

2. Entitled "Kūkan no bungaku e," the essay was first serialized in the journal *Bungaku-kai* from September 1979 to January 1980, and is included in his seminal collection of essays, Maeda Ai, *Toshi kūkan no naka no bungaku* (Tokyo: Chikuma shobō, 1992). Many of the most important essays from this collection are translated into English in *Text and the City: Essays on Japanese Modernity*, ed. James A. Fujii (Durham, N.C.: Duke University Press, 2004).

3. Recent waves of scholarly interest in Abe's writing have expanded the critical understanding of his work. Scholarly monographs include Thomas Schnell-bächer, *Abe Kōbō, Literary Strategist: The Evolution of His Agenda and Rhetoric in the Context of Postwar Japanese Avant-garde and Communist Artists' Movements* (München: Iudicium, 2004); Toba Kōji, *Undōtai Abe Kōbō* (Tokyo: Ichi-yōsha, 2007); Nina Cornyetz, *The Ethics of Aesthetics in Japanese Cinema and Literature: Polygraphic Desire* (London; New York: Routledge, 2007); Christopher Bolton, *Sublime Voices: The Fictional Science and Scientific Fiction of Abe Kōbō* (Cambridge, Mass.: Harvard University Asia Center, 2009); Margaret S. Key, *Truth from a Lie: Documentary, Detection, and Reflexivity in Abe Kōbō's Realist Project* (Lanham, Md.: Lexington Books, 2011); and Richard Calichman, *Beyond Nation: Time, Writing, and Community in the Work of Abe Kōbō* (Stanford, Calif.: Stanford University Press, 2016).

4. The novel itself was only one form taken by this work. As Abe describes in a roundtable discussion originally published with the novel, "*Moetsukita chizu o megutte*," the work began when he first published the short story "Kābu no mukō" ("Beyond the Curve") in 1965, then after two years of continual modification and development, published *Moetsukita Chizu* ("The Ruined Map"). *Abe Kōbō zenshū*, vol. 21: 313–320. The short story "Beyond the Cure" appears in *Beyond the Curve*, trans. Juliet Winters Carpenter (Tokyo; New York: Kodansha International, 1991). Subsequent to the publication of the novel, Abe drafted a screenplay that was the basis of the 1968 film *Moetsukita chizu*, directed by Teshigahara Hiroshi. While the novel is the focus of this chapter, it is important to recognize that Abe's "oeuvre" is constituted by dynamic traversals of genre and medium, and in particular, the collaborative framework established between Teshigahara and Abe must be considered a crucial component in shaping the trajectory these traversals took. Tomoda Yoshiyuki has exhaustively explored this dynamic and collaborative aspect of their works in Japanese in *Sengo zen'ei eiga to bungaku: Abe Kōbō x Teshigahara Hiroshi* (Kyōto: Jinbun Shoin, 2012).

5. Odagiri Takushi has explored the development of a "textualist" mode of criticism in Maeda's subsequent volume *Introduction to Literary Texts* (*Bungaku tekusuto nyūmon*, 1988), in "Maeda Ai's Predicate Theory," in *Japan Review* 22 (2010): 201–212.

6. Joseph A. Murphy has taken an illuminating look at Maeda's efforts to incorporate topology into literary criticism in "Maeda Ai: Topology and the Discourse of Complexity in Japanese Literary Criticism," in *Metaphorical Circuit: Negotiations Between Literature and Science in Twentieth-century Japan* (Ithaca, N.Y.: East Asia Program, Cornell University, 2004).

7. Abe himself was quite invested in mobilizing topological thought in his fiction at this time, as evidenced by the form and contents of the short story "Ningen sokkuri," published in 1966 just prior to *The Ruined Map*. Furthermore, Abe described topological thought to be a crucial means of confronting the residual instincts of belonging. He notes how he used it in the plot of the short story to provide contemporary readers an "antidote" to the facile forms of identity evidenced by wearing badges and discourses of "Japanese-ness." "Anata ni toporojii teki kōshō o—kizoku hon'nō e no chōsen shōsetsu 'Ningen sokkuri'" ("For your topological laughter: the story "Just-like a Human" that defies the instincts of belonging"), *Abe Kōbō zenshū* 20: 492.

8. Abe Kōbō, *Suna no onna* (Tokyo: Shinchōsha, 1962); *The Woman in the Dunes* (New York: Alfred A. Knopf, 1964); *Tanin no kao* (Tokyo: Kōdansha, 1964); *Face of Another* (New York: Alfred A. Knopf, 1966); *Hako otoko* (Tokyo: Shinchōsha, 1973); *The Box Man* (New York: Alfred A. Knopf, 1974). Each of these novels was translated by E. Dale Saunders.

9. For a fascinating account of the transformation of Shinjuku Station's West Exit Plaza from a public square (*hiroba*), to a "flow plaza" governed by traffic laws, see Jordan Sand's, "Hiroba: The Public Square and the Boundaries of the Commons," in *Tokyo Vernacular: Common Spaces, Local Histories, Found Objects* (Berkeley: University of California Press, 2013).

10. Seo Hong describes the reasons for this lack of attention having to do with the emphasis of Abe's efforts falling upon the literary style of this work rather than the narrative content itself. Seo Hong, "Moetsukita chizu ni okeru hanpukku hyōgen," *Kindai bungaku shiron* 42 (December 2004): 49–57.

11. Maeda Ai, "Kūkan no bungaku e," in *Toshi kūkan no naka no bungaku* (Tokyo: Chikuma shobō, 1992), 568.

12. Maeda Ai, 570. In this influential essay, Maeda furthermore outlined the possible contours of an urban fiction practice in order to counteract the myriad attempts to confine and constrain emergent strains of experimental literature, precisely despite or because of the disorientations 1970s literary works were inflicting upon prior generations of critics such as Okuno Takeo (1926–1997). "If we consider Okuno's *Archetypal Landscape in Literature* (*Bungaku ni okeru genfūkei*) to be an attempt to resuscitate 'the language of an ancient collectivity' [*kyōdōtai*] within contemporary urban space, then Abe Kōbō's series of works from *The Woman in the Dunes, Face of Another,* and *The Ruined Map* were attempts to

create a new language of the city by effecting the drastic dissolution of the city as a landscape." "Kūkan no bungaku e" ("For a Literature of Space") in *Toshi kūkan no naka no bungaku*, 561–562.

13. *The Ruined Map*, 7. I will use the existing English translation whenever possible, except where I have retranslated passages in order to better illustrate the original language when noted.

14. Isoda Kōichi's *Sengoshi no kūkan* (Tokyo: Shinchōsha, 1983), and other commentators have discussed the gender relations, consumer–commodity habits, and dietary changes that corresponded with the generalization of *danchi* lifeways. Wakabayashi Mikio's essay provides a useful overview of the conditions surrounding the formation of the image of the *danchi* as modern and rational living space in, "Sumukoto no shinwa to genjitsu" in *Kōgai no shakaigaku: gendai o ikiru katachi* (Tokyo: Chikuma Shinsho, 2007), 109–155. Numerous books from the nostalgia industry have engaged these lingering reminders of other lifeworlds. Today, these aging estates currently serve as vehicles of property speculation as the redevelopment of these sites promises to "update" or renew many of these dilapidated estates. The diverse manifestations of the housing estate linger as enduring traces whose various forms disclose many strata of Japan's rapidly urbanized social space. In the essay, "The Wages of Affluence: The High-Rise Housewife in Japanese Sex Films," *Camera Obscura* 27, 1 (79): 1–29, Anne McKnight explores how the figure of the *danchi* rose to prominence in a number of cinematic works during the 1960s, and spawned its own genre of soft-core pornography in the 1970s *Danchi Zuma* series films. We might situate the novel's representation of the *danchi* as occupying a position between those of Hani Susumu's *She and He* (*Kanojo to kare*) of 1963 and Wakamatsu Kōji's *Secrets Behind the Walls* (*Kabe no naka no himegoto*) of 1965, in terms of the thematic and material rendering of the *danchi*.

15. Amanda C. Seaman has described the novel's attention to suburbanization as a process of "geographical defamiliarization" in her article "Oases of Discontent: Suburban Space in Takahashi Takako and Abe Kōbō," *U.S.-Japan Women's Journal* 43 (2012): 48–62.

16. Maeda describes this as the erotic space or refuge of interior space in "Kūkan no bungaku e." Moreover, his readings of Gotō Meisei's work describe the expanding manifestations of literary practice engaged with the shifting contours of social space, with Abe situated as the "founding father" of these forms of literary practice. That the figure of the *danchi* housing developments play such a central role in Maeda's urban literary genealogy is significant for consideration of the geopolitics of literary production.

17. This substitution moreover is doubled by the reader who follows after the protagonist. The detective himself draws attention to this structural substitution

by citing a work entitled "The Memoirs of a Sleuth," "no good hunter pursues his quarry too far." Rather he puts himself in his quarry's place as he looks for the path of flight; by pursuing himself he corners his quarry." *The Ruined Map*, 176. Although no Japanese translation of the exact title Abe refers to exists, this is most likely Abe's reworking of *The recollections of a policeman*, originally published as William Russell, *Recollections of a Detective Police-Officer* (Boston: Wentworth, 1856).

18. Seo Hong's essay "Moetsukita chizu n ni okeru hanpukku hyōgen" delineates a variety of discontinuities and repeating phrases that structure this work.

19. *The Ruined Map*, 8.

20. *The Ruined Map*, 20.

21. *The Ruined Map*, 24.

22. *The Ruined Map*, 79. Here, the "municipal cooperative movement" refers to the consolidation of municipalities that accompanied urban growth and restructuring of boundaries.

23. The most prominent literary example of the reimagining of this particular landscape is Kunikida Doppo's 1898 short story "Musashino," ("The Musashi Plain") in *River Mist and Other Stories*, trans. David G. Chibbett (Tokyo; New York: Kodansha International Ltd., 1983). Kota Inoue has pointed out the definitive role of modern literary practice in rendering coherent the expansive social space of the emergent Japanese empire, particularly in the suburban social space that we find being dismantled in the detective's remapping here. Kota writes, "the consolidation of Japan as a modern empire requires the silencing of certain groups of people (the colonized, the poor, women, etc.) while creating the illusion of the unity of all forty million imperial subjects. 'Musashino,' in which a sense of unified community is built upon the silence of the villagers, encapsulates this colonial relation between center and the periphery in its narrating of the suburban landscape." Unpublished dissertation, "The Suburb as Colonial Space in Modern Japanese Literature and Cinema," (University of California, Irvine, 2004), 67. This poignant reading builds from critical reconsiderations of Kunikida's work, such as those found in Karatani Kojin's *Origins of Modern Japanese Literature*, and Seiji Lippit's "The Double Logic of Minor Spaces," in *Minor Transnationalism*. These critical readings have demonstrated the significance of reimagining like Kunikida's in rendering coherent the ever expanding geopolitical vision of imperial modernity. It is thus one important aspect of Abe's efforts here to produce a literary topos derived from this very same terrain, revealing the geopolitical recoding of a place as it is integrated into a different order.

24. *The Ruined Map*, 84.

25. As David W. Plath has traced in his overview of the emergence of the *maika* (or, "My Car") discourse and the generalization of the car during the Showa era

(1925–1989) in Japan, the mechanized identity of the self with the promise of mobility in the car "triggered a remapping of not just transportation routes but also the line of human sociability." "My-Car-isma: Motorizing the Showa Self," in *Showa: The Japan of Hirohito*, ed. Carol Gluck and Stephen Graubard (New York: Norton, 1993), 229–244.

26. It is not too difficult to roughly align the map included within the novel with the Yotsuya ward of Fuchū-city, near the site of the Chūō Expressway's Kunitachi Fuchū interchange, completed in the same year the novel was published. However, it seems the text is not directly indexing a precise location, but it is instead delineating a set of relations undergoing change, the flux in local property relations disclosed through the expansion of the freeway system. Nonetheless, the novel is poignantly prescient regarding the future (the present) of the area, as we can discern from contemporary maps that little has deviated from its predicted fate, as piecemeal residential housing developments pepper the small-scale agricultural fields, seemingly resilient to large-scale changes.

27. *The Ruined Map*, 85.

28. *The Ruined Map*, 88.

29. *The Ruined Map*, 107.

30. *The Ruined Map*, 119

31. *The Ruined Map*, 119.

32. *The Ruined Map*, 100.

33. *The Ruined Map*, 118.

34. Edward Fowler, *San'ya Blues: Laboring Life in Contemporary Tokyo* (Ithaca, N.Y.: Cornell University Press, 1996).

35. For a fascinating 2006 film documentary of the history of Osaka's legendary *yoseba*, including footage of the 1961 Nishinari riot that erupted after a day laborer was hit by a car, see *Mapping the Future, Nishinari*, distributed by Zakka Films.

36. The plight of day laborers remains a deeply compelling locus of inquiry, playing a crucial role in both of the largest mobilizations of labor procurements in the infrastructural and construction projects undertaken in the name of the 2020 Tokyo Olympics, and the massive decontamination of radioactive materials in the wake of the ongoing release of radioactive contamination following the meltdown of the Fukushima Dai'ichi reactor in 2011.

37. The detective describes the women's violation as a ceremony that evokes an image of dismembered pieces of meat. Thus, the detective's safe escape is tied to the "sacrificial" female bodies, a trope that Maeda Ai and other critics find is shared among many of Abe's texts. This notion of ceremonial sacrifice harkens back to an enduring gender relation within modern literary practice, as exemplified directly in Tamura Taijirō's 1946 short story "Nikutai no mon" (1947, "Gate

of the Flesh"). For a discussion of this work and the trope of women as sacrificial saviors of males, see Douglas Slaymaker, *The Body in Postwar Japanese Fiction* (London: RoutledgeCurzon, 2004).

38. *The Ruined Map*, 174.

39. *The Ruined Map*, 175.

40. *The Ruined Map*, 175.

41. "Chizu to keiyaku: Abe Kōbō Moetsukita ron," *Nihon kindai bungaku*, Dai 81 Shū (November 2009): 208–223.

42. *The Ruined Map*, emphasis added, 177.

43. *The Ruined Map*, 190.

44. This is demonstrated by the detective's movements as a driver. The automobile takes on an increasingly significant role in the plot to discover the client's missing husband as well as the detective's own "escape" into the world of the disappearing. It is what brings him to the riverside and facilitates his narrow escape. Namigata Tsuyoshi has an interesting discussion of the car as the shell of the narrator's subjectivity in "Abe Kōbō Moetsukita chizu ron," *Tsukuba Studies in Literature* 14 (1997): 152–131. Although this allows us to consider the implications of this mode of transportation on the detective's actions, it overlooks the shifting vantage point secured in the detective's movements.

45. *The Ruined Map*, 157–162. In discussions with critics and journalists around the time of the novel's publication, Abe described doing actual interviews with taxi drivers. In a roundtable discussion and other interviews, Abe repeatedly mentioned a story of a prominent New York politician who disappeared then was later discovered to be working as a taxi driver. Abe's interest in taxi drivers, which clearly builds upon his much earlier interest in professional drivers and driving in general, serves to illuminate the central transformative role of the anonymous drivers who gather at the Camellia. See the roundtable discussion on *Moetsukita Chizu*, and related contemporary interviews with Abe collected in *Abe Kōbō zenshū* 21 (313–322, 419–429).

46. *The Ruined Map*, 263–265.

47. One can find uncanny resonance with the mobilization of increasingly precarious forms of labor in "ride sharing" platforms such as Uber and Lyft, where the crux of the conflicts over the juridical status of drivers as "users" or "employees" belies the much bigger problems of precarity and vast disparities in the distribution of risk and profit within the dominant economies of such platforms.

48. *The Ruined Map*, 269–270.

49. We saw this pump image earlier and it re-emerges after the detective loses his memory in his misrecognition of the sketch map of S-station as some sort of pump device. This offers an interesting contrast to the "pump" and vascular movement of water through sand "discovered" by the protagonist in *Suna no*

onna. There the pump held an important role inwardly as potential social knowledge, whereas here the city as gigantic pump embodies the unknowable sociality of otherness that constitutes urban social space.

50. In an early essay by Karatani Kōjin, Abe is considered to have simply obtained an illusory sense of liberation without confronting the radical implications for collective social practice his own work suggests. "Chizu wa moetsukitaka: Ōe, Abe ni miru sōzōryoku to kankei ishiki," in *Ifu suru ningen* (Tokyo: Tōjusha, 1979), 287–295. Nakano sees the question lying with the misrecognition of the form of community Abe was rejecting in "Chizu to keiyaku: Abe Kōbō Moetsukita ron."

51. Abe Kōbō, "Toshi ni tsuite," *Abe Kōbō zenshu* 20: 399.

52. For a fascinating discussion of how topological inquiry has been mobilized to explore the novel changes in the operation of power by affording dialogues among discourses of political theory and social sciences, see John Allen's *Topologies of Power: Beyond Territory and Networks* (Abingdon, UK: Routledge, 2016).

53. Félix Guattari traveled to Tokyo in 1983 and published a series of texts and interviews based on his visit. These have been recently translated into English in the collection *Machinic Eros: Writings on Japan* (Minneapolis, MN: Univocal, 2015), 16. Guattari's insights capture a moment of possibility that seems increasingly remote, but as a result increasingly inviting.

3. LANDSCAPE VOCABULARIES: *FOR A LANGUAGE TO COME* AND THE GEOPOLITICS OF READING

1. Ongoing efforts to reappraise, reintroduce, and reexamine Nakahira's works led by critic Yasumi Akihito and critic-curator Kuraishi Shino have had a monumental impact on restoring Nakahira Takuma's status as one of the most influential writers, photographers, and thinkers of the 1960s and 1970s. The bibliographic record of their efforts does not fully capture the importance of their contributions, yet demonstrates the accelerating growth of interest in Nakahira they have facilitated: Yasumi edited the first detailed reappraisal of Nakahira's work in a special issue on the Provoke Era in *Deja Vu* 14 (October 1993); contributed the main essay "Nakahira Takuma: Facing the Critical Point of Photography" to the Nakahira volume of Iwanami Photographers of Japan book series, *Nihon no shashinka 36: Nakahira Takuma* (Tokyo: Iwanami Shoten, 1999); provided the first English-language essay on Nakahira, "Journey to the Limits of Photography: The Heyday of Provoke 1964–1973," for a collector's edition reprint of Japanese photobooks *The Japanese Box* (Göttingen: Steidl; London: Thames & Hudson, 2001); the essay, "Kioku to bōkyaku no kishi: shashinka wa nani o mayasu no ka" ("The Border Between Memory and Forgetting: What does the Photographer Ignite?"), *Bijutsu Techo* (April 2003); "Kiroku/kioku no sākyurēshon: Nakahira

Takuma o meggute" ("The Circulations of Documentary/Memory: On Naka-hira Takuma"); *Gendai Shashin no riariti* (Tokyo: Kadokawa Gakugei Shuppan, 2003); "Imeiji no reido: Nakahira Takuma Genten fukki—Yokohama" ("Degree Zero of the Image: Nakahira Takuma's Genten Fukki-Yokohama"), *Nakahira Takuma Genten fukki: Yokohama* (Tokyo: Osiris, 2003); coedited the collection of Nakahira's writings, *Mitsuzukeru hate ni hi ga . . .: hihyō shūsei 1965–1977* (Tokyo: Osiris, 2007); provided the commentary for the paperback republica-tion of Nakahira's 1973 collection, "Kaisetsu" in *Naze, shokubutsu zukan ka: Nakahira Takuma eizō ronshū* (Tokyo: Chikuma Gakugei Bunko, 2007); and coauthored, "Nakahira Takuma, sono kiseki to toi"("Questioning the Trajec-tory of Nakahira Takuma") with Kuraishi Shino, *Nakahira Takuma: Kitarubeki shashinka* (Tokyo: Kawade Shobo Shinsha, 2009). Kuraishi Shino curated the monumental exhibition of Nakahira's work, *Nakahira Takuma Genten fukki: Yokohama*, providing the essay, "Nakahira Takuma Genten fukki: Yokohama no gaiyō to kōsei" ("Outline and Formation of Nakahira Takuma Genten fukki: Yokohama") *Nakahira Takuma Genten fukki: Yokohama*; the essay, "Michi no kitei: 1970 nendai ni okeru Nakahira Takuma no tekusuto he no oboegaki" ("Prescriptions of the Unknown: a Note on Nakahira Takuma's Texts in the 1970s"), in *Bijutsu Techo* (April 2003); and many other important essays that touch upon aspects of Nakahira's work.

2. Terayama Shūji's *Gendai no Seishun-ron* (later published as the infamous col-lection *Iede no susume* [in praise of running away from home]) in "Kangaesaser-areru ikutsuka no omoitsuki," *Gendai no me* (August 1963); Tanigawa Gan's *Kage no ekkyō o megutte*, "Wazukani nokotta 'kakumeisha' no fūbō," *Gendai no me* (September 1963); and Matsumoto Toshio's *Eizo no hakken* in "Bunseki shit-sukusu rojikku," *Gendai no me* (April 1964).

3. Tōmatsu Shōmei, in contrast to Nakahira, has enjoyed a long and favorable reception outside of Japan. Most recently, Jonathan Reynolds has provided a detailed study of the full scope of Tōmatsu's work in an illuminating account of the expanded intellectual and cultural horizons that informed Tōmatsu's oeuvre. *Allegories of Time and Space: Japanese Identity in Photography and Architecture* (Honolulu: University of Hawai'i Press, 2015).

4. Steven Ridgely describes the subject of the novel to be that of "boxing, explored through the frame of violence as communication," *Japanese Counterculture: The Antiestablishment Art of Terayama Shūji* (Minneapolis: University of Minnesota Press, 2011), xxi.

5. In addition to Ridgely's definitive study, Miryam Sas has explored the broad cul-tural milieu illuminated by Terayama's diverse works in *Experimental Arts in Postwar Japan: Moments of Encounter, Engagement, and Imagined Return* (Cam-bridge, Mass.: Harvard University Asia Center, 2011).

6. *1968 Photography: Photographs that stirred up debate, 1966–1974* (*Nihon shashin no 1968: 1966~1974 futtōsuru shashin no mure*) (Tokyo: Tokyō-to Shashin Bijut-sukan, 2013).

7. Tsuchiya Seiichi, "The whereabouts of the 'record' discovered: reflections on A Century of Photography" in *1968 Photography: Photographs that stirred up debate, 1966–1974*, trans. Ruth McCreery, xiv.

8. Gyewon Kim, "Reframing 'Hokkaido Photography': Style, Politics, and Documentary Photography in 1960s Japan," *History of Photography* 39(4) (October 2015): 348–365.

9. This point is elaborated in detail in Kohara Masashi's essay, "The Cycle of Provocation: *Provoke's Path*," in *1968 Photography*, xxiii–xxxiii.

10. Gyewon Kim, "Paper, Photography, and a Reflection on Urban Landscape in 1960s Japan," *Visual Resources* 32:3–4 (2016): 230–246. Yuko Fujii's PhD dissertation makes an exhaustive art historical engagement with the journal, including an important study of longer photographic histories that informed the work of *provoke* photographers and those they influenced. "Photography as process: a study of the Japanese photography journal *provoke*" (City University of New York, 2012).

11. "Dōjidaiteki de aru to wa nanika?," collected in *Mitsuzukeru hate ni hi ga . . .*, 55–88.

12. *Asahi Camera* 56 (October 1968), collected in Nakahira Takuma, *Toshi fūkei zukan: magazine work 1946–1982* (Chōfu: Getsuyōsha, 2011), 55–62.

13. Another photograph of this figure appeared two months later in a special issue of *Bijutsu techo*, though composed differently, neatly framed horizontally, centered along the middle axis of the train car, greatly reducing the tension of the former photograph. *Toshi fūkei zukan*, 82–83.

14. *Toshi fukei zukan*, 62.

15. "Dōjidaiteki de aru to wa nanika?," *Mitsuzukeru hate ni hi ga . . .*, 86.

16. As Karatani Kōjin's reading of Marx has discussed, this "fatal leap" embodies the crisis form of the commodity itself. We can similarly situate Nakahira's (re) definition of photography here to be a pursuit of a critical language based upon this form of crisis embedded within the communicative act itself. See Karatani's *Transcritique: On Kant and Marx*, trans. Sabu Kohso (Cambridge, Mass.: MIT, 2005), 106.

17. Simply entitled "Image, Language" ("Eizō•kotoba") in *For a Language to Come*, the essay immediately followed the essay "language, silence" ("Kotoba•chinmoku"). The only other material these two collections shared was a selection of Nakahira's essays on Jean-Luc Godard.

18. "Has Photography Been Able to Provoke Language?" ("Shashin wa kotoba o chōhatsu shietaka") originally published in *Nihon dokusha shinbun* (March

1970), the essay was included in the collection *Mitsuzukeru hate ni hi ga . . .,* 105–109. My original translations of this essay are included in *For a Language to Come* (Tokyo: Osiris, 2010), 5–7 and *Provoke: Between Protest and Performance: Photography in Japan 1960–1975.*

19. "Has Photography Been Able to Provoke Language?" Slightly modified from original translation.

20. The republished 2010 version of *For a Language to Come* maintains this structure by printing the essays as a separate insert. Although the essays are different from the original version, the structure as an assemblage remains.

21. It is interesting to note that as an uncoded text it is difficult to sustain the most common aesthetic distinctions applied to photographic media. For instance, the text cannot be read as "objective" in the sense of directly accessing the material realities recorded. Nor is it merely "subjective" in the sense of either producing inaccessible meanings only significant to Nakahira as "author," nor solely up to the viewer to passively glean whatever private meanings they like. Despite, or perhaps because of, such difficulties, reception of the text nonetheless tends to force one or the other of the distinctions rendered unstable by the text.

22. This disordering of language is one of the defining aspects of the form of poetic language Roland Barthes described in *Writing Degree Zero*, one moreover that Nakahira's essays make clear he was intimately familiar with. "Modern poetry is a poetry of the object. In it, Nature becomes a fragmented space, made of objects solitary and terrible, because the links between them are only potential. Nobody chooses for them a privileged meaning, or a particular use, or some service; nobody imposes a hierarchy on them, nobody reduces them to the manifestation of a mental behavior, or of an intention, of some evidence of tenderness, in short. The bursting upon us of the poetic word then institutes an absolute object; Nature becomes a succession of verticalities, of objects, suddenly standing erect, and filled with all their possibilities: one of these can be only a landmark in an unfulfilled, and thereby terrible world. These unrelated objects—words adorned with all the violence of their irruption, the vibration of which, though wholly mechanical, strangely affects the next word, only to die out immediately—these poetic words exclude men: there is no humanism of modern poetry. This erect discourse is full of terror, that is to say, it relates man not to other men, but to the most inhuman images in Nature: heaven, hell, holiness, childhood, madness, pure matter, etc." Roland Barthes, *Writing Degree Zero*, trans. Annette Lavers and Colin Smith (New York: Hill and Wang, 1977), 50.

23. "The collapse of an immobilized point of view: Thoughts on William Klein's *New York*," ("Fudō no shiten no hōkai: Uiriamu Kurain Nyūyōku kara no hassō"), originally published in 1967, included in *Mitsuzukeru hate ni hi ga . . .,* 22. It is telling

that it was not the content of Klein's photography that inspired Nakahira, but a critical fluidity of form.

24. Of course today when we seek to claim such texts to be "political," we must at minimum address a number of problems, including the radically constrained definitions of the political that operate at present, as well as asking for whom such claims are made. In fact, without a more rigorous delineation of the crises and critical practices that arose in contestation of the Cold War's proliferating forms of violence, unleashed at the local, regional, and global levels, we risk simply amplifying on a discursive level the acts of violence committed in the name of capitalist/socialist state power(s). To demonstrate, as this book does, that the Cold War remaking of Japan posed both aesthetic and geopolitical crises for a wide range of cultural practices, is but one such attempt to begin to grasp the different and differential forms of violence that mark both historical and contemporary transformations of capitalist state power.

25. To name just a few of the historical "events" and mass spectacles that were planned and unplanned to occur during the year 1970, first and foremost the renewal of the United States-Japan Security Treaty Expo 1970, which was in part planned to prevent another mass mobilization of the anti-United States-Japan Security Treaty protests during 1960; the inception of the National Railways' Discover Japan campaign; the dramatic Japanese Red Army Faction's JAL *yodo-go* air hijacking; and the spectacle of Mishima Yukio's suicide. The danger of narratives derived from such events is that they totalize the myriad historical struggles that surround each of these in order to enclose a safe inevitability of fixed "meaning" to what were public spectacles deeply fraught with contradictory significations, both at the time and afterwards. But even this partial listing suggests a dominant shift in the nature of state power and the changing nature of the responses seeking to confront this power.

26. The essay "Fūkei e no hanran" first appeared in the journal *Graphication* in June of 1970, and Nakahira first used the term "landscape" (*fūkei*) as a title for his photographs in the February 1970 issue of the journal *Design*. The essay and photographs were included in *For a Language to Come*.

27. Yuriko Furuhata, *Cinema of Actuality: Japanese Avant-Garde Filmmaking in the Season of Image Politics* (Durham, N.C.: Duke University Press, 2014), 139.

28. "Fūkei e no hanran," *Mitsuzukeru hate ni hi ga . . .*, 127–128. There are slight differences between the versions of the essays that appear in *For a Language to Come* and *Mitsuzukeru hate ni hi ga . . . Hihyō Shūsei 1965–1977*. The 2007 collection reverts to the versions as they first appeared, while Nakahira had made subtle changes to the versions collected in *For a Language to Come*. This translation represents a slightly revised version of my own translation first published in the 2010 edition of *For a Language to Come*.

29. The a priori urban discourses Nakahira confronted here bring to light an important aspect of this transformative historical period in that the supposedly antipower discourses that engaged the urban terrain relied upon distinctly uncritical notions of community, modernity, and politics. The popularity of such discourses is illustrated by the best-selling status Marxist historian Hani Gorō's *Toshi no ronri* ("The Logic of the City") during the late 1960s. Thus, it is significant that the violence that Nakahira confronted at once moved beyond the given meanings of the city toward a much more powerful magnitude of order, which secures the landscape, and moves within the perceptive faculties of the observer who faces, and thus secures this landscape, as discussed below.

30. For example, the essay "What is it to be Contemporary?" described the practical compliance of self-described social-justice photojournalists and the generalized media complicity mobilized in the police assault on Zenkyōtō activists (the predominant form of decentralized student movements in the late 1960s, an abbreviation of *Zengaku kyōtō kaigi* [All Campus Joint Struggle Committee]).

31. Setsu Shigematsu has situated the emergence of Japan's radical women's liberation movement within this accentuated moment. Confronting not only police violence on the front lines of the struggle but also internal suppression within the male-dominated student movements, the vital perspectives of *ūman ribu* afford a much-needed expansion of the domain of the "political." For instance, we discover the movement's articulation of "an epistemic turn between sex and political subjectivity, rearticulating the meaning of women's liberation by reconceiving of the sexed-body and sexual subjectivity as integral to revolution. Revolution was to be understood as a living and lived practice in which the subject struggled to transform society and the self and the self's relationship with the other—not a future utopia." "Introduction: Ūman Ribu as Solidarity and Difference," in *Scream from the Shadows: The Women's Liberation Movement in Japan* (Minneapolis: University of Minnesota Press: 2012), xxi.

32. The Kanda *kaihō-ku* was a brief student barricade of Meiji Boulevard, a major street near Meiji University, Nihon University, and Chūō University in central Tokyo, which was occupied during the police assaults on Yasuda Hall, and inspired by the student occupation of the Latin Quarter in Paris during the May 1968 uprisings.

33. "Fūkei e no hanran," *Mitsuzukeru hate ni hi ga . . .*, 129–130.

34. Taki Kōji, "Kitarubeki kotoba no tame ni," originally published in *Desain* (December 1970), collected in *Kotoba no nai shikō* (Tokyo: Tabata Shoten, 1972), 93.

35. Nakahira retrospectively describes this moment in a pivotal essay, "The Documentary Illusion: From the Document to the Monument," which first appeared in the July 1972 issue of *Bijutsu techo*. "By generously accepting the defiant sentiment and feeling in our images that we thought may have been defiant at the

time, the technique of blur and shake that resulted from the raw experience of life that we arrogantly believed to be found in a direct encounter between the world and the self, was transformed instantly into a kind of design and inversely our defiance was made benign as a result of this. Around the time of the National Railways's absurd tourism campaign, Discover Japan, advertised on a large scale, a friend joked, 'Provoke is getting huge, even the railways are using blurred and shaken images.' This was no joke. That was instead proof of this." "Kiroku toiu gen'ei: dokyumento kara monyumento e," *Mitsuzukeru hate ni hi ga . . .*, 234.

36. Nakahiri Takuma, "Morokko, ehagaki no fūkei" ("Morocco, a picture postcard landscape"), 1971, 194.

37. Nakahira's continual critique of travel, the travel industry, or photographers who only shot oversees on the one hand, and his consistent call for movement and nomadic wandering on the other, found in many different forms of writings throughout the 1970s, confronted the commodified movement of the dislocated masses who were now encouraged to "discover" the consumable traces of their "native places" that had been dismantled and remade in pursuit of rapid economic development. Tomiko Yoda has engaged with the limits of Nakahira's critique of the Discover Japan campaign to illuminate the novel production of subjectivities indexed by the campaign in her groundbreaking essay, "Girlscape: The Marketing of Mediatic Ambience in Japan," in *Media Theory in Japan*, ed. Marc Steinberg and Alexander Zahlten (Durham and London: Duke University Press, 2017). In addition, Marilyn Ivy has explored the transformative spatial-temporal relations this campaign demonstrated in *Discourses of the Vanishing: Modernity, Phantasm, Japan* (Chicago: University of Chicago Press, 1995), 29–65.

38. "Fūkei e no hanran," *Mitsuzukeru hate ni hi ga . . .*, 131.

39. The resonance of Jacques Ranciere's notion of *Dissensus* with Nakahira and other practices explored in this work has as much to do with the aesthetic problems posed by the upheaval of May 1968, as it does with the shared experiences of the geopolitics of the Cold War that informed each moment differently. See Kristin Ross's work on the "afterlives" of 1968 that continues to inform the misrecognition and erasure of not only the aesthetic and geopolitical problems disclosed by May 1968, but also how we might begin to further elaborate these uncanny resonances across a variety of contexts, *May '68 and its Afterlives* (Chicago: The University of Chicago Press, 2002).

40. Most strikingly, this critical use of the term makes available an important conceptual lens for rereading notions of landscape across diverse histories of Japanese literary modernity. On the one hand, we can project the crux of the problem of landscape "back" into modern Japan's origins. The primary instance of landscape in this sense of the term can be traced to Shiga Shigetaka's *Nihon Fūkei-ron*, an influential encouragement of mountaineering and "gentlemanly"

aesthetics. On the other hand, we can project the discoveries of landscape "forward" to the emergence of the term within literary criticism of the 1970s, first in Okuno Takeo's *Bungaku ni okeru genfūkei: harappa, dōkutsu no gensō* (Tokyo: Shūeisha, 1972), then in Maeda Ai's response to Okuno in *Toshi kūkan no naka no bungaku*, and perhaps mostly prominently, in Karatani Kojin's *Origins of Modern Japanese Literature*. As Richard Okada's fascinating reading of both moments demonstrates, the literary genealogy of the term captures the aporia of modernist literary production, as a part of—and apart from—the geopolitics of empire. "'Landscape' and the Nation-state: A reading of *Nihon Fūkei Ron*" in *New Directions in the Study of Meiji Japan*, ed. Helen Hardacre and Adam Kern (Leiden; New York; Köln: Brill, 1997), 90–107. Furthermore, it is perhaps more clearly this sense of landscape that Maeda Ai engaged with in his reading of Abe's *Moetsukita chizu*, discussed in the previous chapter, in order to counteract the myriad attempts to confine urban literature to the modern literary landscape Karatani discovered, precisely despite or because of the disorientations 1970s literary works were inflicting upon prior generations of critics such as Okuno Takeo (1926–1997). "If we consider Okuno's *Bunkagku ni okeru genfūkei* (*Archetypal Landscape in Literature*) to be an attempt to resuscitate 'the language of an old collective social body (kyōdōtai)' within contemporary urban space, then Abe Kōbō's series of works from *The Woman in the Dunes*, *Face of Another*, and *The Ruined Map* were attempts to create a new language of the city by effecting the drastic dissolution of the city as a landscape." "Kūkan no bungaku e" ("For a Literature of Space"), in *Toshi kūkan no naka no bungaku* (Tokyo: Chikuma shobō, 1992), 561–562. Thus, the signification of landscape within literary discourse in the 1970s was in some sense a contestation over the implications of the transformed contours of Japanese social space and the possibilities of literary practice, which likely was a direct outcome of the interrogation of landscape initiated by Matsuda and Nakahira discussed here.

41. As discussed in the next chapter, Nakahira's essay "The Documentary Illusion: From the Document to the Monument" ("Kiroku toiu gen'ei: dokyumento kara monyumento e"), in *Bijitsu teicho* (1972), embodied a culmination of his response to the entanglement of Japan's urban and media environments. An important element of this was the rapid rise of television in the second half of the 1960s that had displaced the photograph as the dominant image medium in Japan. At the same time, the Japanese camera industry had succeeded in becoming a global industry and secured the generalization of photography with more affordable, higher quality, smaller sized, and standardized camera technologies. For an overview of the technical developments of the Japanese camera industry, see Fujita Naomichi, "Kamera-Kankōzairyō no hattatsu" ("Cameras: the Development of Photosensitive Materials"), in *Nihon gendai shashinshi 1945–1970* (Tokyo: Heibonsha, 1977), 480–491.

42. *Naze shokubutsu zukan ka: Nakahira Takuma eizōron-shū* (Tokyo: Shōbunsha, 1973).

43. Gō Hirasawa, "Kaisetsu: fūkei-ron no genzai," in *Fūkei no shimetsu, Zōho shinpan* (*The Extinction of Landscape*, revised and expanded edition) (Tokyo: Koshisha, 2013), 319–320.

44. *Kikan firumu* 13 (December 1972), 142.

45. Abe Kōbō, The Ruined Map, trans. E. Dale Saunders (New York: Knopf, 1969), 164.

46. Adachi Masao describes the difficulties they faced as "revolutionaries" in much the same terms in the dialogue with Nakahira, "The Demolition Plan for a Theory of Media," first published in one of the final issues of *Film Criticism*, "Medeia-ron e no kaitai puran," *Eiga hihyō* (December 1973): 93.

4. AN ILLUSTRATED DICTIONARY OF URBAN OVERFLOWS

1. Abe Kōbō, *The Box Man*, trans. E. Dale Saunders (New York: Knopf, 1974), 41–42. I have modified the translation to reflect the original, as in chapter 2 of this volume. Saunders's translations are accurate but often lose definition in the abstraction of language that Abe employed in passages such as this.

2. Atsuko Sakaki, "Anonymously Yours: Abe Kōbō's Engagement with Photography" in *The Rhetoric of Photography in Modern Japanese Literature: Materiality in the Visual Register as Narrated by Tanizaki Jun'ichirō, Abe Kōbō, Horie Toshiyuki and Kanai Mieko* (Leiden: Brill, 2016), 93.

3. Walter Benjamin, "The Work of Art in the Age of Its Technological Reproducibility: Second Version (1936)," in *Walter Benjamin: Selected Writings Volume 3, 1935–1938*, ed. Marcus Bullock and Michael W. Jennings (Cambridge, Mass.: Belknap Press, 1996), 117.

4. Kaja Silverman, "Introduction," in *The Miracle of Analogy or the History of Photography, part 1* (Stanford, Calif.: Stanford University Press, 2015), 11.

5. Silverman deftly reads Benjamin's earlier understanding of photography found in the "Little History of Photography" as well as its contemporaneous criticism of "left-wing melancholy" against his own celebrations of technological reproducibility of his later writings. Therefore, excavating Benjamin's earlier understanding of photography, which Silverman identifies as the encounter of a look and a world that has anticipated it, where "the present discovers itself within the past, and the past is realized within the present," as informing the later messianic notion of history. Silverman, 4–8. As such, as linkages of varying magnitudes of similarity and difference, Silverman moreover makes the compelling claim that photography models Maurice Merleau-Ponty's notion of the "chiasmus." "Photography models it for us through the inversion and lateral reversal of the camera obscura's image

stream, the positive print's reversal of the reversal through which its negative was made, the two-way street leading from the space of the viewer to that of the stereoscopic image, cinema's shot/reverse shot formation, and the cross-temporal practices of some contemporary artists. I say 'model' because we, too, are bound to each other through reversible reversals, and because it is there and only there, that the promise of social happiness can still be glimpsed." Silverman, 12.

6. See Richard Calichman's translation of Abe's earlier essay, "The Frontier Within" ("Uchi naru henkyō"), originally published in *Chūō Kōron* in 1968. Calichman also offers a useful discussion in the introduction to the volume on how the "margins within" operate to consolidate particular forms of power, and how for Abe, grasping the structuring of relational forms constituted an ethical ground for becoming in the world. *The Frontier Within: Essays by Abe Kōbō*, trans. Richard Calichman (New York: Columbia University Press, 2015).

7. *Naze shokubutsu zukan ka: Nakahira Takuma eizōron-shū* (Tokyo: Shōbunsha, 1973). Here I have translated the English equivalent of *eizō*, or "image," to the more expanded notion of "visual media" in order to reflect the conceptual scope of Nakahira's essays in the collection.

8. Nakahira Takuma, "Afterword" ("atogaki"), *Naze shokubutsu zukan ka*, 253.

9. The specific essay that incited this claim was "The Documentary Illusion: From the Document to the Monument" ("Kiroku to iu gen'ei: dokyumento kara monyumento e"), Nakahira, 62, originally published in *Bijutsu techō* (July 1972), discussed later in this chapter. It is interesting to note that the subsequent and enduringly partial reception of Nakahira's work seems to merely reiterate the convictions behind this claim, despite, or perhaps because of, the outpouring of criticism and photographic work that Nakahira produced to dismantle these very problematic assumptions.

10. While the writings of thinkers such as Walter Benjamin, Frantz Fanon, Hans Magnus Enzensberger, and Herbert Marcuse appear among the essays of the collection, the title essay touches upon the writings of Alain Robbe-Grillet. In English, these are collected in Robbe-Grillet's *For a New Novel: Essays on Fiction* (Evanston, Ill.: Northwestern University Press, 1992). Nakahira's method of self-critique mobilized in the title essay was also "prototyped" in earlier essays, but perhaps the essay which most explicitly indexes the methods of *Zenkyōtō* activists as a model was the longest of the fragmentary essays of Section two, "Concepts Wrought from Date and Place: July, 1971, Journalism, Zenkyōtō, Expression" ("Hizuke to basho kara no hassō: 7.1971 jānarizumu, Zenkyōtō, hyōgen"), in *Naze shokubutsu zukan ka*, 181–187.

11. For an example of how this "clarity" is read as a return to "realism," for instance, see Philip Charrier's essay on Nakahira's *Why an Illustrated Botanical Dictionary?* Charrier traces an illuminating speculative genealogy across what he

claims are traces of the decisive influence of Jean-Paul Sarte's existentialism and earlier Japanese photographic realist discourses in Nakahira's desire to restore the "clarity" of the photographic subject. Philip Charrier, "Nakahira Takuma's 'Why an Illustrated Botanical Dictionary?' (1973) and the quest for 'true' photographic realism in post-war Japan," in *Japan Forum*, 2017.

12. Nakahira Takuma, *Naze shokubutsu zukan ka*, 20.

13. There is a resonance with Guy Debord's critiques in *The Society of the Spectacle*, where he noted, "The spectacle erases the dividing line between the self and world, in that the self, under siege by the presence/absence of the world, is eventually overwhelmed; it likewise erases the dividing line between true and false, repressing all directly lived truth beneath the real presence of the falsehood maintained by the organization of appearances." Guy Debord, *The Society of the Spectacle*, trans. Donald Nicholson-Smith (New York: Zone, 1994), 153. Yuriko Furuhata has noted the affinities between Nakahira and Debord in the introduction to *Cinema of Actuality: Japanese Avant-Garde Filmmaking in the Season of Image Politics* (Durham, N.C.: Duke University Press, 2013), 8.

14. Nakahira Takuma, *Naze shokubutsu zukan ka*, 24–25.

15. Nakahira Takuma, *Naze shokubutsu zukan ka*, 27–28.

16. Nakahira Takuma, *Naze shokubutsu zukan ka*, 31–32.

17. It is important to recall the rather obvious fact that even for those at the time, a coherent totalized reading of the changes at hand was just as inaccessible to them as it is a reading of our own present to us.

18. Matsuda Masao, *Fukanōsei no media* (Tokyo: Tabata Shoten, 1973), Adachi Masao, *Eiga e no senryaku* (Tokyo: Shōbunsha, 1974), Tsumura Takashi, *Media no seiji* (Shōbunsha, 1974), Miyauchi Kō, *Fūkei o ute: daigaku 1970–75 Miyauchi Kō Kenchiku ronshū* (Tokyo: Sagami shobō, 1976).

19. For a rich account of the shifting contours of the radical left's criticism of media in the struggle against capitalist state power, see Miryam Sas's essay, "The Culture Industries and Media Theory In Japan," in *Media Theory in Japan*, ed. Marc Steinberg and Alexander Zahten (Durham, N.C.: Duke University Press, 2017).

20. Setsu Shigematsu's history of women's liberation in Japan illuminates the profoundly fraught dimensions of given narratives of the Red Army incident: "The URA's [United Red Army] use of violence in the name of the revolution has been regarded as a disturbing and tragic event that marked the downfall of the Japanese New Left. To this day, the causes, residues, and scars of this self-destructive phenomenon have haunted many of those involved in the political movements of that era." Shigematsu moreover explores the intensely gendered dimensions of how the "event" was monumentalized in the chapter "*Ribu's* Response to the United Red Army: Feminist Ethics and the Politics of Violence," in *Scream from the Shadows: the Women's Liberation Movement in Japan*

(Minneapolis: University of Minnesota Press, 2012), 139. For another fascinating account of the gender-encoded narratives of the "end" of the New Left, see Chelsea Schieder's work on the evolutions of the figures of the leftist female activists in Japan and in particular, " 'Gewalt Rosa': The creation of the terrifying, titillating female student activist," in "Coed Revolution: The Female Student in the Japanese New Left, 1957–1972" (PhD diss., Columbia University, 2014). For more general accounts of the "afterlives" of the 1972 event, see Patricia G. Steinhoff's article, "Memories of New Left Protest," *Contemporary Japan* 2013; 25(2): 127–165, and Yoshikuni Igarashi's "Dead Bodies and Living Guns: The United Red Army and its Deadly Pursuit of Revolution, 1971–1972," *Japanese Studies* 27, 2 (September 2007): 119–137.

21. Shigematsu has detailed the entangled genealogies of Zenkyōtō and *uman ribu* movements in the early 1970s, noting how the everyday (*nichijōsei*) as the localized loci of the reproduction of power was interrogated by the women's liberation movement, seeking "to question the common sense of daily living and the way one's subjectivity and political consciousness were constituted by one's daily existence." *Scream from the Shadows: the Women's Liberation Movement in Japan* (Minneapolis: University of Minnesota Press, 2012), 46.

22. This work gained attention due to a series of publications and exhibitions, commencing with the 2012 Osiris book *Circulation: Date, Place, Events*, the exhibition of selected prints in 2012 and 2013 gallery shows and the 2015 exhibition *For a New World to Come*, curated by Yasufumi Nakamori at the Museum of Modern Art, Houston. In 2017, the Art Institute of Chicago exhibition, "Takuma Nakahira: Circulation," produced a "recreation" of one instance of *Circulation*, as curated by Matthew S. Witkovsky. This exhibition undertook an "archeological" effort to recreate one instance of the full installation. It was based on thorough research of the available records and installation views of the 1971 exhibition in Paris, and included new prints from the negatives to assemble a selected instance of the installation. The differences among these "versions" suggest the manifold and open-ended potential of the original installation, drawing our attention to the wholly *other* understanding of photography it offers. Thus, even as the specificities and differences of each version do matter, in its diverse "afterlives," Nakahira's *Circulation* continues to offer a novel understanding of photography.

23. The essay was first published as "Morocco, a picture postcard landscape" ("Morokko, ehagaki no fūkei"), accompanied by both color and monochrome photographs in the journal *Graphication* (December 1971). It was included in *Why an Illustrated Botanical Dictionary?* as "Returning from Africa" ("Afurika kara kaeru").

24. "Photography, A Single Day's Actuality," "The Exhaustion of Contemporary Art," and "Returning from Africa," in *Takuma Nakahira Circulation: Date, Place, Events* (Tokyo: Osiris Co., Ltd., 2012).

25. Although Nakahira did not travel to Paris with any complete installation plans, he did appear to have conceived of the expanding format prior to his arrival. Unfortunately, due to a shortage of money due to unexpected costs of commuting to the exhibition space by taxi during a transport strike, as well as the other challenges he encountered in both the developing stage and exhibiting stage of the process, the installation was ceased by Nakahira prior to reaching its intended scale. "Nakahira Takuma: sentō-tekina peshimisuto," in the column "Intabiyū hyōron: gendai no shashin sakka," *Asahi Camera* (August 1972): 156–159.

26. "The Exhaustion of Contemporary Art," originally published in *Asahi Journal* (December 10, 1971), and collected in *Why an Illustrated Botanical Dictionary?*, 88.

27. Nakahira's methodology bears an orientation like that of the cinematic mode of remediation identified by Yuriko Furuhata as a crucial dimension of the "cinema of actuality" of the late 1960s to early 1970s, exemplified by filmmakers such as Wakamatsu Kōji, Ōshima Nagisa, and Adachi Masao. Noting the difference between cinematic and journalistic temporality, Furuhata argues that this mode of remediation "halts the flow of the journalistic economy, reorients its direction, and commands critical attention from the spectator as it plays up the temporal gap between these two modes of image consumption and circulation." Furuhata, "Remediating Journalism: Politics and the Media Event," *Cinema of Actuality*, 109. Whereas the remediations Furuhata describes were situated in a self-reflexive interval between cinematic and journalistic visual regimes, Nakahira's installation forged a similar mode of traversal by self-reflexively transporting the deluge of everyday flows that constitute the everyday urban and media environments into the non-everyday domain of the international art exhibition.

28. For a fascinating discussion of *Circulation* and the role it played within the longer evolutions of Nakahira's work that continued until around 2011, see Yasumi Akihito's essay, "Optical Remnants: Paris, 1971, Takuma Nakahira," in *Circulation: Date, Place, Events*.

29. I have traced the connective role played by the installation in the essay, "On *For a Language to Come, Circulation*, and *Overflow*: Takuma Nakahira and the Horizons of Radical Media Criticism in the Early 1970s," in *For a New World to Come: Experiments in Art and Photography in Japan, 1968–1979* (Houston, Tex.: Museum of Fine Arts, 2015). Kuraishi Shino was the first to introduce the *Overflow* exhibition in his overview essay, "Outline and Structure of 'Nakahira Takuma: Degree Zero—Yokohama,'" in *Nakahira Takuma: genten fukki—Yokohama = Nakahira Takuma: Degree Zero—Yokohama* (Tokyo: Osiris, 2003), 130–136.

30. Next to the words "New Yorker," we see the phrase "aru saro," an abbreviation of the term "arubaito saron," a kind of hostess cabaret that employed part-time female performers. At the edge of the nude sign we can make out the words of a sign affixed to a pole that reads, "Minato-ward Crime-Safety Light" ("Minato-ku

Bōhandon"). Another photograph of what appears to be the same location with a different hand-painted sign based on the appearance of the same pole signage was published in a series entitled, "Illustrated Natural History Dictionary: The City" ("Hakubutsu Zukan: Toshi"), *Kamera Mainichi* (August 1972), the month prior to the "New Yorker" photograph that was published in the installment, "City-Landscape" ("Toshi-Fūkei"), *Asahi Journal* (September, 29, 1972).

31. Two photographs of *Overflow* in fact first appeared in "Atami," in the March 1969 issue of *Asahi Camera*, the first published examples of Nakahira's use of color photography.

32. The *Asahi Journal* series continued with "An Illustrated Natural History Dictionary" ("Hakubutsu Zukan"); "City" ("Toshi") parts one, two, and three; "Home" ("Ie"); "TV" ("Terebi"); and "City-Landscape" ("Toshi-Fūkei"). The color urban series then continued with the twelve color images from the 1974 covers of the magazine *Modern Architecture* (*Kindai Kenchiku*) and the 1975 *Asahi Camera* series "Urban Traps-Urban Shades," ("Toshi-Kansei, Urban Shades"). For a concise description tracing the contours of this urban trajectory see Kuraishi's "Outline and Structure of 'Nakahira Takuma: Degree Zero—Yokohama,'" in *Nakahira Takuma: genten fukki—Yokohama = Nakahira Takuma: Degree Zero—Yokohama* (Tokyo: Osiris, 2003), 130–136.

33. That is to say, these dynamic explorations of urban forms cannot be separated from the increasing amount of media criticism Nakahira produced during this period—these were in a perpetually interrogative relationship, questioning each other while differentially materializing diverse dimensions of the transformed conditions he was confronting. While I focus here more directly upon the urban photography of this period, my approach to these works is informed by Nakahira's media critiques, and as we shall see these converge in very concrete and significant ways around 1973 and after in the subsequent chapter.

34. "Shokubutsu Zukan," *Asahi Journal* (August 20, 27, 1971).

35. "Toshi III," *Asahi Journal* (March 17,1972).

36. "Toshi II," *Asahi Journal* (Feb, 11, 1972).

37. Here the city is itself shown to be a privileged term within a fossilized and codified language, which like "history," no longer corresponds to the new scales of contradictions and asymmetries of urbanized social space. Thus, it is clear that his attempt to dismantle the homogenous landscape into interrelated fragments is in fact an intensification, not the abandonment, of Nakahira's earlier pursuit of an "irruptive discourse." Furthermore, it demonstrates that the historical process through which even critical language became fossilized is an important element of the processes of capitalist urbanization through which this landscape was articulated.

38. "Toshi no kansei," *Asahi Journal* (November 17, 1972). This phrase "healthy city" alerts us to the increasing dominance of an urban planning discourse during this

period that is tightly bound up with development priorities of the state seeking to contain the ever-intensifying expanse of contradictions and costs of growth.

39. *Asahi Journal* played an important role in this moment as a platform for photographers such as Nakahira, Moriyama Daidō, and Fukase Masahisa (1934–2012), as well as works of manga such as Sasaki Maki's experimental manga and Akasegawa Genpei's *Sakura Gaho* series. Ryan Holmberg has explored Sasaki's *Asahi Journal* work in the fascinating essay, "Hear no, speak no: Sasaki Maki manga and *nansensu*, circa 1970," *Japan Forum* 21,1 (2009): 115–141. Such print publications serve as a reminder that the valuation of photography as "art" objects has developed on the continued disavowal of the different domains traversed by the circulation of photographic images. As we saw in the last chapter, *Asahi Journal* was one among many journals Nakahira continued to publish for, and print journals remained the primary platform for both his photography and writings throughout the late 1960s and early 1970s.

40. "Why Jazz Now? Preface to a Theory of Place" ("Nani o imasara jazu nanoka: ba-ron josetsu"), collected in *Naze shokubutsu zukan ka?* 2007, 215–216.

41. Along with the so-called Nixon Shock (which, in the Japanese context, indexes both the resumption of diplomatic ties with the People's Republic of China, and the move away from the gold standard), the first "oil shock" had a decisive impact on the restructuring of the Japanese political economy in the 1970s. The language monumentalizing such events betrays an understanding of the geopolitical as a closed system of thermodynamic forces seeking equilibrium. However, while a historical understanding of the Cold War as a totality consisting of devastating military conflicts, catastrophic ecological depletions, and political economic plundering has yet to emerge, it should suffice to suggest that the terminology of "equilibrium," "shocks," and "pressures," is entirely insufficient.

42. As Shigematsu importantly points out, the desire for "encounter" was not merely aesthetic, but increasingly figured in the women's liberation movement's efforts to interrogate the everyday where the conditions of possibility for other relations among selves, other, and material things were increasingly depleted: "The *ribu* movement did not aim to eliminate, injure, or annihilate the other but rather to create different conditions for the encounter with the other. The point of liberation was to create better conditions that would enable the self to encounter the other more freely." *Scream from the Shadows: the Women's Liberation Movement in Japan*, 61.

43. Yuko Fujii "Kōji Taki: A Theorist-Photographer," *For a New World to Come: Experiments in Art and Photography in Japan, 1968–1979*, 92.

44. Kuraishi Shino touches upon the collaborative nature of Taki's series in his overview essay "Outline and Structure of 'Nakahira Takuma: Degree Zero-Yokohama,'" in *Nakahira Takuma: genten fukki*. According to this volume's

meticulous bibliography compiled by Ishizuka Masahito, "The City" series included seventeen installments that included Nakahira's black and white photographs. While in many cases these appear to be unpublished photographs, there are many examples of incorporating previously published photographs as well in the series. In addition to collaborating on Taki's *Asahi Journal* series, Nakahira would participate in a number of published dialogues and roundtables with Isozaki and Kimura between 1973 and 1975. Moreover, Yasumi Akihito and Kuraishi discuss Nakahira's work with these figures in an invaluable dialogue, which offers a concise introduction to the depth and breadth of Nakahira's work, found in the volume of critical essays and reprinted primary sources, *Nakahira Takuma: Kitarubeki shashinka* (Tokyo: Kawade Shoboshinsha, 2009), 2–31. They furthermore note how this interdisciplinary consideration of urban form presaged the explosion of interest in urban theories and discourses in the 1980s amidst the massive real estate speculation-fueled "bubble" economy.

45. *Asahi Journal* (March 15, 1974). The final installment features Nakahira's first photograph, the ominous expanse of the *danchi* housing development from 1964.

46. A comprehensive study of Taki Kōji's later work is beyond the scope of this chapter. Useful surveys of Taki's broad-ranging work and a comprehensive bibliography can be found in *Taki Kōji to kenchiku*, edited and published by Nagashima Akio, 2013.

47. "Anākisuto wa kenchikuka ni narieruka," *Kindai kenchiku* (June 1974). For this special issue on the topic of the Marunouchi district adjacent to the imperial palace, Nakahira also contributed photographs of diverse modern Japanese architectural "masterpieces" of the Marunouchi area. While formally these photographs could be described as standard architectural photography, in light of this critical essay, it is unclear how they would contribute to the actually existing practice of architecture.

48. "Anākisuto wa kenchikuka ni narieruka."

49. "Anākisuto wa kenchikuka ni narieruka."

50. This essay also affords a useful insight into Nakahira's own relationship to the notion of landscape and subsequent shift away from this term: "To digress a bit, two or three years ago I often spoke about the so-called 'theories of landscape.' I played only a small part in this but if I made another attempt to interpret this it would be like this. The 'landscape' that wraps the outer surface of the contemporary city smoothly and beautifully spreads out uniformly. The dualism of relating the city against the village found in this is in fact merely a formal category of superficial relations, for what we call the village, the 'frontiers,' the 'native,' these are just the reverse side of the pretext that has been penetrated by the logic of monopoly capital. The parts that are called 'pre-modern' surely can only exist

as forms that must support monopoly capital today. The problem is where to and how to shred this 'landscape' into pieces made impermeable by its uniform beauty. Adachi and Matsuda have formulated this 'theory of landscape' through the making of their incomplete film 'AKA Serial Killer' [. . .] despite lacking as clear a theory as them, I have affirmed my own 'theory of landscape' through the camera's finder. Talking about their 'theories of landscape' again now may be meaningless. They have entered into their practice with their knowledge of the 'landscape.' I too have started crossing into my own mode of practice at last." "Anākisuto wa kenchikuka ni narieruka."

51. "Anākisuto wa kenchikuka ni narieruka."

52. "Anākisuto wa kenchikuka ni narieruka."

53. Although he does not introduce this term here, as we have already seen, the "illustrated dictionary" outlined in *Why an Illustrated Botanical Dictionary?* as well as the *Asahi Journal* installments modeled a self-reflexive approach that sought an embedded locus of inquiry that confronted its own discursive location within the larger totality of social relations of production.

54. It is interesting to note how many of the same projects and problems continue to sustain ongoing efforts at "reconstruction," which has come to be the principal activity of governance in Japan today, despite (or because of) the impossibilities to "recovery" exposed by the magnitude of the Fukushima Dai-ichi reactor meltdown disaster.

55. The images appeared in two different review essays, one at the time of the exhibition, and one a few months later. The editors of *Asahi Camera* covered the exhibition in a somewhat critical review essay entitled, "Eight Years Later, a 'Photographers Today' Exhibition: 'Fifteen Photographers' at the National Museum of Modern Art" ("Hachinen buri no 'kyō no shashinka': Kokuritsu Kindai Bijutsukan• 'jūgonin no shashinka"), *Asahi Camera* (September 1974): 74–79. And later, Ōshima Hiroshi's survey, "Photography Exhibition as Media" ("Medeia toshite no shashinten"), *Asahi Camera Zōkan kindai shashin no shūen gendai no shahin '75* (April 1975).

56. Many of these same portraits were an important part of the screenings of the Ogawa Productions documentary film *Sanrizuka-Heta Village*, one of the most compelling of the Sanrizuka films the cooperative produced in wake of the bitter struggle over the building of the Narita Airport. *Forest of Pressure: Ogawa Shinsuke and Postwar Japanese Documentary*, Abé Mark Nornes's exhaustive study of Ogawa includes many images of both Naitō's photography and Kitai Kazuo's work, another participant in the 1974 exhibition. Marilyn Ivy has explored the allegorized aporia of Japanese modernity encountered in Naitō's work in the groundbreaking chapter, "Dark Enlightenment: Naitō Masatoshi's Flash," in *Photographies East: The Camera and its Histories in East and Southeast Asia*, ed. Rosalind C. Morris (Durham, N.C.: Duke University Press, 2009), 229–257.

57. Takanashi Yutaka's work was published in his self-published photobook *Toshi e* (Tokyo: Izara Shobō, 1974), the same year it appeared in this exhibition. *Toshi e* has typically been translated into English as "Towards the City," but as the original English title given in the 1974 exhibition demonstrates, it can be rendered in the plural as "To the Cities." As the exhibition catalogue acknowledged, Taki Kōji also played a role in the selection of photographers who participated in the exhibition. In many ways the exhibition can be read as the formalization of photography's status as an art object, and in particular the institutionalization of *Provoke*'s interventions into the practice of photography. As such, the exhibition itself revealed many of the problems that Nakahira had been actively criticizing in his writings at the time, and thereafter. This, in part, may offer a clue regarding his silence regarding *Overflow* and his decision to destroy much of his own negatives, prints, and notes around this time. One glaring limitation of the exhibition is indexed in the contradictions between the title "Fifteen Photographers Today," a title that is not inflected by gender or nationality, and the resultant selection of fifteen male Japanese photographers. That the given of frames of reference for photography remains nationalized and gendered in this manner even today is one of the most compelling problems facing historiographies of photography.

58. While outside the historical and geographical frame of Nakahira's installation, it is significant that *Overflow* resonates with contemporary discourses of new materialism in many interesting ways. Jane Bennett's description of the vitality of matter comes to mind here and opens another possible line of inquiry into the question of "reading" the residual materialities we encounter in *Overflow*: "All forces and flows (materialities) are or can become lively, affective, and signaling. And so an affective, speaking, human body is not *radically* different from the affective, signaling nonhumans with which it coexists, hosts, enjoys, serves, consumes, produces, and competes." Jane Bennett, *Vibrant Matter: A Political Ecology of Things* (Durham, N.C.: Duke University Press, 2010), 117.

59. In a question-and-answer exchange after a talk given at one of Tōmatsu Shōmei's Workshop events, Nakahira touches briefly upon *Overflow*, describing it as a "strategic failure" ("senjutsu daun"), compared to *Circulation*. Nakahira, "Photography is deception!!" ("Shashin wa sajutsuda!!"), *Workshop* 2 (December 1974): 14.

60. While the image of a fin de siècle photographer does not immediately lend itself to a radically transformed critical inquiry into urban and media environments, Eugène Atget's role in repeatedly reshaping our understanding of photography and its social dimensions cannot be overstated. From his influence on the surrealist movement to the pivotal role Atget plays in Walter Benjamin's well-known essay, "The Work of Art in the Age of Its Mechanical Reproducibility," his work

continues to inspire awakenings to the vast capacities of photography as a critical medium. For a critical examination of Atget's works see, Molly Nesbit, *Atget's Seven Albums* (New Haven, Conn.: Yale University Press, 1992).

61. First published as "Eugène Atget: Toshi e no shisen aruiwa toshi kara no shisen," *Asahi Camera* (November 1973). It was later included in the book coauthored by Nakahira Takuma and Shinoyama Kishin, *Ketto shashin-ron* ("Duel on Photography") (Tokyo: Asahi Shimbunsha, 1977), with minor revisions by the author. My original translation, based upon the version appearing in *Ketto shashin-ron*, was published as "Eugène Atget: Looking at the City or, the Look from the City" in the 2010 republication of *For a Language to Come*. A French translation of this essay was included in a collection of writings about Atget that included essays by writers, photographers, and curators that have shaped the reception of Atget, *Les silences d'Atget: Une anthologie de textes*, ed. Luce Lebart (Paris: Textuel, 2016). Within the context of the reception of Atget's work in Japan, Nakahira's essay was notable for the way it challenged the myth of Atget the artist, and engaged with the form of mediation found in his work. Ōshima Hiroshi's meticulous study *Atget's Paris, Aje no Pari* (Tokyo: Misuzu shobo, 1998), represents an exceptionally rich engagement with Atget's work.

62. This is made stunningly clear in the opening chapters of Nesbit's, *Atget's Seven Albums*, as well as Shelley Rice's *Parisian Views* (Cambridge, Mass.: MIT Press, 1997). It is important to note that Nakahira's essay moreover produces a striking resonance between seemingly discrete historical moments, post-Commune France and post-1970 Japan (or post-Haussmann Paris and post-Olympics Tokyo on another historical register), in the development of a photographic media of critical knowledge of and about urban materiality. As moments that both immediately followed decisive, irreversible shifts in the transformative possibilities of political action as well as the urban social spaces from which they erupted, Nakahira's essay thus illuminated the profoundly *other* (other to the homogenized "sealed-up" space-time of the urbanized landscape materialized by Japan's Cold War urbanization) dimensions of seeing embedded between attraction and repulsion. While it would be reductive to conflate the differences of such disparate moments together, it is nonetheless instructive to consider ways in which such histories can be seen together as part of an incomplete whole. Much of the benefits of such an attempt are made clear in Kristin Ross's *Communal Luxury: The Political Imaginary of the Paris Commune* (London: Verso, 2016).

63. Nakahira Takuma, "Eugène Atget: Toshi e no shisen aruiwa toshi kara no shisen," *Asahi Camera* (November 1973).

64. Takuma, "Eugène Atget."

5. PHOTOGRAPHY AS THRESHOLD AND PATHWAY AFTER REVERSION

1. The recent contributions of a number of critics and scholars have greatly expanded the reception of Nakahira Takuma's work to rigorously engage with the postreversion relations among Okinawa, the mainland, and the islands in between. In Japanese see, Kuraishi Shino, "On the Border: Takuma Nakahira's Photography of the Amami and Tokara Islands" ("Kokkyō: Nakahira Takuma no Amami, Tokara no Shashin"), *Bungaku to Kankyō: The Journal of the Association for the Study of Literature and Environment in Japan* 18 (2015): 5–15; Yasumi Akihito, "Kaisetsu: Guntō, bohi, mujin: Nakahira Takuma 1974–1978," in *Nakahira Takuma: Okinawa, Amami, Tokara 1974–1978* (Tokyo: Miraisha, 2012). Nakazato Isao engages with Nakahira's Okinawan work in his book *Fotoneshia: me no kaikisen Okinawa* (Tokyo: Miraisha, 2009). Takara Ben, a poet, discusses Nakahira's journeys to Okinawa in *Okinawa seikatsu-shi* (Tokyo: Iwanami Shoten, 2005). Kohara Masashi examined the trajectories of Nakahira's Okinawa photography in the important essay, "To the Southern Islands/From the Southern Islands II" ("Nantō e/ Nantō kara, shita"), *10+1* 50 (2008): 39–43. In English, see the author's essay, "Takuma Nakahira and the Photographic Topographies of Possibility," in *Spaces of Possibility: Korea, Japan, In, Between, and Beyond the Nation*, ed. Andrea Arai and Clark W. Sorensen (Seattle: University of Washington Press, 2016), 273–289.

2. While many critics have variously described an "inward turn" and contracting forms of relation with the "outside" that accompanied the rise of a consumer culture following a decline in so-called politically engaged cultural practices, others have celebrated the diversification of platforms and participatory forms of cultural production in this period. For example, Karatani Kojin has described 1970 as a pivotal turning point, if not the end, of a particular discursive space that conditioned the production of literature in Japan. Noting the changes in the economic and geopolitical orders of the 1970s as the impetus for Japan's emergence as an economically powerful nation on the world stage, on the level of thought and discourse, Japan receded within its interiority. "Every kind of information from the outside had been transmitted and consumed, but the 'outside' did not exist." "The Discursive Space of Modern Japan," trans. Seiji Lippit, *boundary 2* 18, 3, Japan in the World (Autumn 1991), 218. It remains to be understood how we might grasp the geopolitical and aesthetic contours of these changes together with a critical understanding of how the concentrated urban and media ecologies informed such practices.

3. In Japanese, "reversion" is rendered by the terms *fukki* and *henkan*, suggesting the return, recovery, or restoration of something lost. However, the use of such

terms depends solely upon the bilateral United States–Japan military-economic framework, which has displaced Okinawa from the terms of Okinawa's reversion. A fascinating collection of recent writings from the so-called postreversion generation of Okinawan writers offers diverse critical perspectives commemorating forty years of reversion, *Tōsō suru kyōkai: Fukkigo sedai no Okinawa kara no hōkoku, Chinen Ushī* (Tokyo: Miraisha, 2012).

4. Nakahira, "My Naked Eye Reflex: 1974, Okinawa, Summer" ("Waga nikugan refure: 1974, Okinawa, natsu"), in *Mitsuzukeru hate ni hi ga . . .: Nakahira Takuma hihyō shūsei 1965–1977* (Tokyo: Osiris, 2007), 351–352.

5. Nakahira was critical of so-called social-justice photographers whom he considered to be merely using photography as a means of "illustrating" preexisting ideas. For instance, in the 1969 essay, "What is it to be Contemporary?," Nakahira questioned photographers who went to Okinawa not to photograph the actual specificities they as individuals would encounter there, but instead to photograph scenes that illustrated their stereotyped ideologies of U.S. imperialism and the unfortunate state of Okinawa under military rule. Nakahira decried such instrumental forms of photography, saying, "this is to not see Okinawa at all, but instead to see only the meaning of Okinawa." "Dōjidaiteki de aru to wa nani ka," in *Mitsuzukeru hate ni hi ga . . .*, 78.

6. *Nakahira Takuma: Okinawa, Amami, Tokara 1974–1978* (Tokyo: Miraisha, 2012).

7. Okinawa writer Takara Ben (b. 1949) has described what he perceives to be the definitive impact of Nakahira's visits to Okinawa on all of his subsequent photography, see "Waga Nakahira Takuma," in *Tamafuri: Ryūkyū bunka geijutsu-ron* (Tokyo: Miraisha, 2011), 181–188.

8. These events formed the basis for his 1972 essay, "The Documentary Illusion: From the Document to the Monument" ("Kiroku to iu gen'ei: dokyumento kara monyumento e"), which demonstrated how the police had increasingly utilized media spectacles such as this one. This essay was originally published in *Bijutsu techō* (July 1972) and was included in the collection, *Naze shokubutsu zukan ka: Nakahira Takuma eizōron-shū* (Tokyo: Shōbunsha, 1973).

9. "Kiroku to iu gen'ei: dokyumento kara monyumento e," in *Naze shokubutsu zukan ka* (2007), 44.

10. Nakahira, "Photography is deception!!" ("Shashin wa sajutsuda!!"), *Workshop 2* (December 1974).

11. "Kiroku to iu gen'ei: dokyumento kara monyumento e," in *Naze shokubutsu zukan ka* (2007), 42. The essay makes lengthy engagements with Walter Benjamin's writings, which were translated into Japanese from the late 1960s.

12. "Kiroku to iu gen'ei: dokyumento kara monyumento e," 51–52.

13. For a discussion of the architectural projects of Ocean Expo '75, see Vivian Blaxell, "Preparing Okinawa for Reversion to Japan: The Okinawa International

Ocean Exposition of 1975, the US Military and the Construction State," *The Asia-Pacific Journal* 29, 2, 10 (July 19, 2010).

14. "Okinawa-wasurerareyuku kichi no sonzai," *Asahi jānaru* (July 12, 1974): 76–77.

15. "Okinawa-wasurerareyuku kichi no sonzai," 77.

16. The original terms, "Ooraka rando" and "jetto rakuraku ukiuki tabiji," are suggestive of an earlier moment in Okinawa's codification within the domestic air tourism economy. It not only preceded the tropicalization of Okinawa as Japan's Hawai'i, here being associated with Kyushu instead, it also reflected the novelty of domestic air travel developing at the time. Japanese sociologist Tada Osamu has charted the production of Okinawa's tropical imagery as a popular tourist destination after reversion. See his book-length study, *Okinawa imēji no tanjō: Aoi umi no karuchuraru sutadīzu* (Tokyo: Tōyō Keizai Shinpōsha, 2004), for a critical exploration of the reconstruction of the Okinawan landscape as well as its cultural encodings. In English, Tada provides a brief look at Hawai'i's role as a model for Okinawa in the essay, "Constructing Okinawa as Japan's Hawai'i: From Honeymoon Boom to Resort Paradise," *Japanese Studies* 35, 3 (2015): 287–302. Historian Gerald Figal has fully elaborated the history of Okinawa's remaking through military and tourism visions in the book, *Beachheads: War, Peace, and Tourism in Postwar Okinawa* (Lanham, Md.: Rowman and Littlefield, 2012).

17. A precedent for this reportage approach, with a number of crucial differences, can be found in Nakahira's mentor Tōmatsu Shōmei's photobook, *Okinawa Photobook: It's not that there are bases in Okinawa but that Okinawa is in the bases* (*Okinawa Shashinshū: Okinawa ni kichi ga aru no dewa naku kichi no naka ni Okinawa ga aru)* (Tokyo: Shaken, 1969).

18. Nakahira Takuma, "Poverty on Display" ("Chinretsu sareru hinkon"), *Asahi jānaru* (May 3, 1974): 78–80.

19. Nakahira Takuma, "The outflowing of the young workforce" ("Ryūshutsu suru wakai rōdōryoku"), *Asahi jānaru* (May 10, 1974): 74–77.

20. Nakahira Takuma, "My Naked Eye Reflex: 1974, Okinawa, Summer" ("Waga nikugan refure: 1974, Okinawa, natsu"), in *Mitsuzukeru hate ni hi ga . . .*, 352.

21. It bears mentioning that in addition to Walter Benjamin's writings on photography and Hans Magnus Enzensberger's *The Consciousness Industry*, the writings of Frantz Fanon played a crucial role in Nakahira's thinking at this time. The possession of language indexed here clearly derives from Fanon as similar points of reference can be found in Nakahira's earlier essay, "Documentary Illusion," as well as the "Poverty on Display" *Asahi Journal* installment touched upon above.

22. As Okinawan poet Takara Ben has described, the nature of Nakahira's changing photographic praxis after his travels to Okinawa was as a kind of perpetual escape from such contradictions. "The Nakahira who shot city night scenes had

gone. Perhaps he was intending to escape from both Japan and the self." Takara Ben, *Okinawa seikatsushi* (Tokyo: Iwanami Shoten, 2005), 120–121.

23. "Amami: nami to haka to hana, soshite taiyō," *Asahi Camera* (February 1976).

24. "Amami: nami to haka to hana, soshite taiyō," *Asahi Camera* (February 1976).

25. "Amami: nami to haka to hana, soshite taiyō," *Asahi Camera* (February 1976). Although his assertion of a multiethnic Japan sounds fairly commonplace now, the inception of this project came at the historical juncture between the resurgent journalistic discourses of a unique, ahistorical, homogeneous Japanese-ness or Nihonjin-ron, and the emergent contours of neoliberal globalization and Japan's readvancement into East and Southeast Asia as a regional economic "superpower," as discussed by Karatani Kōjin in "The Discursive Space of Modern Japan."

26. Philip Gabriel's critical introduction to Shimao Toshio's vast body of fiction and nonfiction work importantly notes the integral role the notion of "Yaponesia" played in questioning Okinawa's reversion, both before and after it was carried out. Thus, it is no accident that Nakahira's interest in Amami was piqued by Shimao's writings. Nakahira was clearly situating his Amami series as participating, however from a different approach and later historical moment, in the debates that once surrounded reversion, perhaps seeking to imaginatively rekindle a much-needed questioning which, as his earlier reportage demonstrated, was tapering off in the embrace of the postreversion landscape as natural and given from those on the left. See J. Philip Gabriel, *Mad Wives and Island Dreams: Shimao Toshio and the Margins of Japanese Literature* (Honolulu: University of Hawai'i Press, 1999). Kuroda Kio (1926–1984) was an important poet activist whose work can be explored in such collections as *Shi to han shi: Kuroda Kio zen shishū zen hyōronshū* (Tokyo: Keisō Shobō, 1968), *Fusei to dakkai: Kuroda Kio hyōronshū* (Tokyo: San'ichi Shobō, 1972), *Higan to shutai* (Tokyo: Kawade Shobō Shinsha, 1972), *Shizen to kōi: hyōron, taidan-shū* (Tokyo: Shichōsha,1977), and *Hitori no kanata e* (Tokyo: Kokubunsha, 1979).

27. The breadth of the contributions to a 1978 special issue of the journal *Kaie: atarashii bungaku no techō* devoted to Shimao attests to the diversity of scholarly and intellectual contexts to which his work spoke. Of particular interest are the inclusion of major Okinawan writers Ōshiro Tatsuhiro (b. 1925) with thinkers such as Arakawa Akira (b. 1931), Okamoto Keitoku (1934–2006), and Kawamitsu Shin'ichi (b. 1932), who often clashed over the import of Shimao's notion of Yaponesia for a critical appraisal of reversion. *Kaie: atarashii bungaku no techō* (Tokyo: Tōjusha, 1978). For a discussion of the antireversion critiques of Arakawa and Kawamitsu, see Shinjō Ikuo, "Hanfukki hankokka-ron no kaiki," *Sengo Nihon sutadīzu 2: 60–70 nendai*, ed. Narita Komori et al. (Tokyo: Kinokuniya shoten, 2009). In English, see Michael Molasky, "Arakawa Akira: The Thought and Poetry

of an Iconoclast," in *Japan and Okinawa: Structure and Subjectivity*, eds. Glen Hook and Richard Siddle (London: Routledge, 2003), and Miyume Tanji, *Myth, Protest and Struggle in Okinawa* (London: Routledge, 2006), 97–98. However, as Davinder Bhowmik points out, "*Theory of Yaponesia* is a travel narrative that recycles old stereotypes rather than denaturalizing them. Shimao's repetition of hackneyed ideas such as the gentleness of island culture, the outward kindness and inward volatility of islanders, and the slowed-down time of the islands conceals the multifaceted reality of the Ryukyus." Bhowmik, "Colonial Desire and Ambiguity in Shimao Toshio's Theory of Yaponesia," in *Writing Okinawa: Narrative Acts of Identity and Resistance* (London: Routledge, 2008).

28. Kuraishi Shino, "On the Border: Takuma Nakahira's Photography of the Amami and Tokara Islands" ("Kokkyō: Nakahira Takuma no Amami, Tokara no Shashin").

29. Tōmatsu Shōmei, *Taiyō no enpitsu: Okinawa umi to sora to shima to hito, soshite Tōnan Ajia e* (Tokyo: Camera Mainichi, 1975). This work had been first serialized in the pages of diverse photographic periodicals from 1973 to 1975. While Nakahira and Tōmatsu's relationship was close, it is clear that Nakahira's postreversion work is in many ways a dynamic critique of the assumptions behind the ethnographic gaze exhibited by Tōmatsu. Kohara Masashi has posed a useful contrast between Tōmatsu and Nakahira's Okinawa photography in "Tōmatsu Shōmei to Nakahira Takuma no Okinawa," *Saizō* (February–April, 2017). Jonathan Reynolds has richly explored the Okinawa work of Tōmatsu in *Allegories of Time and Space: Japanese Identity in Photography and Architecture* (Honolulu: University of Hawai'i Press, 2015). Tōmatsu's monumental photobook was republished in an expanded and revised form as *Shinpen taiyo no enpitsu* (Kyoto: Akakasha, 2015), with important new essays by Itō Toshiharu and Imafuku Ryūta.

30. Kohara Masashi has also examined the ethnographic aspects of this work in "To the Southern Islands/From the Southern Islands I" ("Nantō e/ nantō kara, ue"), *10+1* 49 (2007): 63–65. Kunio Yanagita's *Kaijō no michi*, and Taro Okamoto's *Okinawa Bunkaron: wasurerareta Nihon* are indexed in many ways throughout Tōmatsu's ethnographic photographs and writings that accompanied them. The larger history of modernist aesthetics and colonial desire, although beyond the scope of the current chapter, is clearly an important component at play here.

31. "Amami: nami to haka to hana, soshite taiyō."

32. In fact, Nakahira's travels to the Amami Islands would seem to have preceded the main wave of the production of ethnographic knowledge about these islands. For an English-language survey of the development of Amami Studies, see Kuwahara Sueo's "Research Issues in the Culture and Society of the Amami Islands," in *The Islands of Kagoshima*, ed. Kei Kawai, Ryuta Terada, and Sueo Kuwahara (Kagoshima University Research Center for the Pacific Islands, 2013).

33. The role of photography in constituting colonial power and the corresponding disciplinary formations within the production of knowledge has been a rich area of critical inquiry. In the context of East Asia see Rosalind C. Morris's introductory essay in *Photographies East: The Camera and its Histories in East and Southeast Asia*, ed. Rosalind C. Morris (Durham, N.C.: Duke University Press, 2009), 1–28, for a useful discussion of stakes of such an inquiry. For a vivid portrait of the codetermination of colonial and photographic histories more broadly, see Zahid Chaudhary's *Afterimage of Empire: Photography in Nineteenth-Century India* (Minneapolis: University of Minnesota Press, 2012).

34. The resonances between Nakahira's and Shimao's work should not obscure key differences and deeper similarities between them. Beyond the obvious difference in context, medium, and scope of each engagement with this intermediary zone, their shared emphasis on the gaze, exhausting of the gaze, and overcoming the relations regulated by the seeing subject's autonomous induction into a dominated or closed circuit of meaning is notable. The religious overtones of Shimao's hallucinatory visuality however make for a stark contrast with the perpetual dispelling of religiosity found in all of Nakahira's work.

35. Kuraishi further locates the origins of the "illustrated dictionary" form that would characterize Nakahira's photography since the early 2000s with the Amami text, in "Kokkyō: Nakahira Takuma no Amami, Tokara no Shashin," 12.

36. As discussed in the previous chapters, not only has the partial reception of Nakahira's work overwhelmingly focused on the black and white photography that served as the material of *For a Language to Come*, Nakahira's own narrative of entering a "slump" thereafter described his changed attitudes toward the prospects of a critical photographic praxis, much of which informed *Why an Illustrated Botanical Dictionary?*. In this way, we might then add to this periodization an important point of inflection around 1975, which informed the thresholds explored in his travels to Amami as well as the critical developments of novel ways of seeing modeled in his writings of 1976–1977.

37. In addition to the contributions outlined in this chapter, Nakahira published the photographic piece "Urban Shades-Urban Pitfalls" ("Toshi-Kansei") (January 1975), four additional essays, and actively participated in roundtable discussions on photography. In this sense, we can regard *Asahi Camera* as a crucial platform for the development of Nakahira's work at this time. At the same time, Nakahira continued to publish his writings and photography in a wide range of print media, including notable contributions to such venues as *Playboy Japan* and *Contemporary Poetry Notebook* (*Gendaishi techō*), including a series of cover photographs for the lesser known *Nishi igaku* from 1976–1978.

38. Suzuki Shirōyasu's work has received little scholarly attention, but he remains an influential visual artist and poet. Suzuki's work often contained the phrase

"extremely private" ("Kyukushiteki"), as found in the title of his essay collection, "Extremely Private Contemporary Poetry, an Introduction," in *Kyokushiteki gendaishi nyūmon* (Tokyo: Shichōsha, 1975). Starting in the mid-1970s, Suzuki's "private films," along with the work of documentary filmmaker Hara Kazuo, according to Abé Mark Nornes, heralded "a new direction, a path Japanese documentary has followed to the present day. Hara Kazuo and Suzuki Shirōyasu are the pioneers of what has come to be called private film (*puraibeto firumu*) in Japan, a new production mode based on the solitary work of a singular filmmaking subject." "The Postwar Documentary Trace: Groping in the Dark," *positions: east asia cultures critique* 10, 1 (Spring 2002): 63. Nakahira would discuss the resonance of Suzuki's notion of the "extremely private" with his own way of seeing material things at the heart of a renewed photographic praxis in an essay published in the same issue of *Asahi Camera* as the Amami text, "The 'self' can only be materialized negatively" ("'Watashi' wa jōkyō o hikiukete koso naritatsu"), the second installment of the serialized collaboration with Shinoyama Kishin "Duel on Photography" ("Kettō shashin-ron"), *Asahi Camera* (February 1976), and was later collected in the 1977 volume *Kettō shashin-ron* (Tokyo: Asahi shinbun-sha, 1977).

39. The overlap of Nakahira and Taki Kōji's work into the mid-1970s continued in parallel collaborations with photographer Shinoyama Kishin, each contributing groundbreaking critical essays for two seminal works, *Ie: The Meaning of the House* (Tokyo: Ushio shuppansha, 1975), and *Kettō shashin-ron*.

40. We can detect notes of Michel Foucault's *Order of Things* here in modeling the discursivity of encyclopedic knowledge. The Japanese translation was published in 1974 as *Kotoba to mono: jinbun kagaku no kokogaku* (Tokyo: Shinchō-sha, 1974).

41. As with Taki's influential work on urban form and architecture, which we saw emerging from collaborations with Nakahira in the previous chapter, Taki would later develop this approach to the discursivity of the photographic text initiated here into major works of criticism, such as *Nūdo shashin* (Tokyo: Iwanami Shoten, 1992), and *Shōzō shashin: jidai no manazashi* (Tokyo: Iwanami Shoten, 2007).

42. First published in the May and June issues of *Asahi Camera*, collected in *Kettō shashin-ron*.

43. "Shisen no tsukiru hate," *Mitsuzukeru hate ni hi ga . . .,*" 412.

44. "Shisen no tsukiru hate," *Mitsuzukeru hate ni hi ga . . .,*" 418–419.

45. "Shisen no tsukiru hate," *Mitsuzukeru hate ni hi ga . . .,*" 428.

46. Moreover, it is important to note how Nakahira had previously used the term in the "Rebellion Against Landscape" essay, originally published with the title, "Fire at the limits of my perpetual gaze . . ." ("Mitsuzukeru hate ni hi ga . . ."). There it indexed the flames of an unnamed transformative force located at the limits of

a perpetual gaze, embedded within the landscape that confronted and engulfed the viewer, as discussed in chapter 3.

47. The essays that Nakahira contributed to the "Duel on Photography" series consistently traversed both contemporary and historical moments when seeing itself became a critical threshold in the workings of power.

48. In addition to the *Asahi Camera* installment discussed below, Nakahira's Tokara photographs appeared as "The Southern Limits of Yamato" ("Yamato nangen") in the March 1977 issue of the journal *Ryūdō*, as well as on the covers of the minor monthly health journal *Nishi igaku* from February 1977 to June 1977. Kuraishi Shino estimates that Nakahira took 570 color slide photographs and ten rolls of black and white photographs while traveling in the Tokara Islands, much more than what he photographed on Amami, "On the Border: Takuma Nakahira's Photography of the Amami and Tokara Islands," 9.

49. The results of these travels were published in the Japanese edition of *Playboy* magazine between July 1976 and May 1978, with Nakahira providing photographs for Nakagami Kenji's serialized fiction work, "The Streets!" ("Machi yo!"), later included in Nakagami's collected works without the accompanying photographs. *Nakagami Kenji zenshū* 8 (Tokyo: Shūeisha, 1996). Nakagami's collaborations with photographers would continue with Araki Nobuyoshi in *Monogatari Souru* (Tokyo: PARCO Shuppan, 1984), and Shinoyama Kishin in *Rinbusuru Souru* (Tokyo: Kadokawa Shoten, 1985). Anne McKnight provides a fascinating account of Nakagami's expanded geopolitical imaginary at play in his continued travels from the late 1970s into the 1980s in her chapter, "The 38th Parallax: Nakagami in/and Korea," in her monumental study *Nakagami, Japan: Buraku and the Writing of Ethnicity* (Minneapolis: University of Minnesota Press, 2011).

50. As Anne McKnight notes, South Korea, and the collaborations with photographers who traveled with him there, played a crucial role for Nakagami's expanded literary critique. "Between 1978 and 1985, Nakagami visited Korea seven times and traveled extensively from his base in Seoul. Korea would become one of the largest subjects in his oeuvre. Nakagami initially imagined Korea as an alternative to Japanese modernity but became disillusioned with the revival of nativist culture by leftist intellectuals because they abandoned its roots in outcast culture when they mobilized its cultural forms for antiauthoritarian protest. Although his initial expectations do not pan out, his interest is vindicated by the vitality of street life in Seoul and the new styles of writing and photography that he engages to capture Korea as a whole." "The 38th Parallax: Nakagami in/and Korea," in *Nakagami, Japan: Buraku and the Writing of Ethnicity*, 171.

51. Nakahira Takuma, "Kokkyo Tokara rettō: mujinka suru shimajima," *Asahi Camera* (March 1977). Tanigawa Gan's essay, "Death Watch Beneath the Palms" ("Birōjū no shita de no shi tokei") was first published in *Chūō Kōron*

(August, September, 1958), and collected in *Kosakusha sengen* (Tokyo: Chūō Kōron-sha, 1959).

52. Nakahira Takuma, "Kokkyo Tokara rettō: mujinka suru shimajima."

53. In Japanese, see Araki Yasutoshi, *Sākuru-mura no jiba: Ueno Hidenobu, Tanigawa Gan, Morisaki Kazue* (Fukuoka: Kaichōsha, 2011) for a detailed look at the rich activities of these writers.

54. In English, Brett de Bary has richly engaged with Morisaki's work in the essay, "Morisaki Kazue's 'Two Languages, Two Souls': Language, Communicability, and the National Subject," in *Deconstructing Nationality*, ed. Brett de Bary, Toshio Iyotani, Naoki Sakai (Ithaca, N.Y.: East Asia Program, Cornell University, 2005). For an introduction to Ishimure's work in English-language scholarship, see the fascinating collection of essays, *Ishimure Michiko's Writing in Ecocritical Perspective: Between Sea and Sky*, ed. Bruce Allen and Yuki Masami (Lanham, Md.: Lexington Books, 2016).

55. See the introduction by Iwasaki Minoru, "Tanigawa Gan to sengo seishin no senseiryoku," in *Tanigawa Gan serekushon: sengo shisō o yominaosu*, ed. Iwasaki Minoru and Yonetani Masafumi (Tokyo: Nihon Keizai Hyōronsha, 2009).

56. Wesley Sasaki-Uemura touches upon Tanigawa's legacy in his groundbreaking essay, "Tanigawa Gan's Politics of the Margin in Kyushu and Nagano" *positions: east asia cultures critique* 7, 1 (1999): 129–163. For the ways Tanigawa's revolutionary margins were a considerable influence on Nakagami, see a dialogue between Tanigawa and Nakagami that appears in a collection of Nakagami's interviews and roundtables, "Taishō kōdōtai to roji no ronri: mu no zōkei," in *Nakagami Kenji hatsugen shūsei, 2 taidan* (Tokyo: Daisan Bunmeisha, 1995). Moreover, Kawanaka Ikuo has explored the import of Tanigawa's writings for Nakagami in the volume, *Nakagami Kenji-ron, dai san kan: gensō no mura kara* (Tokyo: Choeisha, 2016). This decentered critique from the margins is thus engaged with what Seiji Lippit has described as the "double logic of minor spaces" in postwar literary discourse, which confronts the nation form as "an attempt to represent a space situated on the borderlines of national community that escapes this process of appropriation—that is, a space that evades the double structure of abjection and incorporation, both of which merely reinforce the phantasmal boundaries of the nation." "The Double Logic of Minor Spaces," in *Minor Transnationalism*, ed. Francoise Lionnet and Shu-mei Shih (Durham, N.C.: Duke University Press, 2005), 286.

57. "Birōjū no shita de no shi tokei," *Kosakusha sengen*, 161.

58. Gavin Walker has provided an eloquent engagement with Tanigawa's poetry and thought as approached for its resonance with a wide range of political thought. Describing the paradoxical pursuit of fictional loci of relating that abound in his writings, Walker notes, "Tanigawa's work can function not as a guide but as a

historical-material trace of the figuration of the origin, an antimemory that still calls for new forms of recombination, new ways of relating in an immanent, poetic zone that cannot be rediscovered or returned to but that must be created and inscribed anew." "Tanigawa Gan and the Poetics of the Origin," *positions: east asia cultures critique* 25, 2 (2017): 380.

59. In this sense, the depopulation of peripheral areas was a crucial aspect of Japan's Cold War remaking, which along with the rationalization of other sectors of Japan's economy, such as energy restructuring that produced a shift from coal to petrochemical and nuclear energy, further depleted the self-sufficiency of local communities in the name of conforming to U.S. geopolitical priorities.

60. This is not to say that Tanigawa was somehow opposed to the ostensible goals of reversion, the removal of all U.S. base facilities, and the rejection of Japan's remilitarization. But rather, Tanigawa persistently challenged the organizational assumptions of centralized networks of opposition movements such as the reversion movement that betrayed the necessary questioning of given identifications and images of national community induced by such hierarchical forms (where not only were Okinawans and other non-"reverted" islanders somehow nonbeings without "national identity," but the supposed collective desire for the "mother country" of Japan reproduced the colonial discourse of assimilation and moreover reinforced the boundaries of the Cold War nation-state).

61. "Birōjū no shita de no shi tokei," *Kosakusha sengen*, 212.

62. While Tanigawa's critique of this double structure helps situate his engagement with Tokara and the transformative possibilities he discovers on Gajajima, Nakazato Isao has moreover treated Tanigawa's concern with this double structure as a thematic figure that permeated his writings and culminated in his 1961 critical essay, "The Double Structure of Japan" ("Nihon no nijū kōzō") in "Kaisetsu," *Tanigawa Gan serekushon: Sengo shisō o yominaosu 2, Genten no genshisha*, 399.

63. "Birōjū no shita de no shi tokei," *Kosakusha sengen*, 214.

64. Kuraishi Shino, "Kokkyō: Nakahira Takuma no Amami, Tokara no Shashin," 10.

65. Nakahira Takuma, "Kokkyo Tokara rettō: mujinka suru shimajima."

66. Kuraishi Shino, "Kokkyō: Nakahira Takuma no Amami, Tokara no Shashin," 10.

67. Many of the photographs from Nakahira's Tokara journey were unpublished. Some of these have been included in the collection *Nakahira Takuma: Okinawa, Amami, Tokara 1974–1978*, including the ones I describe here.

6. RESIDUAL FUTURES

1. Takuma Nakahira, "Preemptive Strike: Looking and Reading" ("Sensei no ichigeki: miru koto to yomu koto"), *Waseda bungaku* (October 1977), quoted from *Mitsuzukeru hate ni hi ga . . .*, 494–495.

2. Christopher Bolton, *Sublime Voices: The Fictional Science and Scientific Fiction of Abe Kōbō* (Cambridge, Mass.: Harvard University Asia Center: Distributed by Harvard University Press, 2009), 221.

3. Abe Kōbō, *Secret Rendezvous*, trans. Juliet W. Carpenter (New York: Knopf, 1979), 73.

4. Bolton, 232.

5. Paul Roquet offers an expansive perspective that affords *both* an account of the emergent of neoliberal biopolitical regimes of control operative in ambient subjectivation as well as the marginal degree of autonomy these afford. In addition, this double vision invites us to explore how techniques of the self in fact traverse modernity and its aftermath. "The social and cultural shifts beginning in the late 1970s have less to do with the collapse of grand narratives and much more to do with emerging techniques of self-care, somatic techniques that run prior to and in some ways independent of narrative or even political identification." *Ambient Media: Japanese Atmospheres of Self* (Minneapolis: University of Minnesota Press, 2016), 13.

6. Roquet, 178.

7. Marié Abe, *Resonances of Chindon-ya: Sounding Space and Sociality in Contemporary Japan* (Middletown, Conn.: Wesleyan University Press, 2018), 192.

8. Isozaki Arata, "Kumo no senryaku, arui wa kihō no haikyo ni," in *Spider's Strategy* (Tokyo: Osiris, 2001) unpaged.

9. Jane Bennett, "Systems and Things: On Vital Materialism and Object-Oriented Philosophy," in *The Nonhuman Turn*, ed. Richard Grusin (Minneapolis: University of Minnesota Press, 2015), 233.

10. https://twitter.com/akagishuji

11. Akagi Shuji, *Fukushima Traces 2011–2013*, trans. Dan Abbe (Tokyo: Osiris, 2015).

12. In August of 2016, Akagi's work was exhibited along with a series of symposia in the exhibition, "Akagi Shuji + Kuroda Kio: Shusa dekonta 2016," at the Hachinohe City Museum of Art.

13. Peter C. van Wyck, *Signs of Danger: Waste, Trauma, and Nuclear Threat* (Minneapolis: University of Minnesota Press, 2005), xi.

14. van Wyck, xii.

15. Mitsuhiro Yoshimoto, "Nuclear Disaster and Bubbles," in *Planetary Atmospheres and Urban Society After Fukushima*, ed. Christophe Thouny and Mitsuhiro Yoshimoto (Singapore: Palgrave Macmillan, 2017).

16. From the publisher's press release for *Fukushima Traces 2011–2013*.

17. Félix Guattari, "Ecosophical Practices and the Restoration of the 'Subjective City,'" in *Machinic Eros: Writings on Japan*, ed. Gary Genosko and Jay Hetrick (Minneapolis: Univocal Publishing, University of Minnesota Press, 2015), 113.

Index

Page numbers in *italics* indicate figures.

Aa, kōya. See Ah, Wilderness

Abe, Marié, 196

Abe Kōbō, 12, 111, 221n3, 222n10, 227n50, 236n6; body of work, 48–49; Bolton on, 194–195; ceremonial sacrifice and, 225n37; collaboration and, 221n4; as literary pioneer, 223n16; taxi drivers and, 226n45; Teshigahara and, 221n4; topos and, 222n7, 224n23. *See also Ruined Map, The*

Adachi Masao, 125, 212n16, 235n45, 239n27, 243n51

afterlives: of Cold War, 8, 211n11, 233n39; of radical leftist thought, 125–126

"Afurika kara kaeru." *See* "Returning from Africa"

agriculture, 39, 57, 60, 66, 80

Ah, Wilderness (Aa, kōya) (Terayama Shūji), 84

Aikura Hisato, 212n16

Akagi Shuji, 203–207, *205*, 256n12

Akasegawa Genpei, 241n39

A.K.A. Serial Killer (film), 10, 11, 243n50

Allegories of Time and Space (Reynolds), 250n29

Alliez, Eric, 216n5

Amami Islands, 13, 154, *167, 170*, 249n26, 251n36; with gaze of viewer, 169; "illustrated dictionary" and, 163, 169; as (in)visible boundary, 162–172; "naked-eye reflex" and, 165, 172

"Amami: Waves, Graves, Flowers, and the Sun" (Nakahira Takuma), 162, 165–166, *167*

Anime Machine, The (LaMarre), 210n5

"Another Country" (photographic series, Asahi Journal), 132

anti-ANPO movement, 178–180

Arakawa Akira, 249n27

architecture, 140; "electro-graphic," 138; with student revolts, 142; Taki Kōji and influence on, 252n41. *See also Modern Architecture*

Asahi Camera (magazine), 88, 240nn31–32, 243n55, 244n60; "Amami: Waves, Graves, Flowers, and the Sun," 162, 168; Nakahira Takuma and, 172, 251n37

Asahi Graph (magazine), 5, 84, 88

Asahi Journal (news magazine): *danchi* in, 242n45; "illustrated dictionary" in, 243n53; Okinawa in, 151; as platform

Asahi Journal (continued)
  for photographers, 88, 132, 136, 137,
    143, 240n32, 241n39
Asama Mountain Lodge incident, 125
Atget, Eugène, 146–148, 160, 175, 195,
    244n60, 245n61
Atget's Paris, Aje no Pari (Ōshima
    Hiroshi), 244n60
Atget's Seven Albums (Nesbit), 245n62
Attack the Landscape (Miyauchi Kō), 125
audio surveillance system, 195

Barthes, Roland, 91–92, 99, 230n22
Beckman, Karen, 36, 218n23
Benjamin, Walter, 114, 156, 235n5, 236n10,
    244n60, 247n11, 248n21
Bennett, Jane, 202, 244n58
Beyond Nation (Calichman), 221n3
"Beyond the Curve." *See* "Kābu no mukō"
Bhowmik, Davinder, 250n27
Bijutsu techo (magazine), 229n13, 232n35,
    234n41, 236n9
Bolton, Christopher, 194–195, 221n3
Box Man, The (Abe Kōbō), 50, 54; "From
    Within the Mirror," 113; nonselective
    visuality in, 115–116, 131, 132;
    photographic visuality in, 115
"bubble" economy, 197, 242n44
burial methods, Amami Islands, 166

Calichman, Richard, 221n3, 236n6
camera: industry with photography,
    234n41; SLR, 156
"Can an Anarchist become an Architect?"
    (Nakahira Takuma), 140
Carpenter, Juliet Winters, 221n4
Cazdyn, Eric, 209n2
Central Terminal Station. *See* CTS
Century of Photography, A (exhibition),
    84–85
ceremonial sacrifice, 225n37
Certeau, Michel de, 7
Chattopadhyay, Swati, 16
"chiasmus," 235n5
children, traffic war and, 219n25
Christo, 103–104
Chūō Kōron (journal), 236n6

Cinema of Actuality (Furuhata), 11,
    213n16, 237n13, 239n27
Circle Village (*Sākuru mura*) (poetry
    journal), 177
Circulation: Date, Place, Events
    (Nakahira Takuma), 126, 143, 238n22;
    infrastructure and, 127; republication
    of, 199; as text, 127–128, 132
city, 244n57; circulatory system of,
    56–57; as deadly glass bottle, 28, 33;
    depictions of, 28, 30, 140, 217n17;
    "healthy," 135, 240n38; language and,
    134, 240n37; "symphony" films, 35,
    218n22; violence of, 101, 232n29
"City, The" ("Toshi") (*Asahi Journal*),
    137–139, 242n44
coal miners, 68, 178–179
"cognitive mapping," 211n12
Cold War, 23–24, 45–47, 111, 211n7,
    255n59; afterlives, 8, 211n11, 233n39;
    in context, 2, 6–7, 16, 87, 137;
    determinism, 210n5; in East Asia,
    197; endocolonization and, 216n5; *The
    Ruined Map* and, 65–66; violence and,
    231n24. *See also* reversion
Cold War remaking, 50, 178, 207, 210n5;
    Amami Islands and, 164; capitalism
    and, 137; depopulation and, 255n59;
    with expanded ecologies, 15–16,
    18; geopolitics and, 8–9, 21–22, 23,
    43, 65–66, 87, 231n24; "illustrated
    dictionary" and, 13; infrastructure
    of, 11, 13, 14, 16, 19, 24, 193; media
    and, 87; Okinawa and, 152, 154; with
    "permanent revolution of gaze," 13–14;
    post-, 202; PR film and, 30; seeing
    and, 148; of social spaces, 51; Tokara
    Islands and, 180–181, 183; topological
    visuality and, 12; traffic war and, 39,
    47; tranverse readings and, 7
colonial power, photography and, 251n33
Communist Party of Japan, 27, 180,
    212n13
construction: Narita Airport, 137, 243n56;
    in *The Ruined Map*, 62–64
consumer culture, 246n2
Contemporary Eye (magazine), 84

Contemporary Poetry Notebook
  (*Gendaishi techō*), 251n37
Cornyetz, Nina, 221n3
CTS (Central Terminal Station), 152, 157
culture, 163, 166; consumer, 246n2;
  difference, 165, 168, 169, 171; media, 9;
  Okinawan, 164; uniforms and, 138

danchi (housing developments), 51, 95,
  223n16; in *Asahi Journal*, 242n45; as
  modern living space, 223n14; in *The
  Ruined Map*, 53–58, 61, 62, 65
Danchi Zuma series films, 223n14
*Death and Life of Great American Cities,
  The* (Jacobs), 213n20
"Death Watch Beneath the Palms"
  (Tanigawa Gan), 177, 179
Debord, Guy, 237n13
decontamination: of Fukushima Dai'ichi
  reactor, 205, 225n36; photography,
  206; Van Wyck on, 203–204
defamiliarization, 17, 115–116, 223n15
Design (magazine), 88, 231n26
detective (fictional character): ceremonial
  sacrifice and, 225n37; escape and flight
  of, 226n44; reflections of, 223n17. *See
  also Ruined Map, The*
determinism, Cold War and, 210n5
Deutsche, Rosalyn, 215n31
disappearance, with *Ruined Map, The,*
  50–51, 65
Discourses of the Vanishing (Ivy), 233n37
Discover Japan campaign, 106–107,
  231n25, 233n35, 233n37
"Documentary Illusion, The" (Nakahira
  Takuma), 155, 159, 232n35, 234n41,
  236n9, 247n8
Domon Ken photography prize, 198
"Double Logic of Minor Spaces, The"
  (Lippit, S.), 224n23
dreams, photography and, 175
"Duel on Photography" (Shinoyama
  Kishin and Nakahira Takuma), 173,
  177, 190, 253n47

East Asia, Cold War in, 197
Easterling, Keller, 20

ecologies, expanded, 14–19
"Ecologies of Japan" (*"Nihon no seitai"*)
  (photography series), 88–90
Edo period, 181
Eiga hiyō (film journal), 212n16
endocolonization, 216n5
Engineer's Assistant, An, 29, 31
Enzensberger, Hans Magnus, 236n10,
  248n21
escape: from expression, 84–87; in *The
  Ruined Map*, 69–73, 223n17, 226n44
*Ethics of Aesthetics in Japanese Cinema
  and Literature, The* (Cornyetz), 221n3
"Eugène Atget" (*Asahi Camera*), 244n60
"Execution of Personal Autonomy, The"
  (Komatsu Hiroko), *201*, 201–202
Extrastatecraft (Easterling), 20

Face of Another, The (Abe Kōbō), 50,
  222n12, 234n40
Fanon, Frantz, 236n10, 248n21
farmer-activists, 144
Felski, Rita, 7–8, 211n10
Fifteen Photographers Today (exhibition),
  129, 139, 143
Film Quarterly (*Kikan firumu*), 109
flight, in *Ruined Map, The*, 69–73, 223n17,
  226n44
flow plaza, 214n22, 222n9
folk guerilla movement, 214n21
folk songs, 163
For a Language to Come (Nakahira
  Takuma), 12–13, 83, 188, 230n20;
  Circulation installation and, *126*,
  126–128, 132, 143; cover design, 138;
  decentering textuality of, 93–99, *96*;
  interrogative strategies, 108–112;
  landscape and limits of reading, 104–
  108; with photography as provocative
  accumulations for thought, 87–93;
  with revolt against landscape, 99–104;
  "What is it to be Contemporary?," 88,
  232n30
"For a Literature of Space" (Maeda Ai), 48
For a New Novel (Robbe-Grillet), 236n10
For a New World to Come (photography
  exhibition), 129

Forest of Pressure (Nornes), 243n56
Foucault, Michel, 252n40
Fowler, Edward, 68
framing: in photography, 114–115; seeing and, 131
freedom, speed and, 12, 214n21
"From Within the Mirror" (Abe Kōbō), 113
"Frontier Within, The" (Abe Kōbō), 236n6
Fujii, Yuko, 137, 139, 229n10
Fukase Masahisa, 241n39
"Fūkei e no hanran" (Nakahira Takuma), 231n26, 231n28
Fūkei no Shimetsu (Matsuda Masao), 109
fūkei-ron. See landscape, radical discourse of
Fukushima Dai'ichi reactor, 197, 202, 203, 205–207, 225n36, 243n54
Fukushima Traces 2011–2013, 203
Fuller, Matthew, 14
Furuhata, Yuriko, 11, 44, 100, 213n16, 237n13, 239n27

Gabriel, Philip, 249n26
Gajajima, 179–183
gaze: limits of, 172–176, 190; nikugan reflex, 156, 247n4, 248n20; "permanent revolution of," 13–14, 175–177, 185, 190–192; of reader, 97; in The Ruined Map, 50–53, 69–70, 73–75, 77–78; of viewer, 169
Gendai no me, 88
Gendaishi techō (Contemporary Poetry Notebook), 251n37
gender, photography and, 244n57
geopolitics: Cold War remaking and, 8–9, 21–22, 23, 43, 65–66, 87, 231n24; infrastructure and, 11–12; in On the Road, 34, 43–45; sensing, 43–45
geopolitics, of reading: in context, 81–83; for decentering textuality, 93–99; escape from expression and, 84–87; interrogative strategies and, 108–112; limits, 104–108; with provocative accumulations for thought, 87–93; with revolt against landscape, 99–104
"Girlscape" (Yoda), 233n37

glass bottle, city as deadly, 28, 33
Gotō Meisei, 223n16
Graphication (journal), 231n26, 238n23
Guattari, Félix, 15, 80, 207, 227n53

hallucinatory visuality, 251n34
Halpern, Orit, 214n23
Hani Gorō, 213n17, 232n29
Hani Susumu, 23, 34, 223n14
Hanran. See Overflow
Hara Kazuo, 252n38
Harvey, David, 215n31
"Has Photography Been Able to Provoke Language?" ("Shashin wa kotoba ochōhatsu shietaka") (Nakahira Takuma), 91–92
Hawai'i, as model for Japan's military-tourist development of Okinawa, 248n16
"healthy city," 135, 240n38
Heike clan, 181–182, 184
"Heta Village" (Naitō Masahito), 144
Hiraoka Masaaki, 212n16
Hirasawa, Gō, 109
hiroba (public square), 12, 222n9
Holmberg, Ryan, 241n39
Hong Kong, 177
Hörl, Erich, 15
housing developments. See danchi

"I am King" (Nakahira Takuma and Tōmatsu Shōmei), 84
"Illustrated Botanical Dictionary" ("Shokubutsu zukan") (Nakahira Takuma), 132
"illustrated dictionary" (zukan), 113–116; Amami and, 163, 169; defined, 13; with ecologies in flux, 125–128; evolution of, 132–137, 243n53; interrogatives, 117–121; juxtaposition and, 124, 144; knowledge, commodification of, 136–137; landscape and, 124, 125, 134–135; "naked-eye reflex" and, 161–162; Overflow installation, 129, 129–130, 131, 132, 133, 139, 145, 146–149; visuality and, 121–124. See also Why an Illustrated Botanical Dictionary?

Image of the City, The (Lynch), 213n20
Indonesia, 164
infrastructure, 8, 137, 214n21; *Circulation*
    installation and, 127; of Cold War
    remaking, 11, 13, 14, 16, 19, 24, 193;
    decentering textuality and, 95–96; flow
    plaza and, 214n22; geopolitics and,
    11–12; media, 9, 111, 118, 127–128, 161,
    176, 178, 192, 194, 199; networks, 16; PR
    film and, 29–30; role of, 5–6, 20–21;
    self and, 196; Tokyo Olympics (1964),
    225n36; traffic wars and, 20, 25–26;
    with traffic wars and Cold War, 46–47;
    with traffic wars and geopolitical, 43,
    45; traffic wars as topos and, 35, 37–38;
    urban/rural difference and, 212n15
interrogative strategies: *For a Language
    to Come*, 108–112; state power and,
    136; *Why an Illustrated Botanical
    Dictionary?*, 117–121
Ishimure Michiko, 178
Ishizuka Masahito, 2, 242n44
Isoda Kōichi, 223n14
Isozaki Arata, 43–44, 138, 199, 242n44
Ivy, Marilyn, 209n1, 233n37, 243n56
Iwanami Film Production Studios, 23, 28,
    216n7

Jacobs, Jane, 213n20
JAL *yodo-go* air hijacking, 231n25
Jameson, Fredric, 211n12, 215n31
Japan, as "superpower," 249n25
Japanese Documentary Film (Abé Mark
    Nornes), 27
Japanese Red Army, 231n25, 237n20
Japanese Self Defense forces, 152
Jilani, Sarah, 218n22
juxtaposition, "illustrated dictionary" and,
    124, 144

*Kabe no naka no himegoto. See Secrets
    Behind the Walls*
"Kābu nomukō" ("Beyond the Curve")
    (Abe Kōbō), 221n4
Kakumoto Ryōhei, 21, 213n20, 215n3
Kanda liberated district, 103–104, 232n32
Kanemura Osamu, 197–201

Kanojo to kare. See She and He
Karatani Kojin, 224n23, 227n50, 229n16,
    234n40, 246n2
Kawamitsu Shin'ichi, 249n27
Kawanaka Ikuo, 254n56
Kepes, György, 214n23
Key, Margaret S., 221n3
Kikan firumu (*Film Quarterly*), 109
Kim, Gyewon, 85
Kindai Kenchiku. See Modern Architecture
Kinkle, Jeff, 9, 211n12, 214n24
Kitai Kazuo, 243n56
Klein, William, 97–98, 230n23
knowledge: commodification of, 136–137;
    "metacritical" production, 173; through
    photographic visuality, 136; of urban
    nebula, 137–143
Kohara Masashi, 250n29
Komatsu Hiroko, 201–203
Kōsōkuka no owari (Kakumoto Ryōhei),
    213n20
Kota Inoue, 224n23
Kotobukicho, day laborers of, 68
Koza City (Okinawa), 164
Kuchinoshima Island, 184
"Kūkan no bungaku e" (Maeda Ai), 221n2,
    223n16
Kunikida Doppo, 224n23
Kunitachi Fuchū interchange, Chūō
    Expressway 225n26
Kuraishi Shino, 82, 164, 183, 227n1,
    239n29, 241n44, 251n35
Kuroda Kio, 163, 164, 172, 213n17, 249n26
Kuroki Kazuo, 27, 34

laborers: coal miners, 68, 178–179;
    Okinawan, 160; "ride sharing," 226n47;
    taxi drivers, 30–32, 34, 35–42, 44,
    73–75, 226n45; Tokyo Olympics and,
    225n36
LaMarre, Thomas, 210n5
landscape, radical discourse of (*fūkei-
    ron*), 252n46; connotations, 233n40;
    "illustrated dictionary" and, 124, 125,
    134–135; with limits of reading, 104–
    108; Nakahira and, 100–102, 109, 111,
    135, 231n26, 242n50; revolt against,

landscape, radical discourse of (*fūkei-ron*)
(*continued*)
99–104; state power and, 10–11, 116,
125; as term, emergence of, 234n40;
violence of, 101–102
language: city and, 134, 240n37; new,
49; photography and, 90–92; poetic,
230n22; urban, 77–80, 222n12. *See also*
For a Language to Come
"Last train" ("*shūdensha*") (Nakahira
Takuma), 88–90, 94
Latin Quarter, Paris, 232n32
Lazzarato, Maurizio, 216n5
Lefebvre, Henri, 18, 215n32
leftist thought, "afterlives" of radical,
125–126
women's liberation movement, (*ūman
ribu*), 232n31, 237n20, 238n21, 241n42
"Limits that Consume the Gaze, The"
("Shisen no tsukiru hate") (Nakahira
Takuma), 173–174, 176, 190
Lionnet, Francoise, 224n23
Lippit, Seiji, 224n23, 254n56
Lippit, Yukio, 14–15
Literature in Urban Space (Maeda Ai), 49
"Little History of Photography"
(Benjamin), 235n5
Lived House, The (Taki Kōji), 139
"Logic of the City, The." *See Toshi no ronri*
Lynch, Kevin, 213n20, 214n23

Machinic Eros: Writings on Japan
(Guattari), 227n53
Maeda Ai, 48, 49, 51–52, 79, 234n40;
danchi and, 223n16; on urban fiction,
222n12
Mapping the Future, Nishinari (film),
225n35
Marcuse, Herbert, 138, 236n10
Marunouchi district, 242n47
Marx, Karl, 229n16
materialism, 202, 244n58
Matsuda Masao, 10, 100–101, 108–109,
212n16, 213n17; landscape and, 243n51;
media and, 125
Matsumoto Toshio, 27, 34, 84,
217n14

Matsunaga Yū, 154–155, 174
McKnight, Anne, 223n14, 253nn49–50
media: culture, 9; ecologies, 2, 5, 14, 81,
123, 147, 246n2; infrastructural, 9,
111, 118, 127–128, 161, 176, 178, 192,
194, 199; photography as form of, 121;
photojournalism and police, 102–103,
232n30; police and, 247n8; power,
125; social, 199, 203; state power
and, 237n19; with systematization of
sensory capacities, 147, 174
Media of Impossibility (Matsuda Masao),
125
Meiji Boulevard, 232n32
Meiji Restoration (100th anniversary), 85
Merleau-Ponty, Maurice, 235n5
Metaphor of the Eye (Taki Kōji), 139
Metropolitan Police Traffic Bureau, 21,
26–27, 28, 33
military, U.S., 13, 152, 179
Minamata disease, 23, 178
Minimata (film, 1971), 23
Minor Transnationalism (Lionnet and
Shih), 224n23
Mitsuhiro Yoshimoto, 206
Miyauchi Kō, 125
Mizuki Kaoru, 213n17
"mobile tent theatre," 138
Modern Architecture (*Kindai Kenchiku*)
(magazine), 139, 240n32, 242n47
Moetsukita chizu (Abe), 138, 221n4,
234n40
Moetsukita chizu (film), 221n4
Morisaki Kazue, 178
Moriyama Daidō, 82, 84–85, 86, 172,
241n39
Morocco, 127, 177
municipal cooperative movement, 59,
224n22
Murphy, Joseph, 222n6
"Musashino" ("Musashi Plain, The")
(Kunikida Doppo), 224n23
Museum of Modern Art, Houston,
238n22

Nagayama Norio, 100
Naitō Masahito, 144

Nakagami Kenji, 177, 253nn49–50
Nakahira Takuma, 12–13, 17, 231n28, 236n9, 244n60, 247n8, 253n47; Amami and, 162–172, *167*, *170*, 249n26, 251n36; *Asahi Camera* and, 172, 251n37; Atget and, 146–148; bibliographic record of, 2, *3*, *4*, 5, 227n1; escape from expression, 84–87; gaze and, 172–176, 190; influence of, 252n39; influences on, 87, 91–92, 184; on knowledge, commodification of, 136–137; "landscape" and, 100–102, 109, 111, 135, 231n26, 242n50; legacy, 81–83; Marunouchi district and, 242n47; with Matsunaga Yū, in support of, 155, 174; "naked-eye reflex" and, 156–157, 160–162, 165, 172; with Okinawa, 150–162, *153*, *158*; at Paris Biennale (1971), 126, 239n25; "permanent revolution of the gaze" and, 192; photographic visuality and, 13–14, 116, 118, 139, 142, 148, 193–194; with photography, role of, 90, 123, 233n37; on police and photojournalism, 102–103; with *Provoke*, 85–86; on seeing, 193; with self-critique, 117–118, 120–121, 236n10; Shimao Toshio and, 251n34; on social-justice photographers, 247n5; Tokara Islands and, 177–179, 183–186, *187*, 188, *189*, 253n48, 255n67; as Yugi Akira, 84. *See also* "Amami: Waves, Graves, Flowers, and the Sun"; "Can an Anarchist become an Architect?"; *Circulation: Date, Place, Events*; "Documentary Illusion, The"; "Duel on Photography"; *For a Language to Come*; "Fūkei e no hanran"; "Has Photography Been Able to Provoke Language?"; "Illustrated Botanical Dictionary"; "Last train"; "Limits that Consume the Gaze, The"; *Nakahira Takuma: Okinawa, Amami, Tokara 1974–1978*; "National Border The Tokara Archipelago"; "Okinawa: The Bases That Will be Forgotten"; *Overflow*; "Preemptive Strike: Seeing and Reading"; "Rebellion Against the Landscape"; "Returning from Africa"; "Urban Shades-Urban Pitfalls"; *Why an Illustrated Botanical Dictionary?*
Nakahira Takuma: Degree Zero-Yokohama (retrospective, 2003), 82
Nakahira Takuma: Okinawa, Amami, Tokara 1974–1978 (Nakahira Takuma), 154
Nakano Kazunori, 71, 72
Nakanoshima Island, 184
Nakazato Isao, 255n62
"naked-eye reflex," 156–157, 160–162, 165, 172
Namigata Tsuyoshi, 226n44
Narita Airport, 137, 243n56
"National Border The Tokara Archipelago" (Nakahira Takuma), 177
National Museum of Modern Art, Tokyo, 129
National Railways, 106, 231n25, 233n35
nebula. *See* urban nebula, knowledge of
Nesbit, Molly, 245n62
"New Encyclopedia of Photography," 172–173
New York (Klein), 97–98, 230n23
Nihon dokusho shinbun (newspaper), 88
Nihon Fūkei-ron (Shigetaka), 233n40
"*Nihon no seitai*." *See* "Ecologies of Japan"
"Nikutai no mon" (Tamura Taijirō), 225n37
ningen johatsu (people who vanish into thin air), 50–51
"Ningen sokkuri" (Abe Kōbō), 222n7
Nishinari riot (1961), 68, 225n35
Nixon Shock, 241n41
nonselective visuality, 115–116, 131, 132
Nornes, Abé Mark, 210n3, 243n56, 252n38
nuclear waste, 203–204, 225n36. *See also* decontamination

Odagiri Takushi, 221n5
Ogawa Productions, 243n56
"oil shock," 241n41
Okada, Richard, 234n40
Okada Tadahiko, 85–86
Okamoto Keitoku, 249n27
Okamoto Tarō, 165

Okinawa: in *Asahi Journal*, 151; culture, 164; laborers, 160; Nakahira Takuma and, 150–162, *153*, *158*; reversion of, 13–14, 150–162, 246n3; student protests, 154–155; "Third Annexation of," 152; tourism and, 248n16; (re)versions of, 152–162

Okinawa Photobook (Tōmatsu Shōmei), 248n17

Okinawa Sea Expo '75, 157, *157*, 160

"Okinawa: The Bases That Will be Forgotten" (Nakahira Takuma), 157

Okuno Takeo, 222n12, 234n40

Olympics. *See* Sapporo Winter Olympics; Tokyo Olympics

On Remodeling the Japanese Archipelago (Tanaka Kakuei), 142

On the Road (Tsuchimoto Noriaki PR film), 199; city in, 28, 30; Cold War and, 23–24, 45–47; in context, 11–12; deconstructed, 22–23, 26–30; geopolitics and, 34, 43–45; historical conditions of, 22; influence of, 219n24; rejection of, 21; taxi drivers in, 30–32, 34, 35–42, 44; as topos, 35–42, *38*, *42*; traffic war traversed in, 24–26, *26*; traversals, 32–34; x-ray scene, 31–33, 218n19

"optical unconscious" (Benjamin), 114

Order of Things (Foucault), 252n40

Origins of Modern Japanese Literature (Karatani Kojin), 224n23, 234n40

Ōshima Hiroshi, 244n60

Ōshima Nagisa, 239n27

Ōshiro Tatsuhiro, 249n27

out-of-focus photography (*are-bure-boke*), 82, 86, 88

Overflow (*Hanran*) (Nakahira Takuma), 13, 128, *131*, 132, *145*, 168; beginnings, 135; criticism of, 244n59; as disorienting, 132; with elements reassembled, 133; "illustrated dictionary" and, *129*, 129–130, *131*, 132, 133, 139, *145*, 146–149; without logical presentation, 130–131; materialism and, 244n58; with naked eye reflex, 146–149; photography, 13, 128–132, *129*, *131*, 133, 139, *145*, 146–149,

244n59; seeing incompleteness and, 143–146; structure, 130–131; title, connotations, 129

Paris Biennale (1971), 126, 239n25

Paris du Temps Perdu (Atget), 148

Parisian Views (Rice), 245n62

Pencil of the Sun, Okinawa and S.E. Asia, The (Tōmatsu Shōmei), 164–165

people who vanish into thin air (*ningen johatsu*), 50

"permanent revolution of the gaze," 13–14, 175–177, 185, 190–192

Philippines, 164

photobook: decentering textuality of, 93–99, *96*; with gaze of reader, *97*. *See also For a Language to Come*

photographers: social-justice, 247n5; workshops for, 198–199, 244n59

photographic visuality, 201; in *The Box Man*, 115; knowledge through, 136; Nakahira Takuma and, 13–14, 116, 118, 139, 142, 148, 193–194

photography: of Atget, 146–148; Benjamin and, 235n5; camera industry and, 234n41; *Circulation* installation, *126*, 126–128, 132, 143; "The City" series, 137–139; colonial power and, 251n33; decontamination, 206; dreams and, 175; *Fifteen Photographers Today* exhibition, 129, 139, 143; as form of media, 121; framing in, 114–115; gender and, 244n57; as incomplete, 90–91; language and, 90–92; *For a New World to Come* exhibition, 129; out-of-focus style, 82, 86, 88; *Overflow* installation, 13, 128–132, *129*, *131*, 133, 139, *145*, 146–149, 244n59; *Paris du Temps Perdu*, 148; power and, 126–128; as provocative accumulations for thought, 87–93; role of, 84–87, 109, 123, 176, 233n37; Tokyo College of Photography, 198. *See also* Nakahira Takuma

photojournalism: Okinawa student protests and, 154–155; police and, 102–103, 232n30

Plath, David W., 224n25
Playboy Japan (magazine), 251n37, 253n49
Poe, Edgar Allan, 78
poetic language, 230n22
Poetics of Things, The (Taki Kōji), 139
police: media and, 247n8; Metropolitan
  Police Traffic Bureau, 21, 26–27, 28, 33;
  with Okinawa student protests, 154–
  155; photojournalism and, 102–103,
  232n30; violence, 137, 139, 232nn31–32
Politics of Media, The (Tsumura Takashi),
  125
Politics of the City, The (Taki Kōji), 139
poverty, 138
power: Japan as capitalist state power,
  249n25; media, 125; photography and,
  126–128; photography and colonial,
  251n33; state, 10–11, 116, 125, 136, 138,
  237n19
"Preemptive Strike: Seeing and Reading"
  (Nakahira Takuma), 193
PR film, 29, 31; city depicted in, 28,
  30; Cold War remaking and, 30;
  documentary aesthetics and, 22,
  27, 29–30, 34, 43, 45, 219n24;
  documentary film and, 11, 22–23,
  27, 34, 36, 217n12; evolution of, 27,
  219n24; role of, 217n12. *See also On
  the Road*
private film (*puraibeto firumu*), 252n38
Provoke (magazine), 82, 85–86, 88, 91, 106,
  137, 244n57
public square (*hiroba*), 12, 222n9
pump image, in *Ruined Map, The*, 56, 78,
  226n49
puraibeto firumu (private film), 252n38
pure time, 71–72

Raine, Michael, 217n14
Rancière, Jacques, 212n13, 233n39
reading, 193; incompleteness in *The
  Ruined Map*, 58–61; transverse, 7–11.
  See also geopolitics, of reading
"Rebellion Against the Landscape"
  (Nakahira Takuma), 100, 252n46
recovery: Fukushima Dai'ichi reactor,
  206–207, 243n54; myths of, 29,

206; "reversion" and, 246n3; Tokyo
  Olympics (1964) as moment of, 29, 46,
  202, 205, 219n32, 220nn33–34
remaking. *See* Cold War remaking
resonance, dynamic relationality of, 196
"Returning from Africa" ("Afurika kara
  kaeru") (Nakahira Takuma), 238n23
reversion: connotations, 246n3; of
  Okinawa, 13–14, 150–162, 246n3;
  Tanigawa Gan and, 255n60; Tokara
  Islands, 179; violence of, 184–185
Reynolds, Jonathan, 228n3, 250n29
Rice, Shelley, 245n62
Ridgeley, Steven, 210n3, 228n4
Robbe-Grillet, Alain, 236n10
Roquet, Paul, 196, 256n5
Ross, Kristin, 211n11, 212n13, 233n39
Ruined Map, The (Abe Kōbō), 12, 234n40;
  badge and, 66; Camellia anomaly
  in, 73–77; ceremonial sacrifice
  and, 225n37; Cold War and, 65–66;
  construction in, 62–64; *danchi* in,
  53–58, 61, 62, 65; detective in, 223n17,
  225n37, 226n44; disappearance
  with, 50–51, 65; environments of
  abstraction, 53–58; escape and flight
  in, 69–73, 223n17, 226n44; failing
  gaze in, 50–53, 69–70, 73–75, 77–78;
  municipal cooperative movement
  in, 59, 224n22; new language and,
  49; pump image in, 56, 78, 226n49;
  pure time and, 71–72; reading
  incompleteness, 58–61; ruptures and
  rituals, 62–69; taxi drivers in, 73–75;
  as topos, 50, 63, 65–69, 79–80; urban
  language and, 77–80, 222n12; urban
  writing and, 48; violence in, 67–68,
  74–77; *yoseba* in, 68–69
rural homelands (*furusato*), 209n1, 212n14
Ryūdō (journal), 186, 253n48

Sakai, Naoki, 210n4, 211n7
Sakaki, Atsuko, 114
Sakura Gaho manga series (Akasegawa
  Genpei), 241n39
Sākuru mura. See Circle Village
Sand, Jordan, 12, 214n22

Sanrizuka-Heta Village (documentary film), 243n56
Sanya, 68, 80
Sapporo Winter Olympics (1972), 137
Sartre, Jean-Paul, 237n11
Sas, Miryam, 210n3, 228n5
Sasaki Maki, 241n39
Sasaki Mamoru, 212n16
Sasaki-Uemura, Wesley, 254n56
Saunders, E. Dale, 222n8, 235n1
Sawaragi Noi, 203
Schivelbusch, Wolfgang, 215n3
Schnellbächer, Thomas, 221n3
Seaman, Amanda C., 223n15
Secret Rendezvous (Abe Kōbō), 194–195
Secrets Behind the Walls (*Kabe no naka no himegoto*) (Wakamatsu Kōji), 223n14
seeing: framing and, 131; incompleteness, 143–146; Nakahira Takuma on, 193. *See also* visuality
Sengo zen'ei eiga to bungaku: Abe Kōbō x Teshigahara Hiroshi (Tomoda Yoshiyuki), 221n4
Seo Hong, 222n10, 224n18
"Shashin wa kotoba ochōhatsu shietaka." *See* "Has Photography Been Able to Provoke Language?"
She and He (*Kanojo to kare*) (Hani Susumu), 223n14
Shibuya area, 32, 39, 218n20
Shiga Shigetaka, 233n3
Shigematsu, Setsu, 232n31, 237n20, 238n21, 241n42
Shih, Shu-mei, 224n23
Shimao Toshio, 163, 165, 249n26, 251n34
Shinjuku, 12, 14–15, 51, 214n22, 222n9
Shinoyama Kishin, 143–144, 173, 177, 190, 244n60, 252n39
"Shisen no tsukiru hate." *See* "Limits that Consume the Gaze, The"
"*Shokubutsu zukan.*" *See* "Illustrated Botanical Dictionary"
Shōwa era (1925–1989), 224n25
"*shūdensha.*" *See* "Last train"
Signs of Danger (Van Wyck), 203–204
Silverman, Kaja, 114–115, 235n5

Singapore, 164, 177
single-lens reflex (SLR) camera, 156
social-justice photographers, 247n5
social media, 199, 203
Society of the Spectacle, The (Debord), 237n13
Soja, Edward, 215n31
"Someday O.K. Prince will Come" (Kanemura Osamu), 198
Sorensen, André, 209n1
South Korea, 253n50
Spain, 177
speed: freedom and, 12, 214n21; traffic wars and, 20–21
Speed and Politics (Virilio), 214n21
Spider's Strategy (Kanemura Osamu), 197–201, *198, 200*
state power: interrogative strategies and, 136; "landscape" and, 10–11, 116, 125; mass resistance to, 138; media and, 237n19
state violence, 103, 125
Strategies for Cinema (Adachi Masao), 125
Streets Are a Battleground, The (Nakahira Takuma and Moriyama Daidō), 84
students: architecture with revolts of, 142; occupation of Latin Quarter, Paris, 232n32; with Okinawa protests, 154–155; Zenkyōtō movement, 103, 232n30, 236n10, 238n21
Sublime Voices (Bolton), 221n3
Suna no onna. See Woman in the Dunes, The
"Sunny Day, A" (Shinoyama Kishin), 143–144
"surveillance organizations," 138–139
Suzuki Shiróyasu, 172, 251n38, 252n38
Szendi Schieder, Chelsea , 238n20

Tada Osamu, 248n16
Taiwan, 164
Takanashi Yutaka, 86, 144, 244n57
Takara Ben, 247n7, 248n22
Taki Kōji, 84–85, 87, 105, 137, 139, 242n44, 242n46; architecture and influence of, 252n41; gaze and, 172–173; influence of, 252n39; *Toshi e* and, 244n57

Taki Kōji to kenchiku (Nagashima Akio), 242n46
"Takuma Nakahira: Circulation" (exhibition), 238n22
Takuya Tsunoda, 216n7
Tamura Taijirō, 225n37
Tanaka Kakuei, 142
Tanigawa Gan, 84, 213n17, 254n56; influence of, 184; reversion and, 255n60; Tokara Islands and, 177–183, 185–186; Walker on, 254n58
taxi drivers: interviews with, 226n45; in *On the Road*, 30–32, 34, 35–42, 44; in *The Ruined Map*, 73–75
television, rise of, 234n41
"Tell-Tale Heart, The" (Poe), 78
"temporary containment facilities," 206
Terayama Shūji, 5, 84, 87, 213n17
Teshigahara Hiroshi, 221n4
"Third Annexation of Okinawa," 152. *See also* reversion
Toba Kōji, 221n3
Tokara Islands, 13, 154; Gajajima community and, 179–183; in isolation like moments, 176–190; Nakahira Takuma and, 177–179, 183–186, *187*, 188, *189*, 253n48, 255n67; reversion of, 179; Tanigawa Gan and, 177–183, 185–186
Tokyo College of Photography, 198
Tokyo Olympics (1964), 11–12, 21, 29, 45–46, 219n32, 220nn33–35; laborers and, 225n36. *See also On the Road*
Tokyo Olympics (2020), 197, 202, 205
Tōmatsu Shōmei, 84, 228n3, 248n17, 250nn29–30; influence of, 87; Okinawa and, 164–165; with workshop events, 244n59
Tomii, Reiko, 210n3
Tomoda Yoshiyuki, 221n4
topography, 95; geopolitical and, 43–45; of human exploitation, 63; of Okinawa, 157, 158; traffic war and, 30, 34, 35–42, *42*
topological visuality, 48–49; Camellia anomaly and, 73–77; capturing flight and, 69–73; environments of abstraction, 53–58; failing gaze,

seeing through, 50–53; reading incompleteness, 58–61; ruptures and rituals, 62–69; urban language, thresholds of, 77–80
topology, 95; Maeda Ai and, 222n6; with new language, 49; reading incompleteness and, 61; of *The Ruined Map*, 65, 66, 69, 79, 80; textual, 69, 74
topos: Abe Kōbō on, 222n7, 224n23; *The Ruined Map* as, 50, 63, 65–69, 79–80; traffic war as, 35–42, *38*, *42*
Toscano, Alberto, 9, 211n12, 214n24
"Toshi." *See* "City, The"
Toshi e ("To the Cities") (Takanashi Yutaka), 144, 244n57
"Toshi-Kansei." *See* "Urban Shades-Urban Pitfalls" (Nakahira Takuma)
Toshi Kukan no naka no bungaku (Maeda Ai), 234n40
Toshi no ronri ("Logic of the City, The") (Hani Gorō), 213n17, 232n29
"To the Cities." *See Toshi e* (Takanashi Yutaka)
tourism, 106–107, 159, 231n25, 233n35, 233n37, 248n16
traffic war (*kōtsū sensō*): children and, 219n25; defined, 24; speed and, 20–21; topography of, 30, 34, 35–36, *42*; as topos, 35–42, *38*, *42*
Trans-Pacific Imagination, The (Sakai and Yoo), 210n4
transverse readings, 7–11
Truth from a Lie (Key), 221n3
Tsuchimoto Noriaki, 11–12, 21, 199–200, 219n25; with city, depiction of, 28; as filmmaker, 23–24, 217n16, 217n18; geopolitics and, 34; with Metropolitan Police Traffic Bureau directive, 27. *See also On the Road*
Tsuchiya Seiichi, 84–85
Tsumura Takashi, 125
Tsunehisa, Kimura, 138, 242n44
Tsutsui Takefumi, 217n18
Twitter, 199, 203

Uber, 226n47
Ueno Hidenobu, 178

ūman ribu movement (women's liberation movement), 232n31, 238n21
Undōtai Abe Kōbō (Toba Kōji), 221n3
United States-Japan Mutual Security Treaty (1960), 46, 103, 220n34, 231n25
urban fiction, 48, 222n12
urban language, in *Ruined Map, The*, 77–80, 222n12
urban nebula, knowledge of, 137–143
urban phenomena, 1–2, 14
urban/rural difference, infrastructure and, 212n15
"Urban Shades-Urban Pitfalls" ("Toshi-Kansei") (Nakahira Takuma), 251n37
urban writing, 48

Van Wyck, Peter, 203–204
violence: of city, 101, 232n29; Cold War and, 231n24; Japanese Red Army and, 237n20; of landscape, 101–102; police, 137, 139, 232nn31–32; of reversion, 184–185; in *The Ruined Map*, 67–68, 74–77; state, 103, 125
Virilio, Paul, 21, 218n23; infrastructure and, 212n15; on speed, 12, 20, 214n21
visuality: decentered, 116–117, 118; dislocation and, 115–116; hallucinatory, 251n34; magnetic fields of, 121–124; "naked-eye reflex," 156–157, 160–162, 165, 172; nonselective, 115–116, 131, 132; "optical unconscious," 114; photographic, 13–14, 115, 116, 118, 136, 148, 193–194, 201; seeing and, 131, 143–146; in *Why an Illustrated Botanical Dictionary?*, 113–115, 118
"vital materialism," 202

"Wages of Affluence, The" (McKnight), 223n14
Wakabayashi Mikio, 223n14
Wakamatsu Kōji, 223n14, 239n27
Walker, Gavin, 254n58
"What is it to be Contemporary?" (essay), 88, 232n30

Why an Illustrated Botanical Dictionary? (Nakahira Takuma), 83, 109–111; *Circulation* installation and, *126*, 126–128, 132, 143; ecologies in flux, 125–128; framing in, 114–115; illustrating dictionaries, 132–137; interrogatives, 117–121; magnetic fields of visuality, 121–124; naked eye reflex, 146–149; organization of, 119–120; *Overflow* installation, 13, 128–132, *129*, *131*, 133, 139, *145*, 146–149, 244n59; seeing incompleteness, 143–146; urban nebula, 137–143; visuality and, 113–115, 118
Williams, Raymond, 18
Witkovsky, Matthew S., 238n22
Woman in the Dunes, The (*Suna no onna*) (Abe Kōbō), 50, 51, 54, 222n12, 226n49, 234n40
women's liberation movement (*ūman ribu* movement), 232n31, 237n20, 238n21, 241n42
"Work of Art in the Age of Its Mechanical Reproducibility, The" (Benjamin), 244n60
workshops, for photographers, 198–199, 244n59
writing, urban, 48
Writing Degree Zero (Barthes), 230n22

yakuza, 65, 68
Yanagida Kunio, 165
"Yaponesia," 163–164, 172, 249n26, 249n27
Yasumi Akihito, 227n1, 242n44
Yoda, Tomiko, 233n37
Yokohama Museum of Art, 82
Yomiuri Shinbun (newspaper), 154
Yoo, Hyon Joo, 210n4, 211n7
yoseba, 68–69, 225n35
Yu Miri, 203

Zakka Films, 216n6, 225n35
Zenkyōtō student movement, 103, 232n30, 236n10, 238n21
zukan. See "illustrated dictionary"